NEFARIOUS REFLECTIONS

For several decades, psychiatrists, social critics, and writers of other stripes have warned us about the havoc that narcissists wreak in our everyday lives. In this book, social scientist Mark S. Davis maintains that narcissism is much more than individual pathology; indeed, it is a virus that also infects organizations and entire societies. Examining America's history, this book broadens the discussion of narcissism beyond a troubling personality style. It delves into how superiority, exploitation, retaliation, and a lack of empathy contribute to contemporary issues such as race relations, immigration, and the marginalization of those deemed "deviant" or different. By examining the tragic interplay between narcissism and history, this volume offers solutions to answer the question: Can anyone in modern society, informed by its past, devise a treatment plan for a nation's personality disorder?

MARK S. DAVIS is a social scientist who studies narcissism, self- and other-directed violence, criminological theory, criminal justice policy, and research misconduct. His recent books include *Fairness and Crime: A Theory* (2024) and, with Bonnie Berry, *Scholarly Crimes and Misdemeanors: Violations of Fairness and Trust in the Academic World* (2018).

NEFARIOUS REFLECTIONS

On Narcissism and Crime

MARK S. DAVIS

CAMBRIDGE
UNIVERSITY PRESS

Shaftesbury Road, Cambridge CB2 8EA, United Kingdom

One Liberty Plaza, 20th Floor, New York, NY 10006, USA

477 Williamstown Road, Port Melbourne, VIC 3207, Australia

314–321, 3rd Floor, Plot 3, Splendor Forum, Jasola District Centre, New Delhi – 110025, India

Cambridge University Press is part of Cambridge University Press & Assessment, a department of the University of Cambridge.

We share the University's mission to contribute to society through the pursuit of education, learning and research at the highest international levels of excellence.

www.cambridge.org
Information on this title: www.cambridge.org/9781108745772
DOI: 10.1017/9781108777636

When citing this work, please include a reference to the DOI 10.1017/9781108777636

First published 2026

Cover image: Washington Monument and Lincoln Memorial Reflecting Pool at night annamarkiewicz/RooM/Getty Images

A catalogue record for this publication is available from the British Library

A Cataloging-in-Publication data record for this book is available from the Library of Congress

ISBN 978-1-108-47840-3 Hardback
ISBN 978-1-108-74577-2 Paperback

Cambridge University Press & Assessment has no responsibility for the persistence or accuracy of URLs for external or third-party internet websites referred to in this publication and does not guarantee that any content on such websites is, or will remain, accurate or appropriate.

For EU product safety concerns, contact us at Calle de José Abascal, 56, 1°, 28003 Madrid, Spain, or email eugpsr@cambridge.org.

NEFARIOUS REFLECTIONS

On Narcissism and Crime

MARK S. DAVIS

CAMBRIDGE
UNIVERSITY PRESS

Shaftesbury Road, Cambridge CB2 8EA, United Kingdom

One Liberty Plaza, 20th Floor, New York, NY 10006, USA

477 Williamstown Road, Port Melbourne, VIC 3207, Australia

314–321, 3rd Floor, Plot 3, Splendor Forum, Jasola District Centre, New Delhi – 110025, India

Cambridge University Press is part of Cambridge University Press & Assessment, a department of the University of Cambridge.

We share the University's mission to contribute to society through the pursuit of education, learning and research at the highest international levels of excellence.

www.cambridge.org
Information on this title: www.cambridge.org/9781108745772
DOI: 10.1017/9781108777636

First published 2026

Cover image: Washington Monument and Lincoln Memorial Reflecting Pool at night annamarkiewicz/RooM/Getty Images

A catalogue record for this publication is available from the British Library

A Cataloging-in-Publication data record for this book is available from the Library of Congress

ISBN 978-1-108-47840-3 Hardback
ISBN 978-1-108-74577-2 Paperback

For EU product safety concerns, contact us at Calle de José Abascal, 56, 1°, 28003 Madrid, Spain, or email eugpsr@cambridge.org.

Contents

After doing research on aggression and violence for over 30 years I have concluded that the most harmful belief people can have is the belief that they are superior to others (e.g., their religion, race or ethnicity, gender or gender identity, sexual orientation, political party or ideology, school, city, state, country, etc. is the best). This feeling of superiority can lead to the mistreatment of others, which hurts society as a whole. Every person on this planet is part of the human family; no person is superior to any other person.

Brad J. Bushman
School of Communication
The Ohio State University

Acknowledgments

I first must thank the staff at Cambridge University Press. The commissioning editor, Janka Romero, saw promise in my original proposal. When she left for another opportunity, I became a publishing "orphan." Emily Watton graciously adopted me and my project and waited patiently as the book finally came together. She, Anna Hubbard and Jodie Mardell-lines gave me the flexibility and extensions I needed to complete the project. For all their understanding and support, I am grateful beyond words. I also very much appreciate the work of Santhamurthy Ramamoorthy and Thivya Kumarasamy of Lumina Datamatics who took over and shepherded the book the rest of the way into print.

Several individuals read drafts of the manuscript and offered invaluable feedback. Stephanie Milan and Rick Cooper gave it a thorough read and pointed out numerous mistakes and opportunities for improvement. An anonymous reader provided thoughtful suggestions that strengthened the book. Any remaining errors are mine.

I would like to acknowledge my mom, the late Novella Humphrey Davis, for bringing me up in a family that valued words and writing. Instead of becoming a poet like her, I chose prose as my preferred medium of expression. Mom introduced me to the Enneagram, which first sparked my interest in narcissism. I also appreciate that she instilled in me a strong sense of right and wrong.

My sisters are also responsible for my arrival at this point as an author. Many years ago, my oldest sister, Diane Villeneuve, an honors English graduate and poet, gave me an informal short course on effective writing. Try to avoid passive constructions and forms of the verb "to be." Limit modifiers, especially adverbs; make the nouns and verbs do the work for the sentence. Favor short, Anglo-Saxon words over the long, polysyllabic Latinate. Diane also came up with "Nefarious" when I was trying to find just the right adjective for "Reflections" for the title.

My other sister, Elaine Sanchez, has also always been there for me in too many ways to count. I never have to wait long before I get a silly text or call that makes me laugh. Like Diane, she is also a writer, though she is too modest to admit it. Years ago, when an inherited disease damaged my kidneys, Elaine insisted on being the donor. That I have since enjoyed the quality of life I have is due to her selfless gift.

My daughters Heather and Stephanie have always been in my corner. The visits with them and our grandkids recharge me in ways that are hard to describe. Heather remains cheerful no matter what; I should take lessons from her. Stephanie is likewise uplifting and a joy to spend time with. I love them and their kids more than they will ever know.

My wife Jan, who has always been "Greenie" to me, supports me in just about every way possible. It is not easy being the partner of a writer, particularly one whose projects span years. But she faithfully gives me space when I need it, pushes me when I procrastinate, and overlooks the many duties and chores I neglect in the process. I have been lucky to have her as my life partner.

Introduction

The idea that narcissism could be connected to crime struck me years ago when I was given a book on the Enneagram, an ancient Sufi system consisting of nine personality types.[1] As I suspect most people do, I first tried to identify my own personality. If my analysis was correct, I was a type One – The Reformer – what clinical psychology would refer to as obsessive-compulsive disorder. I found the descriptions of all nine types fascinating, but the one that drew my attention most was type Three, what the author termed The Status Seeker.[2] The chapter on the Three clearly portrayed narcissists, and the neutral label came across as an effort to put a charitable spin on what many consider an uncomplimentary set of traits. The book's author, Don Richard Riso, described the characteristics of the Three:

> If they are healthy, Threes are worthy of the admiration of others because they have taken pains to acquire the qualities and skills they seem to embody virtually to an ideal degree. The overwhelming positive self-esteem of healthy Threes has a basis in fact, and they are often highly regarded by others, both in their personal lives and in their careers. Healthy Threes are outstanding, human nature's stars.[3]

The author went on to caution the reader about the type's unhealthier side: "… Threes exploit others so they can maintain what has become a spurious superiority. They are extremely devious if they are in danger of losing the competition between themselves and others in which they see themselves always engaged. They become so jealous that they maliciously try to ruin others to achieve the triumph their narcissistic superiority requires."[4] Riso's chapter on the Three painted a portrait of an individual capable of achieving great success but also inflicting great harm.

Notable Threes in the first edition of Riso's book included Jimmy Carter, Brooke Shields, and Sylvester Stallone, a list later updated to include Alec Baldwin, Oprah Winfrey, and Justin Bieber.[5] Also appearing on the original list were Gary Gilmore, the convicted murderer who in 1977 became the first person executed after the end of the US moratorium on the death penalty,[6] and Ted Bundy, one of the most notorious serial killers in American history. As a graduate student specializing in criminology, I wanted to learn more about this personality.

My graduate training prompted me to search the empirical literature, not on the Enneagram, which was all but nonexistent at the time,[7] but on the Three's mainstream counterpart, narcissism. It was in the literature of social-personality psychology where I found published studies, based on experiments carried out in university labs, which investigated narcissism and its association with a variety of traits and behaviors. Among the revelations were that narcissists tend to consider themselves superior, they feel entitled to special treatment, they exploit others and, when their egos feel threatened, they retaliate angrily, sometimes aggressively.

Once we open our eyes to new psychological knowledge, it's natural to apply it in our own personal world. The government agency in which I worked at the time employed a combination of political appointees and career public servants. One appointee, a woman in her early thirties, landed her job through her father who had been a prominent politician and big-city mayor. My fellow staff members and I were put off by her frequent Friday appointments outside the office, conveniently scheduled in the afternoon to shorten her workday. While our office was an appendage of the Governor's Office, we were physically and practically separated from the state's chief executive. Our entitled colleague would nevertheless announce to constituents that she was from "the Governor's Office," drawing on cachet that was not rightfully hers. My armchair diagnosis found confirmation when this woman, having been blocked from a coveted position by one of our male colleagues, called his father-in-law to inform him that his son-in-law was having an extramarital affair, which brought about an abrupt end to the latter's marriage. As frightening as I found her retaliation, the experience was eye-opening for a young social scientist-in-training who had just witnessed up close narcissistic injury and narcissistic rage.

I personally have struggled with a lifelong obsession with fairness and justice, no doubt part of my "Reformer" baggage. Whereas narcissists seek status and attention, those with an obsessive-compulsive bent tend to be more reserved and focus on rules and fairness.[8] They prefer order in the world and pass judgment on people who threaten that order. In college this obsessiveness led me to major in criminology, which involves, at least in part, the study of extreme and harmful unfairness. A graduate course exposed me to equity theory, a social psychological perspective concerned with imbalances of inputs and outcomes in dyadic exchanges.[9] At the core of equity theory lay two common behavioral responses, exploitation and retaliation, both potential threats to distributive justice. I finally had a theory to help me make sense of my obsession.

My doctoral education took place within a department of sociology well-known for training academic criminologists. Despite the first-rate reputation of the faculty, I found their dismissal of human agency limiting and not in keeping with what I observed in my own social world. After all, people are not simply marionettes dancing at the ends of strings manipulated by amorphous social forces. They can and do make choices about possible courses of action. What my sociological training did accomplish, among many other things, was to instill in me an abiding appreciation of the unique aspects of organizations, social structure, and culture that transcend the individual. Still, I didn't understand why social and behavioral scientists tended to choose one level of explanation and ignore the others. Shouldn't they all be reconcilable?

Throughout graduate school and beyond I found myself dissatisfied with prevailing theories on crime. Some emphasized the importance of society's reactions to crime and criminals[10] over social norms and their violation. Others focused on macro-level social forces such as structural disadvantage but ignored individual differences such as personality. I saw the need for a theory that would build on their respective strengths, overcome their weaknesses, and reconcile the supporting research. A personal requirement was that this new perspective must somehow link narcissism, fairness, and crime.

* * *

Numerous books on narcissism have appeared in the early twenty-first century. *The Narcissism Epidemic.*[11] *The Narcissist You Know.*[12] *The Narcissist Next Door.*[13] These titles and others have given impressive coverage to narcissism's contours and growth and have educated those who were eager for advice on how to cope with this type of personality. *Nefarious Reflections: On Narcissism and Crime*, however, has a different mission. Based on the assumption that narcissism is widespread and growing, it follows three lines of inquiry and tracks their convergence. One is the search for the causes of crime. For more than a hundred years, sociologists, psychologists, economists, anthropologists, geographers, political scientists, legal scholars, and others have sought to clarify criminal behavior through their respective disciplinary lenses. And although criminology has long been dominated by sociology and its more macro view of society, criminologists are once again investigating causes of crime that inhere in the individual. With new forms of data, they have been able to take a fresh and fascinating look at the interaction between the human organism and the environment.[14] This has caused genuine, though understandable, consternation among some criminologists over the possible misuses of biological inferences as in the past[15] and of losing the unique insights of sociology, such as the importance of "neighborhood," in explaining crime.[16] But this trend has freed others to pursue research on heredity, physiology, and personality. Given these developments, do other disciplines such as history have something to offer the contemporary study of crime?

The second line of inquiry brings in norms of fairness and reciprocity. These find expression in both civilized and primitive societies, and they prevail in the most basic of social relations. If a man steals someone else's automobile, he has committed a crime. But independent of any legal proscription, his actions have netted him an undeserved outcome. It is simply unfair. A friend who never reciprocates by picking up the check at a restaurant is a different kind of exploiter. Their behavior is not criminal, but it is irritating because it violates common notions of fairness. And although society considers motor vehicle theft far more serious than failing to pick up a check, both breach fairness norms. The time has come to elevate these norms to a more prominent role in explaining harmful behavior and society's reaction to it than they have played in the past.

Certain forms of crime, then, violate fairness norms codified into laws. But if there were no laws prohibiting these behaviors, wouldn't most people still consider them wrong and harmful? Which social norms do the underlying behaviors violate? A norm against robbery? A norm against fraud? No, it is the violation of fairness norms we object to, whether they are grounded in social propriety or in the criminal law.

Not surprisingly, the third line of inquiry focuses on personality. For decades social-personality psychologists have conducted studies in which narcissistic traits have been identified, refined, and correlated using a wide array of psychometric measures. Might it be possible to translate this body of knowledge into a theory that can inform our efforts to understand, control, and prevent crime?

The working definition of personality need not – and this book argues, *should* not – be limited to individuals. Some scholars maintain that organizations, too, possess narcissistic personalities. It is this broader definition that guides *Nefarious Reflections*. According to management experts Dennis

Duchon and Michael Burns, "Organizations, like people, are motivated to protect their identities and they do this by rewarding behaviors that will sustain a positive sense of self and reduce collective anxieties. The effort to protect identity can become fixated on relieving anxiety, and when this happens, the identity itself takes on the qualities of narcissism."[17] The notion of organizations having personalities may be difficult to grasp, but if we look at personality as "ways of behaving,"[18] we can see that some of these entities do indeed behave narcissistically and criminally.

If organizations can have narcissistic personalities and engage in harmful behavior, why can't social movements or entire nation-states? Individual white supremacists commit specific crimes for which they can be charged. Likewise, the organizations to which many of them belong can be investigated and prosecuted. But the racial animus that motivates them and their members can spread throughout society like a highly contagious virus. Once this occurs, we are confronting something different and far more threatening than just racist individuals or groups.

* * *

It is not the intention of *Nefarious Reflections* to vilify all narcissists or to place the blame for all crime on the shoulders of this personality style. Indeed, some narcissistic individuals possess adaptive qualities that make them well-suited to positions of leadership,[19] regardless of the arena in which they operate. "For all his inner suffering," historian Christopher Lasch once noted, "the narcissist has many traits that make for success in bureaucratic institutions, which put a premium on the manipulation of interpersonal relations, discourage the formation of deep personal attachments, and at the same time provide the narcissist with the approval he needs in order to validate his self-esteem."[20] There would be no entertainment industry without actors and comedians and musicians who do their best work under a spotlight or in front of an audience. A celebrity in his own right, Dr. Drew Pinsky, along with University of Southern California business professor Mark Young, conducted a study in which they compared celebrities to MBA students and members of the public on the Narcissistic Personality Inventory. As predicted, the celebrities scored significantly higher on narcissism than the two comparison groups.[21] Despite the pejorative connotation of the words *narcissism* and *narcissist*, many such individuals are go-getters whose achievements serve as a model to others. Seldom is the world black or white, and along with people possessing a variety of other personality styles, some highly successful, well-adjusted narcissists occupy the vast gray landscape in between.

One could even argue that the so-called maladaptive traits of entitle-ment and exploitativeness are adaptive from the narcissist's perspective.[22] In a dog-eat-dog world, the person who can get around rules and take advantage of available opportunities may well come out on top, whether in the corporate boardroom or in the prison yard. In a situation in which resources are scarce and where competition for them is keen, can't many of us imagine wanting just such an individual to lead us to food, water, shelter, and other necessities? Could this be part of the appeal of someone like Donald Trump?

In both primitive and more advanced societies, collective needs may be better met not through competition but through cooperation, and it is here that we see some of the liabilities of a narcissistic posture. Traditional economists might argue that narcissism is nothing more than what we should expect, *homo economicus* pursuing self-interest at the expense of others. But game theory studies have called this traditional view into question. Economists Ernst Fehr and Herbert Gintis conclude that these research findings "… help us understand why a minority of selfish individuals may make sustaining cooperation in the absence of a pun-ishment mechanism impossible, whereas a minority of strong reciproca-tors may permit cooperation to flourish when a punishment option is available."[23] As a consequence of narcissists' self-centeredness, others may consider a relationship with them simply not worth the investment. They may even punish the narcissistic behavior. So, are these traits really serv-ing the needs of narcissists in the long run? They clearly are not serving the needs of everyone else.

* * *

What began as a straightforward analysis of the role of narcissism in crim-inal behavior broadened to include some relevant history of the United States. Narcissism as a modern social phenomenon may be best under-stood by examining some of the ways in which it has expressed itself in the past. It is as the American story has unfolded that the relationship between narcissism and criminal behavior becomes clearer.

Nefarious Reflections: On Narcissism and Crime serves as a compan-ion volume to the author's *Fairness and Crime: A Theory*,[24] which argues that specific behavioral options – exploitation, retaliation, spite, and cer-tain forms of withdrawal – are most detrimental to society and therefore more likely to be defined as criminal. This book attempts to answer the question: In what ways is narcissism responsible for these maladaptive responses, exploitation and retaliation in particular? *Nefarious Reflections* demonstrates that rather than simply being an off-putting, pervasive personality type that characterizes certain individuals, narcissism is a mindset that underlies much of the behavior society has considered harmful. It picks up where more general works have left off and points out the more damaging consequences of this posture. Through the analysis of both historical and more recent examples, bolstered by findings from several decades of research, this book casts the reader in the role of behavioral scientist, one who can reflect on how and why narcissism wreaks so much havoc and on what society might do to change that in the future.

CHAPTER I

The Character of Contemporary Crime

On the evening of June 17, 2015, worshippers gathered for a prayer service at the Emanuel African Methodist Episcopal Church in Charleston, South Carolina. A little after eight o'clock, a young man entered the church and asked if he could join the group. Everyone was welcome there, so of course he was invited to stay.

After about an hour, the young man pulled out a .45-caliber, semi-automatic handgun and said, "You are raping our women and taking over our country."[1] He then proceeded to shoot the worshippers multiple times, even stopping to reload. When he had finished, nine people lay dead or dying, including Clementa Pinckney, one of Emanuel's senior pastors and a well-respected South Carolina state senator. The victims ranged in age from twenty-six to eighty-seven. Miraculously, three had managed to survive.[2]

The following morning police in Shelby, North Carolina, arrested twenty-one-year-old Dylann Storm Roof. He was returned to Charleston and charged with nine counts of murder and three counts of attempted murder, in addition to federal civil rights charges.[3] If convicted, he could face the death penalty. During his interrogation by FBI agents, Mr. Roof readily admitted to the shooting. Nothing suggested that the young man suffered any pangs of guilt over his carnage. To the contrary, he told the agents he had hoped to start a race war. Roof's personal website displayed neo-Nazi images and portrayed him as an angry white supremacist determined to even the score with blacks, whom he blamed for killing numerous whites.[4]

A memorial service held at the TD Arena on the College of Charleston campus drew a *Who's Who* of dignitaries including Speaker of the House John Boehner, Secretary of State Hillary Rodham Clinton, and President Barack Obama,[5] who delivered the eulogy. In speaking about Senator Pinckney, the President noted: "He was full of empathy and fellowship, able to walk in someone else's shoes and see through their eyes."[6] The perpetrator of these crimes clearly was not.

As is customary in such cases, Dylann Roof underwent an examination to determine his competency to stand trial. He apparently knew the difference between right and wrong, and he had chosen the latter. He confidently announced, "There's nothing wrong with me psychologically."[7] Despite evidence of mental illness, two separate assessments cleared the way for a trial to proceed.[8]

Like multiple murderer Ted Bundy decades earlier, Dylann Roof insisted on representing himself in court. But unlike Bundy, Roof lacked legal training.[9] Either the young man had never heard the admonition that one who serves as his own attorney has a fool for a client[10] or, in his arrogance, he had dismissed it. His ill-considered decision may or may not have changed the outcome. In January 2017, a jury determined that Dylann Storm Roof should be put to death for his crimes.[11] Even with the knowledge that he faced execution, he asserted that "anyone who hates anything in their mind has a good reason for it."[12]

Dylann Roof had not simply committed mass murder. He had purposely targeted members of a race he considered inferior and responsible for many of the problems in America. He had positioned himself above people of color and the sacred house of worship in which they prayed. Dylann Roof had, in essence, played a perverse, vengeful version of God.

* * *

Crime has become an unavoidable aspect of contemporary life. One can hardly read a newspaper, watch TV, or consult sources on the web without a reference to crime or criminals. Police respond to a scene where the body of a murdered man lies in an alley. Two young males rob a gas station at gunpoint. A prominent figure in the federal government stands accused of trading political favors for money. Home shopping networks sell stun guns and personal alarms to keep would-be assailants at bay. True-crime shows dissect the methods and motives of offenders, both infamous and obscure. Prime-time dramas feature specialized teams of law enforcement officers pursuing serial killers and other dangerous criminals. During commercials viewers are marketed doorbell cameras and security lights designed to thwart home invaders and porch pirates. In one way or another, the topic of crime touches just about everyone.

Criminology, one of the youngest of the social and behavioral sciences, attempts to understand crime.[13] Using official statistics, surveys, field experiments, ethnographies, and other methods, criminologists try to unravel these mysteries that have perplexed humankind for millennia. Over the last century, criminology has made impressive progress in the theories it has put forth and the data marshaled to support them. And while it stands as a distinct discipline[14], with its own academic units in hundreds of colleges and universities,[15] it owes a debt of gratitude to several older, more established fields of study, including psychology and sociology. The sociological approach to the study of crime, which dominated twentieth-century criminology and still arguably maintains a firm grip,[16] largely rejects the individual as the appropriate focus of analysis. But throughout the evolution of criminology, a handful of adherents have insisted that psychology offers unique insights not discernible from a sociological viewpoint.[17] In recent decades a growing number of criminologists, inspired by advances in genetics and neurophysiology, have embraced the notion that some explanations for crime might lie not solely within social structure, but also within individuals. Regardless of the lens through which they view their subject matter, criminologists strive to gain new insights into criminal behavior, many with a view toward how to prevent it in the future.

As compelling as sociological explanations of crime may be, particularly when supported by strong empirical data, there are offenses that are difficult to explain by such factors as structural disadvantage or demographic shifts in the population. Some crimes evidence an attitude that says, "My needs and passions are more important than anything else, regardless of the consequences to others." This posture of arrogance and superiority places the perpetrators not only above others, but also above the rules and laws to which members of a free society must agree to abide. And in their wake, these entitled offenders leave behind victims who have forfeited something dear to them, often something that cannot be restored. An analysis of these crimes, including those that have made headlines, may reveal clues about what motivates them.

1.1   Homicide and Physical Assault

Among the crimes considered most serious, those that result in grievous bodily injury or death rank near the top of the list.[18] Of these violent crimes, incidents in which large numbers of people are killed or injured by firearms are particularly egregious. Unfortunately, mass shootings – those in which four or more people are injured or killed – occur with dismaying regularity.[19]

1.1.1 Mass Shootings

The vignette at the beginning of this chapter depicts one of thousands of mass shootings that have taken place in the US in the early part of the twenty-first century. Quite often a male perpetrator uses a semi-automatic handgun or military-style rifle on a so-called soft target consisting of a vulnerable group of victims. Concertgoers. Bar or restaurant patrons. Store shoppers. Students and staff at schools or universities. People gathered in places of worship. Such incidents often end with the shooter being killed by responding law enforcement officers or with the former committing suicide. Occasionally they are taken into custody.[20] Widespread media coverage follows the event as does a public outcry centered mainly on mental health and the availability of certain guns.[21] Politicians offer platitudes about thoughts and prayers for the victims and their families, but little else.[22] All the attention gradually wanes until the next mass shooting, and the cycle repeats itself.

On October 27, 2018, Robert Gregory Bowers walked into the Tree of Life Synagogue in the Squirrel Hill neighborhood of Pittsburgh, Pennsylvania, where worshippers were observing the Sabbath. He had brought an assault-style rifle and three semiautomatic handguns.[23] Parishioners tried to hide and some called 9-1-1. Responding police engaged the shooter in a gun battle in which several officers sustained serious injuries. Bowers, who was wounded in the exchange of gunfire, was taken into custody, but not before he had murdered eleven congregants, including the rabbi, and wounded seven others.

Robert Bowers despised Jews for the role he believed the Hebrew Immigrant Aid Society (HIAS) had played in facilitating the immigration and settlement of Central Americans within the US.[24] In one of his social media posts before the shooting, Bowers noted: "HIAS likes to bring invaders in that kill our people. I can't sit by and watch my people get slaughtered. Screw your optics, I'm going in."[25] To his way of thinking, someone had to strike a blow on behalf of white nationalists. In August 2022, a jury found Bowers guilty of eleven counts of murder and decided he should face the death penalty for his crimes.[26]

On August 3, 2019, Patrick Wood Crusius drove to a local Walmart in El Paso, Texas, armed with an AK-47-style assault rifle.[27] Once in the store, he walked up and down the aisles, shooting at every visible human target. His spree lasted only a few minutes, but when it ended, twenty-three shoppers and store employees lay dead, and twenty-two others were wounded, some critically.[28] Crusius, who was taken alive, faced federal prosecution by the US Attorney. After the defendant was assured that the government would not seek the death penalty, he pleaded guilty to ninety counts of murder and hate crimes. He received the same number of life sentences, all to be served consecutively,[29] guaranteeing he would die in prison.

Crusius had heard President Donald J. Trump make disparaging remarks about people from Latin American countries who had illegally crossed the southern border into the US. Authorities found that Crusius had posted xenophobic rants on his social media accounts.[30] He argued that "… if we can get rid of enough people, then our way of life can be more sustainable."[31] President Trump's expressed disdain for undocumented immigrants, as well as his insistence on building a wall to keep them out, may well have been a blasting cap for Crusius's psychic dynamite. Much like Robert Gregory Bowers in Pittsburgh, Patrick Wood Crusius believed he was standing up for aggrieved whites. Crusius specifically targeted a segment of the population he held in contempt. This inferior stratum of humans was ruining American society, a society that rightly belonged to him and other members of the white race.

These incidents are just a few in a seemingly endless series of mass shootings in the US. They occur with almost predictable regularity, so much so that psychologists suggest that Americans suffer from "psychic numbing," that is, the tendency to emotionally detach when a problem seems overwhelmingly large.[32] Upon closer examination, however, a few features set some of these shootings apart from other forms of gun violence. Dylann Roof had an axe to grind with blacks he believed were responsible for the rape and murder of whites. Patrick Wood Crusius saw Latinx immigrants as inferior and a threat to his preferred way of life. Robert Gary Bowers, like most white nationalists, hated Jews in general, but in his case because they had helped Central Americans emigrate to the US. All these mass shooters considered themselves superior to their victims and concluded they were entitled to kill to preserve white culture. Many mass murders, then, frequently have as the underlying motive the desire to get even for some grievance harbored by the perpetrators or the groups they represent. To kill so many so quickly, an individual must relegate the victims to such a lower status that they represent little more than vermin to be exterminated.

The highly publicized mass shootings in Charleston, Pittsburgh, and El Paso do not represent the lion's share of mass shootings in America. Each one has a different face, different victims, and sometimes different etiology. For the year 2024, there were 503 incidents in the US that fit the definition.[33] What many of these less-publicized mass shootings have in common with their notorious counterparts are offenders who put themselves above those they slaughter and who insist on revenge for some real or imagined slight.

Just as a sense of superiority appears to motivate some mass shootings, so evidently can perceiving oneself as being on the receiving end of it. On May 24, 2022, eighteen-year-old Salvador Ramos slipped into the Robb Elementary School in Uvalde, Texas, through an unlocked door. He had brought an assault rifle and extra magazines of ammunition. Several hundred law enforcement officers representing local, state, and federal agencies rushed to the school, and for over an hour they waited. Finally, a group of them stormed the classroom where Ramos had chosen to make his stand and shot him to death, but critics maintain that law enforcement's hesitation to act sooner gave him the opportunity to kill nineteen students and two teachers and wound numerous other children.[34]

A subsequent investigation found that Ramos had once been a student in the Uvalde school system. While in school, he was considered a loner who had suffered bullying by other children due to his stutter, his short haircut, and his clothes.[35] Salvador Ramos, rather than feeling superior to his classmates, had been made to feel as something beneath them. His crimes at Uvalde Elementary were a misguided attempt to strike back at those who had once looked down on him and made fun of him.

Conventional thinking on mass shootings suggests that those responsible must suffer from serious mental health issues.[36] And indeed, some of them do, as in the case of Adam Lanza, the young shooter at Newtown Elementary School in Connecticut.[37] But just as likely is the unsettling possibility that many of these mass shooters know well the difference between right and wrong, and they conclude that ridding the world of immigrants, people of color, members of the LGBTQ+ community, and others they think have offended them constitutes doing the right thing.

1.1.2 Hate Crimes

The hatred of others has taken forms other than mass shootings. For much of American history there have been groups whose very identity hinges on the hatred of people of color, certain religious groups, and other disfavored segments of society. The Ku Klux Klan (KKK), for example, emerged after the American Civil War in large part to terrorize the recently freed blacks.[38] And while the KKK may be one of the oldest and best-known of the white supremacist groups in the US, there would be numerous others whose charters, formal or informal, promoted hatred and violence toward those they consider to be threats to their culture.

In the late twentieth century, legal analysts and policymakers argued that crimes against persons of color, members of certain religious groups, and the LGBTQ+ community required special protections under the law.[39] So reprehensible were the motives behind such crimes that they stood apart from the threats, instances of vandalism, and acts of violence to which victims are typically subjected. This unique element of hatred prompted legislators in the US to pass laws intended to protect these targeted groups from intimidation and violence and to hold accountable those who would threaten them or do them harm. There had been earlier efforts to pass legislation designed to address offenses motivated by hatred,[40] but it was not until the senseless 1998 murders of Matthew Shepard, a young gay man, and James Byrd, Jr., a young black man, that federal legislation zeroed in on "hate" as an essential element of these crimes.[41]

In August 2017, hundreds of white nationalists and neo-Nazis converged on Charlottesville, Virginia, for a "Unite the Right" demonstration. They had come to protest the planned removal of a statue of Robert E. Lee, the commander of Confederate forces during the Civil War.[42] Carrying torches and marching through the streets, they chanted, "Jews will not replace us." Counter protesters showed up to voice their support for the statue's removal and their condemnation of white supremacy. Authorities had anticipated the potential for conflict, but they had not adequately prepared for it. At one point during the demonstration, a young man, James Alex Field, Jr., intentionally plowed his Dodge Challenger into another vehicle, causing a chain reaction that sent another car into the crowd of counterprotesters, killing a woman, Heather Heyer, and injuring thirty-five others.[43] When asked by a reporter to comment on this tragedy, President Donald Trump, rather than denounce the white nationalists, famously responded that there were "… some very fine people on both sides."[44]

On February 23, 2020, Ahmaud Arbery, a twenty-five-year-old black man, jogged through a suburban neighborhood in Glynn County, Georgia. Three white men, one of whom had a background in law enforcement,[45] suspected Mr. Arbery of recent burglaries in the area. They followed him purportedly to make a citizen's arrest. Two of the men, Greg McMichael and his son, Travis, were armed. The third man, William "Roddie" Bryan, followed the McMichaels in another vehicle and filmed the pursuit with his smartphone. When Mr. Arbery, unable to evade his pursuers, tried to defend himself by wresting the shotgun from Travis McMichael, he was fatally shot.[46] All three men were eventually charged and found guilty of murder by a jury and sentenced to life in prison.[47] A federal jury later found the McMichaels and Bryan guilty of additional offenses for which they received prison sentences.[48] Such crimes, much like the lynching of blacks in the nineteenth and twentieth centuries, appear to target not just specific victims but the classes of people the victims represent.

According to FBI statistics, hate crimes in the US have been on the rise in the twenty-first century.[49] What might account for this increase? Is it the result of more haters? Or have those harboring such sentiments simply become emboldened over time? Hate crime experienced a discernible uptick during the COVID-19 pandemic, much of it aimed at Asians.[50] In early 2020, the world learned that this novel coronavirus had originated in Wuhan, China.[51] President Donald Trump reinforced this connection by referring to COVID-19 as the "China Virus" and "Kung Flu," apparently to lay the blame for the pandemic squarely on the Chinese[52] and possibly to divert public attention from his own administration's confusing response.[53] By the time President Trump was made aware of the virus's arrival in the US, he had already established a track record of disparaging foreigners of color, some of whom hailed from what he referred to as "shithole countries."[54] A few Trump supporters subsequently targeted those they thought fit the profile of "Chinese" people who allegedly bore responsibility for bringing the pandemic to America.[55] It mattered little to the perpetrators that many of their victims were lifelong residents of the US – some not even Chinese – who had played no role whatsoever in importing or spreading the deadly disease.

A discussion of hate crime leads to several conclusions. The white perpetrators blame their victims for having marred the complexion of mainstream American culture. Implicit in this view is that their victims, by virtue of their race, color, national origin, sexual identity, religion, or immigration status, hold little value as human beings. This frees the superior whites to demean, threaten, assault, or even kill those who are, by the haters' assessment, worth less.

1.2 Sexual Assault and Sexual Harassment

Sexual assault has long been part of the violent crime picture in America, and it takes a variety of forms. A female worker on her way home from the office becomes the victim of rape by a stranger. On a hot summer night, a woman who leaves a window open for ventilation creates an opportunity for a sexual predator. A group of drunken college men take advantage of a semiconscious coed who accepts a drink laced with a drug. These forms of sexual assault are all familiar to consumers of contemporary news.

Sexual assault, however, does not always involve street thugs or young men who drink too much. Some sex crimes making the news have been perpetrated by well-educated adults whose positions in the community signify respectability and trust. And their victims include some of society's most vulnerable.

1.2.1   The Crimes of Larry Nassar

Larry Nassar was an osteopathic physician and professor at Michigan State University's (MSU) College of Human Medicine. For eighteen years he also served as team doctor for the USA Gymnastics national team.[56] His responsibilities included performing physical examinations of female athletes for the purpose of diagnosing and treating sports-related conditions.

In 1997 complaints surfaced about Nassar's inappropriate behavior toward members of the gymnastics team.[57] It was not until 2015, however, that USA Gymnastics finally took official action against Nassar. They alleged that he sexually assaulted no fewer than 265 girls and young women during physical examinations, which included the touching of private parts and digital penetration.[58] Astonishingly, in some cases the parents of the gymnasts were present in the room during these assaults. The survivors included Olympic gold medalists Simone Biles, Gabby Douglas, and Ally Raisman.[59]

Confronted with overwhelming evidence against him, Larry Nassar pleaded guilty to multiple charges of sexual assault.[60] At his sentencing, Judge Rosemarie Aquilina read aloud a letter from Nassar in which he complained about his treatment and accused his victims of seeking attention and money. Judge Aquilina responded by saying: "This letter tells me you have not yet owned what you did. You still think somehow you are right, you're a doctor, you're entitled, so you don't have to listen."[61] Nassar received both state and federal prison sentences, with some terms running concurrently, others consecutively. The total number of years would amount to a life sentence for the fifty-four-year-old physician.[62]

Nassar's crimes caused other repercussions. Michigan State University knew about the suspected abuse long before formal charges were filed. Nassar's boss, the former dean of the medical college, also faced criminal charges.[63] As a result of her mishandling of the scandal, MSU's president, Lou Anna Simon, was forced to resign,[64] and she was later charged with lying to police during their investigation.[65] Not surprisingly, MSU faced multiple lawsuits due to its failure to prevent the assaults.[66] The university eventually agreed to pay a $500 million settlement to 332 of Nassar's victims. It would be the largest sex-abuse settlement ever paid by a university.[67]

Larry Nassar's crimes while affiliated with MSU and the USA Gymnastics team reveal several noteworthy characteristics. Nassar occupied a position of authority and trust, one the young female athletes were hardly able to question. He betrayed that trust in one of the worst ways imaginable and then later exhibited arrogance and a complete lack of empathy. The organizations under whose watch the criminal behavior occurred failed to have in place mechanisms designed to protect potential victims, even though there were reasonable expectations the latter could be at risk. Once allegations of sexual abuse surfaced, the organizations tried to protect their image by engaging in efforts to keep them from being made public. Even worse, the organizations' choices enabled Nassar to commit additional crimes. The truth eventually came out, but only after numerous victims suffered sexual exploitation by a predator and by the organizations that gave him cover.

1.2.2   *The Boy Scouts Sex Abuse Scandal*

The Boy Scouts of America (BSA) began in 1910 with an act of the US Congress, which established the organization under federal charter.[68] Through membership in the BSA and participation in a variety of indoor and outdoor activities, boys would acquire useful knowledge and skills that would serve them well their entire lives. As one commentator put it in 1911: "Its members are enlisted to war, not against men, whether civilized or savage, but against savage nature, disease, and the injustice of ignoble case. The cradles of the present still produce their pioneers."[69] From the beginning, the Boy Scouts were destined to do great things.

For many, scouting conjures up Norman Rockwell renderings of happy, innocent boys in olive uniforms eager to help others. Such images graced the covers of *The Saturday Evening Post* and other magazines throughout much of the twentieth century. A BSA promotional slogan from the 1970s declared: "Scouting today's a lot more than you think."[70]

Boy Scouts join local troops led by an adult scoutmaster, sometimes a parent of one of the scouts, who assists troop members in internalizing the scouting philosophy and mastering the skills that earn the boys merit badges. More skills and more merit badges permit scouts to advance through the ranks. Periodically, often during holiday breaks and the summer months between school years, Boy Scout troops attend camps and jamborees where they meet with other troops and ply their knot-tying, fire-building, tent-pitching, cooking, and other skills. At the pinnacle of individual achievement stands Eagle Scout, a respected rank attained by a relative few, including such famous Americans as film director Steven Spielberg, astronaut Neil Armstrong, Supreme Court Justice Stephen Breyer, and President Gerald R. Ford.[71]

The BSA maintains its national headquarters in Irving, Texas, and it is represented around the US by hundreds of local councils. Its considerable financial assets consist of cash from paid dues and donations, investments, and a valuable art collection, including Norman Rockwell originals. The local councils have extensive real estate holdings in the form of camps.

Unbeknownst to most outside the world of scouting, as well as many within, the BSA had long been harboring a dark secret. Throughout the entirety of its existence, numerous scoutmasters had sexually abused thousands of boys in their care. These incidents ranged from inappropriate remarks to unwanted touching to forcible sodomy and rape. Some cases consisted of a single episode; others involved multiple offenses over months and even years. Scouting, indeed, was a lot more than anyone thought.

As a result, the BSA periodically found itself forced to pay financial settlements, which, in most cases, kept the incident from becoming public knowledge. During a case heard before the Oregon Supreme Court in 2012, it was discovered that the BSA had long maintained files of Ineligible Volunteers (IV), former scoutmasters whose behavior prohibited them from future service. A subset of these became known informally as the "perversion files," that is, a list of scoutmasters accused of sex offenses, archival proof the BSA knew it had a serious problem.[72] The earlier legal actions, as well as the existence of the IV files, did little to prevent subsequent instances of sexual abuse by these and other scout leaders.

In 2019, with the growing realization that known sexual abuse cases comprised the tip of the proverbial iceberg, several US law firms joined forces to sue the BSA on behalf of victims and expose their secret to the world.[73] Some of the attorneys took out public ads in newspapers and on TV encouraging former scouts, including those who had been molested decades earlier, to submit their claims for representation. As of November 2021, the number of alleged victims in the combined legal action exceeded 82,000.[74]

Faced with multiple lawsuits and almost certain financial collapse, the BSA sought protection under Chapter 11 of the U.S. Bankruptcy Code.[75]

To maintain viability as an organization, as an alternative to dissolution, the BSA and some of its insurers agreed to contribute $1.8 billion to compensate the victims.[76] Many local scout councils were forced to sell their real estate holdings, including their camps, to pay their respective shares. The terms of the settlement provided for varying amounts to victims depending on the severity of abuse suffered, certain aggravating and mitigating factors, and the statutes of limitation of the victims' states of residency.[77] As of December 2021, the proposed settlement had grown to more than $2.6 billion,[78] and the plaintiffs' attorneys were pursuing yet additional assets from insurers. What would be the largest sex-abuse settlement in US history would represent only a modest payout for many victims, a growing number of whom would not live long enough to see any form of justice.

The sex crimes attributed to trusted adults such as scoutmasters are in one sense the crimes of individuals. The leaders, operating under a high degree of trust, molested boys in their care. They violated that trust and felt entitled to take something they had no right to take. Consequently, these individual offenders bear responsibility for the crimes they commit. Such a person, if truly guilty, should be removed from their position and from the organization and should face prosecution for their crimes.

The Boy Scout scandal, however, represents more than a large collection of pedophiles. The BSA early on identified scoutmasters who had committed sexual acts on the boys in their care. And early on the BSA had made the calculated decision to keep these incidents under wraps. Much like predatory Catholic priests who faced no legal consequences for their sex crimes,[79] offending scoutmasters were in some cases permitted to continue their affiliation on an informal, extralegal probation.[80] In shielding scoutmasters from criminal or civil liability, the BSA, the local councils, and even the sponsoring organizations such as YMCAs and churches[81] became complicit in these crimes. Their arrogance implies that the reputation and financial status of these entities and their affiliates eclipse in importance safety, justice, and healing for tens of thousands of victimized boys. When the organizations with which sex offenders are affiliated have knowledge of the criminal behavior and do little or nothing to address it, are they not willing, culpable co-conspirators?

1.2.3 Sexual Harassment in Government

Andrew Cuomo was born into a political family in New York. His father, Mario, had served as a three-term governor of the State from 1983 to 1994.[82] After graduating from Fordham University and Albany Law School, Andrew Cuomo practiced law with a private firm and eventually became the Attorney General of the State of New York. In 2010 he was elected Governor and twice won reelection.

Andrew Cuomo claimed several successes as governor, including pushing for a cap on property taxes and championing same-sex marriage.[83] One of the more notable achievements would be the passage and signing of legislation designed to protect women from sexual harassment.[84] At the time the bill became law, few realized the hypocrisy Cuomo's accomplishment would represent. If they did realize it, they remained silent.

In 2021, a former member of Cuomo's staff, Charlotte Bennett, accused the Governor of sexual harassment.[85] According to her account, which aired on CBS as an interview with anchor and managing editor Norah O'Donnell, Governor Cuomo had slipped his hand up under Ms. Bennett's blouse, cupping her breast. She interpreted the Governor's unwanted overture as, "The governor's trying to sleep with me."[86] Cuomo vehemently denied the allegation, asserting that "it never happened."[87] Soon after Ms. Bennett's story broke, a female member of the Governor's New York State Police security detail came forward and accused him of having placed his hand on her waist.[88] Other accusations followed.[89]

As a result of the growing number of allegations of inappropriate sexual behavior by Cuomo, New York State Attorney General Letitia James announced that her office would open an investigation.[90] The evidence included the testimony of numerous women, most of whom had worked closely with Mr. Cuomo, as well as documents and video footage.[91] While Ms. James's investigation focused on civil violations, some of the alleged acts could have been charged as misdemeanors, each potentially carrying jail time. Perhaps most importantly, the investigation corroborated the accusers' allegations.[92]

Despite numerous calls for Cuomo to step down – including those by President Joe Biden, Speaker of the House of Representatives Nancy Pelosi, and Senate Majority Leader Chuck Schumer – he resisted. On August 10, 2021, Governor Cuomo finally resigned, effective in two weeks.[93] His Lieutenant Governor, Kathy Hochul, succeeded him and wasted no time in setting a different tone. Behavior of the kind contained in the allegations, she announced, would not be tolerated under her administration.[94]

Prosecutors declined to formally charge Andrew Cuomo with any crimes.[95] Justice for his alleged victims would have to rely on civil remedies, if they obtained any justice at all. Regardless, the acts of which

Andrew Cuomo stood accused represent a powerful man taking liberties he had no right to take from women with less power. Much like the sex abuse in the Boy Scouts, the acts are harmful and wrong, regardless of whether criminal charges are ever filed. If sufficient evidence supports the allegations, the conclusion should be that crimes were committed.

Andrew Cuomo's inferable sense of entitlement took other forms during his time as governor. In early 2020, COVID-19 hit the US hard, and in few places did it take a heavier toll than in the State of New York.[96] Cuomo led the public to believe that his proactive stance toward the pandemic had not only saved countless lives, but also served as a model for other jurisdictions to follow.[97] In time, however, investigative journalists found that his administration had fudged the numbers of New Yorkers dying from the disease. Specifically, the New York State Health Department underreported COVID deaths in nursing homes, a venue whose captive populations experienced high mortality rates.[98] Cuomo's public health success was largely a fiction.

The promotion of this fiction led to yet another ethical lapse. In late 2021, New York State's Joint Commission on Public Ethics (JCOPE) ordered Cuomo to return the more than $5 million he had received as an advance against royalties from his publisher for a book on his handling of New York's COVID-19 crisis. When Cuomo first decided to write the book, he obtained permission from the JCOPE to write it if he did so on his own time and did not use any state resources. Upon investigating the circumstances more closely, authorities determined that Cuomo did indeed work on the book during office hours, as did his staff.[99] As a result of the scandal, Cuomo's publisher, Custom House, an imprint of HarperCollins, chose not to publish the book.[100]

Andrew Cuomo's behavior points to several conclusions. As governor, he wielded a great deal of political power, and he behaved as though he was entitled to skirt rules, norms, and laws. He used his position to harass women within his circle of influence. In doing so, he assigned them to a subordinate position undeserving of respectful treatment. He took from these women something he had no right to take, something they did not voluntarily give. Despite testimony from multiple, credible accusers, he failed to take responsibility for his actions, opting to maintain his innocence and cast himself as the victim of baseless accusations.[101] Instead of issuing an apology for the offenses he allegedly committed, Cuomo apologized for what he said his accusers had misinterpreted,[102] yet another sign of arrogance and a lack of empathy. In fact, when he later decided to recoup a political career, he reasserted his innocence.[103]

Andrew Cuomo's sexual harassment scandal carries an interesting and revealing postscript. An investigation by *The New York Times* uncovered a well-coordinated effort by Cuomo's sister, Madeline, to defend her brother.[104] Specifically, she enlisted a group of her brother's devotees to post nasty tweets about his accusers.[105] Arrogant, entitled offenders, particularly those who are powerful or prominent, sometimes rely on sympathetic supporters who try to protect the former's reputation by denying that the behavior occurred, promoting an alternate version of the facts, or attacking the victims, thereby defending the indefensible.

1.3   Crimes of Deceit

The dictionary defines fraud as "intentional perversion of truth in order to induce another to part with something of value or to surrender a legal right."[106] In recent years the various media have carried stories wherein the perpetrators twisted the truth to take something of value from their victims. And the fact that some of them come from privileged backgrounds makes their criminal behavior even harder to understand.

1.3.1   *Elizabeth Holmes and Theranos*

Elizabeth Holmes was born in New York into an upper-middle-class family. Her father had been a vice president at Enron when the infamous accounting fraud scandal became public.[107] In various ways, Holmes's parents used "back door" tactics and personal connections to advantage their daughter.[108] Elizabeth attended Stanford University but did not graduate. She instead dropped out and started her own biomedical research firm.

In the early 2000s, Elizabeth Holmes announced that her company, Theranos, was developing an innovative way to test blood that required samples as small as a single drop.[109] Traditional blood testing necessitated the drawing of one or more tubes from the patient, an uncomfortable, time-consuming, and expensive process. Her new approach, if successful, would be transformational.

Based on what she claimed were encouraging early results, Elizabeth Holmes attracted the interest of several prominent investors, including media mogul Rupert Murdoch, venture capitalist Tim Draper, and business magnate Larry Ellison.[110] With their financial support, Holmes assured them, she could complete her work on this important medical breakthrough. She also managed to place on the Theranos board of directors some high-visibility figures, including former US Secretaries of State Henry Kissinger and George Schultz.[111] All early indicators suggested that Elizabeth Holmes and Theranos were on the verge of making both medical and business history.

Holmes's world started to unravel when *Wall Street Journal (WSJ)* reporter John Carreyrou investigated Theranos's impressive claims and the underlying technology.[112] He spoke with former company insiders and discovered that the revolutionary process to analyze blood had no scientific basis. His investigation and published pieces, which would eventually form the basis of a bestselling book,[113] proved to be the sunlight that disinfects. Elizabeth Holmes initiated legal action to stop Carreyrou and his paper from publishing their revelations, but to no avail.[114]

Elizabeth Holmes eventually faced federal charges of wire fraud and conspiracy, but her trial was postponed due to the COVID-19 pandemic. She obtained representation by the prominent Washington, DC, white-collar crime law firm Williams & Connolly, and in 2021 her case went to trial. In January 2022, a jury found Elizabeth Holmes guilty of several counts of fraud, each of which carried a possible prison sentence of twenty years.[115] As a federal agent involved in the investigation put it: "Elizabeth Holmes chose fraud over business failure."[116] She was sentenced to serve more than eleven years in prison.[117] Holmes' attorneys subsequently filed an appeal,[118] which she lost in 2025.[119]

Elizabeth Holmes knew that her company's technology could not perform the blood analysis as she had described. She duped numerous unsuspecting supporters, some of whom were successful, respected entrepreneurs. In doing so, she treated them with contempt, wasting their investment dollars and damaging their reputations. When challenged, she insisted she had not misled either investors or patients.[120]

1.3.2 Eric K. Noji

Eric K. Noji was a specialist in disaster medicine who had numerous scientific publications to his credit. He had earned a bachelor's degree from Stanford University and an MD from the University of Rochester. For twenty years he served as a physician-scientist with the Centers for Disease Control and Prevention (CDC).[121] He authored or coauthored dozens of papers that were published in leading medical and public health journals. Everything in Noji's academic background suggested that he possessed both the native ability and the acquired skills to succeed as a medical researcher. In recognition of his professional accomplishments in the field of disaster medicine, he was elected to the prestigious National Academy of Medicine (NAM) in 2004.[122]

It is not known exactly when, but at some point during his career, Eric Noji began plagiarizing the works of others. Computer analyses of suspected plagiarized text confirmed the suspicions of his accusers.[123] To make matters worse, Noji also claimed degrees and honors he had not earned.[124] Competent or not, Eric Noji chose to deceive others by taking ethical shortcuts. His superior, entitled posture was also evident in the content of one of his LinkedIn pages which read: "So much has been said and written about the life and work of Eric Noji, a story so mythic in its epic sweep and inspirational in its chronology of service and unrelenting self-sacrifice on behalf of those who suffer that it is difficult to summarize."[125] It is the sort of praise one heaps on others, not on oneself.

Once Noji's plagiarism and falsification of credentials became public, several physicians and scientists, some of whom had worked with Noji at the CDC and elsewhere, tried to invoke various means of social control, including lobbying the NAM to rescind his membership.[126] After initially resisting these efforts, the NAM eventually decided to remove Noji from their roster, but in their notification to members, they requested that the matter not be discussed publicly, presumably to avoid embarrassment.[127]

Noji's research misconduct could have been prosecuted as state or federal crimes. In federal cases, research fraud involving federal funds most often is charged under making false statements.[128] Inasmuch as US Attorneys routinely prosecute bank robbers, white-collar criminals, and organized crime figures, research misconduct such as Noji's plagiarism likely falls low on their list of priorities. Likewise, state prosecutors who handle felonies including violent and property crimes may have little interest in allocating their limited resources to what they might regard as academic esoterica. In fact, the prosecution of lab-coat crimes such as Noji's is relatively rare.[129]

Few consider research misconduct the scourge of modern society. In the US, the Office of Research Integrity (ORI), part of the Department of Health and Human Services, processes relatively few cases each year. The National Science Foundation (NSF), another sponsor of scientific research in the US, confronts even fewer.[130] Most cases are handled administratively by the ORI and the NSF. Research fraud nevertheless represents a unique type of offense committed by those who appear to have a lot going for them: intelligence, advanced education, and the opportunity to have a well-paying, rewarding career. Cases like Eric

Noji's cannot adequately be explained by criminological theories that point to the various strains that sometimes cause otherwise honest, law-abiding individuals to break the law.[131]

Instances of research misconduct by well-educated, seasoned researchers like Eric Noji imply several sentiments:

> I do not have to produce original work to reap science's rewards. The façade of quality scholarship I have created should be sufficient. The harms associated with my actions – such as the waste of research funds, or the misapplication of my so-called findings, or the misappropriation of someone else's work – are insignificant compared to the creation and maintenance of my image as a superior scholar. Further, I have little empathy for those I may have harmed. And should someone level accusations at me, they should expect me to strike back forcefully, even viciously.

As with other forms of contemporary offending, organizations sometimes play advertent or inadvertent roles in facilitating crimes of deceit such as research misconduct. In Eric Noji's case, the NAM dragged its feet in the face of incontrovertible evidence of his offenses and, when they finally decided to act, they urged their members not to publicly discuss it. The NAM did not engage in wrongdoing, but it could have acted more quickly to address Noji's unethical behavior.

1.4   Crimes of the MAGA Movement

In the first part of the twenty-first century, the world witnessed crimes committed not solely by individuals or organizations but by a broader swath of actors from across society. Prominent among these were certain offenses perpetrated during the first Trump administration. Of these, the events of January 6, 2021, comprise a unique category of crime.

1.4.1   *The January 6th Insurrection*

On November 3, 2020, President Donald J. Trump lost his bid for reelection. Joe Biden won the popular vote and the electoral vote, both by substantial margins. But long before election day, Trump had told his supporters that if he lost the election, it would be due to widespread voter fraud.[132] It was clear he had no intention of accepting anything other than a victory.

As with every other US presidential election, Congress had the responsibility of certifying the results, a process which in 2021 was presided over by Vice President Mike Pence. The date for the certification was

January 6, 2021. That very day, President Trump, along with several prominent allies including former New York Mayor Rudy Giuliani and Alabama Congressman Mo Brooks, appeared before a large crowd of supporters at the Ellipse, a park south of the White House and just blocks from the US Capitol Building. Giuliani played a central role in firing up the crowd. At one point during his remarks, he urged the audience to engage in "trial by combat."[133] Congressman Brooks told Trump's followers that it was "time to take names and kick ass."[134] Many of those in the crowd carried signs supporting Trump and his unfounded claims of election fraud. Trump told his supporters to not only reject the election results, but to march down the street to the Capitol and stop the certification process.[135] He also led them to believe he would be going with them.

Thousands of attendees did follow the President's instructions and marched down to the US Capitol. Some wore antisemitic slogans. One read "6MWE," meaning "six million weren't enough," a reference to the number of Jews killed during the Holocaust.[136] Others bore swastikas, which, by definition and history, signify a hatred of Jews. Scores of outnumbered Capitol and Washington, DC, police officers tried valiantly but unsuccessfully to hold them back. It was not long before members of the mob challenged the officers, pushing and shoving and spraying bear repellent. Some struck officers with their fists, flagpoles, fire extinguishers, and other makeshift weapons. Eventually the mob broke through windows and breached the Capitol. They threatened Vice President Pence, Speaker of the House Nancy Pelosi, and other members of Congress, desecrated the venerated building, and, in the process, did millions of dollars' worth of damage.[137] More importantly, they attempted to upend the peaceful transfer of power, something that had never occurred in the 245-year history of the United States.

In time, heavily armed officers retook the Capitol and restored order. The public would later learn that Vice President Pence and members of Congress had come dangerously close to falling into the hands of the mob. Tragically, one of the intruders, Ashli Babbitt of Colorado, was fatally shot by a security officer as she and others attempted to forcefully enter the Speaker's Lobby.[138] One police officer died because of his injuries, and four others later took their own lives.[139]

Most of the rioters were identified by volunteer sleuths who recognized them on social media or through personal knowledge. The participants found themselves charged with a variety of crimes, including trespassing, vandalism, assault, and seditious conspiracy, a serious federal offense just short of treason.[140] Many of those convicted ended up receiving lengthy prison sentences.[141] Once Donald Trump assumed the presidency for a second time, he granted them all pardons,[142] thwarting justice in the eyes of many and sending the message that if Americans supported him, their actions – no matter how abhorrent – were acceptable.

To assign responsibility for the attempted coup, some analysts, including members of the House Select Committee and Special Counsel Jack Smith, have blamed Donald Trump, who before, during, and after the events repeatedly egged on the attendees. Others have looked to various right-wing organizations such as the Proud Boys and the Oath Keepers whose members were in attendance and participated in the insurrection. But the degree of support the events of January 6, 2021, enjoyed, and continued to enjoy long after, suggests something far more widespread and worrisome than the sentiments of any one person or organization.

The storming of the US Capital stands out for many reasons, but a few aspects deserve highlighting. Trump had encouraged his supporters to come to Washington and protest the results. They were upset because he had lost the election through alleged widespread voter fraud. They were convinced that the voting had been rigged. Election officials had somehow perpetrated fraud. Someone had tampered with voting machines. Consequently, Trump attorneys filed numerous lawsuits in the states where Trump had lost. Even though Trump or his supporters lost the majority of the lawsuits[143] – some presided over by conservative, Trump-appointed federal judges – he still maintained he had won the election.

But the real reasons behind his supporters' anger included their fear of losing their white culture to a growing pallet of people of color – black, brown, yellow, and red – which they felt threatened their lives and livelihood. That the events of January 6 constitute criminal behavior may be debated. What cannot be in doubt is that these acts enjoyed broad support among a large segment of the American people.

1.5 Conclusions

Many of the shootings have been the result of the offenders' attempts to get even for some real or perceived grievance. Sometimes the victims represent a class of individuals the shooter holds in contempt and blames for some personal or social wrong. Examples include the mass murder of Jewish worshippers in the Pittsburgh synagogue and that of Latinx shoppers in an El Paso Walmart. Less lethal but still disturbing are hate crimes against Asians and members of the LGBTQ community who, in the eyes of the offenders, have changed American life and culture to a degree that they become targets of revenge.

The forms of sexual assault discussed in this chapter involve one or more offenders taking something from the victim they have no right to take. Whether the offender is a physician performing an inappropriate, invasive procedure or a Boy Scout troop leader molesting a young scout, these exchanges take advantage of vulnerable victims. Such cases cannot claim poverty or social disadvantage as a cause. Clearly, something else must be at work.

In some sexual abuse cases, there is a point at which the sexually exploitative behavior of entitled individuals moves beyond just an individual problem. Indeed, an organizational or institutional structure frequently facilitates the exploitation. It may minimize the harm done by the exploiter or deny any harm altogether. In yet other instances, the organization actively suppresses evidence of wrongdoing. The Boy Scouts of America, which officially stood for inculcating positive values in boys and young men, became far more concerned with its reputation and financial status. As a result, its actions enabled hundreds of predatory scout leaders to victimize tens of thousands of innocent boys. The fact the BSA maintained "perversion files" serves as evidence of their complicity. Just as individual offenders evidence an air of superiority and entitlement toward their victims, so does the umbrella organization that makes excuses or otherwise shields offenders from facing the consequences of their actions. Arrogant exploiters in such a position can use an equally arrogant organizational apparatus at their disposal to insulate themselves from accountability.

It matters little whether authorities process the incident as a crime, the act results in the same personal and social harm. Former New York Governor Andrew Cuomo may never appear before a criminal court for inappropriately touching staffers, but the women's sense of violation is just as real. The fact that countless sex offenses are handled civilly, informally, or not at all worsens the harm done.

Common threads run throughout several forms of behavior currently defined as criminal. One is that it is either overtly or subtly exploitative. That is, a perpetrator takes from another something to which they are not entitled. Likewise, the scientist who fakes data or steals the intellectual property of others to build and maintain a reputation exploits in a different way. A second thread which sets these exploitative acts apart from many others casts the offender as personally, culturally, or structurally superior, and therefore entitled to what they take from, or do to, the victims. Implicit in this posture of superiority is a shortage of empathy for what the victim may have to endure due to the exploitation. Such superiority is not objective fact but instead a stated or implied status. Mass shooters frequently consider the victims they so easily mow down inferior to themselves. Sexual assailants, whether trusted physicians or scout leaders, exploit inferior others who exist for their perverse pleasure.

Given that many forms of contemporary crime are either exploitative or retaliatory in nature, those interested in etiology might wonder what drives these kinds of crimes. What prompts Boy Scout leaders to sexually abuse young scouts who should be able to trust them? The analysis of contemporary crime suggests a need to feel good, even superior, about oneself, even if it amounts to little more than a façade, convincing images of structure and stability with little or nothing behind them. What permits an actor to maintain an air of confidence – in some cases, outright arrogance – without having a solid foundation of self-esteem born of talent or accomplishment? Psychologists associate a sense of superiority and entitlement, as well as a tendency to exploit others and to retaliate in response to perceived transgressions, with the personality style known as narcissism.

CHAPTER 2

Narcissism from Freud to Facebook

Ms. Y is a middle-aged cancer patient. As a result of distress she was experiencing during treatment, her oncologist referred her for psychological symptoms. Her history included multiple boyfriends with whom she had experienced tumultuous relationships. She had lost custody of a child. During her cancer diagnosis, she had consulted multiple cancer centers around the country, one of which declined to treat her due to what they perceived as her inability to collaborate in the treatment process.

During the intake process she had referred to trainees as incompetent. When asked by a male employee to change her clothes, she referred to the request as sexual victimization, an inaccurate characterization and an extreme reaction to a routine medical request. Based on her history and her recent behavior, the staff diagnosed her with narcissistic personality disorder (NPD).[1]

* * *

2.1 Freud and the Psychoanalysts

Viennese physician and psychiatrist Sigmund Freud argued that the brain, the most important and complex of human organs, was influenced early on by the individual's immediate environment.[2] Among the effects of this environment was what Freud termed narcissism, a condition named for the Greek mythological figure Narcissus, who purportedly fell in love with his own image as reflected in water. This self-love, according to Freud, traced back to an early stage of psychosexual development where there was a failure to adequately distinguish the individual from the mother.[3] The result was one who required an inordinate amount of attention and admiration to prop up a fragile façade.

The treatment for this pathological confusion of the self and the other – psychoanalysis – involved peeling back layers of the patients' lives, taking them back through therapy to early traumas that set the stage for their presenting problems. Such a process could prove traumatic by forcing patients to recall painful past experiences. The ideal result, a methodical renovation of the patient's psyche, would permit healthier functioning in the future.

Subsequent psychoanalysts, some of whom were Freud's protégés or devotees, treated their own patients and continued to theorize about narcissism including Heinz Kohut,[4] who took his medical training in Europe but emigrated to the United States. For much of his career he served on the medical faculty at the University of Chicago and authored several influential books including *The Analysis of the Self: A Systematic Approach to the Psychoanalytic Treatment of Narcissistic Personality Disorders*[5] and *The Restoration of the Self.*[6] Among his noteworthy contributions was emphasizing the importance of parenting in appropriately frustrating the narcissistic tendencies in children and in nurturing empathy.

Karen Horney, another psychoanalyst who came to the United States and practiced in the mid twentieth century, disagreed with Freud and others who grounded the etiology of narcissistic disturbances in the human organization. Environment, according to Horney, particularly that which enveloped the child early on, played a predominant role in narcissistic disorders.[7] This would be an important theoretical development that would provide direction for later empirical studies of parenting and other influences on narcissism.

Another prominent figure in psychodynamic research on narcissism was Otto Kernberg, a psychiatrist and for many years a faculty member at what became Weill Cornell Medicine in New York City. Kernberg made the connection of narcissistic disorders to borderline personality, a disorder in which the individual, most often female, experiences unstable relationships and engages in risky behavior, including suicide attempts. In his seminal work, *Borderline Conditions and Pathological Narcissism,*[8] Kernberg argued that despite the different ways these two disorders presented themselves in adult patients, their defensive structures share similarities, with borderline personality being the more difficult to treat.

There would be other psychiatrists who later would carry the psychiatric torch for narcissism, including Elsa Ronningstam of Harvard Medical School.[9] Ronningstam rejected the Freudian view of narcissistic disorders and instead faulted environmental influences broader than those of parents or other caregivers. When the Diagnostic and Statistical Manual of Mental Disorders (DSM) was undergoing revision in the early 2000s, she argued for the retention of NPD. And she has also worked to help clinicians apply the DSM-5 approach to NPD with their narcissistic patients.[10]

Psychiatrists and psychoanalysts contributed greatly to understanding and treating individual narcissism, particularly NPD. They can identify relevant traits and behaviors, assess the severity of the disorder, and formulate a treatment plan that may or may not involve the use of psychotropic drugs to manage the symptoms. As well-trained in medicine and mental diseases as psychiatrists are, there are limitations to the extent to which they can address narcissism. They diagnose and treat patients who present with symptoms. Patients with subclinical narcissism may never find their way to a therapist. And patients with insufficient or no health insurance may not be able to avail themselves of psychiatric treatment.

Psychiatry in the twentieth century, like other medical specialties, was evolving with a growing number of trainees and practitioners, but it lacked an exhaustive, authoritative inventory of all the mental conditions with which patients could present. Respectability as a science demanded consistency in diagnosis such that a patient seen by a doctor in one jurisdiction would be assessed by the same criteria if seen in another.

2.2   The DSM and Narcissism as a Disorder

Professional interests in narcissism and narcissistic traits trace back to Freud and the early psychoanalysts, but it was not until NPD appeared in the DSM that the community of psychiatrists and psychologists saw fit to formalize it as a recognized disorder. The first edition of the DSM was published by the American Psychiatric Association in 1952,[11] and it would see four more editions, as well as periodic text revisions. This compilation would become the bible for professionals who diagnosed and treated various mental conditions.

Compiling such an inventory of all mental disorders would be no small feat. It would first require putting together a list of all known or suspected disorders. Teams of experts would then have to evaluate each malady, sifting through the vast clinical and research literatures. These experts would have to reach some kind of consensus on the contents. The resulting DSM comprised what was deemed an exhaustive inventory of the various mental disorders upon which a large group of psychiatrists, clinical psychologists, and other mental health experts agreed, and which could be diagnosed and treated.[12] By using standardized definitions and criteria of mental disorders, clinicians from different backgrounds – indeed, different parts of the world – could now consistently diagnose the conditions of those seeking treatment.

The group charged with developing the DSM combed the extant literature of psychiatry and psychology and drafted white papers. Smaller subcommittees held meetings at which they discussed the precise criteria by which each disorder would be defined. The result would represent consensus among mental health experts. The experts identified several categories of mental disorders for inclusion in the DSM. One category, the Axis I disorders, encompassed some of the worst pathologies associated with distortions in thinking and behaving. One such disorder was schizophrenia, wherein the individual so afflicted suffered from delusions. Those individuals sometimes heard voices others did not hear. Another Axis I disorder, manic-depressive disorder, now known as bipolar disorder, described an individual whose emotions ran from the extremes of happiness or irritability to sadness and depression. The Axis I disorders were serious enough that they often called for psychotropic medicines to manage the patient's symptoms. The disorder might also require hospitalization, particularly if the patients might pose a threat to themselves or to others.

Box 2.1 Rules Against Diagnosing the Obvious

Well before he decided to run for president in 2015, Donald Trump exhibited a range of narcissistic traits. Once he made that decision and descended the golden escalator in Trump Tower, his personality was on full display. So well did Donald Trump exemplify narcissism that clinical psychologist George Simon once indicated that he was "… archiving video clips of him to use in workshops because there's no better example …"[1]

Passing professional judgment on someone like Trump, however, presented a dilemma. Senator Barry Goldwater successfully sued mental health professionals who had, without seeing him as a patient, asserted that he was unfit to serve as president. Since then, the so-called Goldwater Rule prohibited professionals from diagnosing from a distance.[2]

The Goldwater Rule notwithstanding, in 2017, a group of mental health experts contributed to *The Dangerous Case of Donald Trump. 27 Psychiatrists and Mental Health Experts Assess a President.*[3] It is a temptation to which many without mental health credentials, including attorney, activist, and Trump critic George Conway, succumbed.[4]

[1] McAdams, D. P. (2016). The mind of Donald Trump. *The Atlantic.* www.theatlantic.com/magazine/archive/2016/06/the-mind-of-donald-trump/480771/ Accessed 8-13-16.
[2] Waxman, O. B. (2017). Why the "Goldwater Rule" keeps psychiatrists from diagnosing at a distance. *TIME*, July 27. https://time.com/4875093/donald-trump-goldwater-rule-history/ Accessed 11-23-2024.
[3] Lee, B. X. (2017). *The Dangerous Case of Donald Trump: 27 Psychiatrists and Mental Health Experts Assess a President.* New York: Thomas Dunne Books, St. Martin's Press.
[4] Zhao, C. (2019). George Conway says Trump is a "malignant narcissist": He's "both mentally disordered and evil." *Newsweek*, August 22. www.newsweek.com/george-conway-says-trump-malignant-narcissist-hes-both-mentally-disordered-evil-1455809 Accessed 7-15-2025.

Among the psychological conditions included in the DSM is a category termed personality disorder. They consist of "… a way of thinking, feeling and behaving that deviates from the expectations of the culture, causes distress or problems functioning, and lasts over time."[13] The DSM-5, the most recent version of the DSM, currently lists the following ten personality disorders: antisocial personality disorder; avoidant personality disorder; borderline personality disorder; dependent personality disorder; histrionic personality disorder; NPD; obsessive-compulsive personality disorder; paranoid personality disorder; schizoid personality disorder; and schizotypal personality disorder. Each personality disorder has its own distinguishing features and traits. Each expresses itself in different estimated prevalence rates.

Personality disorders carry real-life consequences for those so afflicted. Relationships, including those with intimates, pose a particular challenge. It is not uncommon for such individuals to have difficulties with coworkers, particularly those exhibiting traits and behaviors at odds with their own. A manager with OCD, for example, will likely be irritated by a subordinate whose desk is in a state of disarray and who seems oblivious to deadlines.

An individual diagnosed with antisocial personality disorder might be labeled "crazy" by laypersons because they not only carried out a mob contract to kill another, but they also dismembered the victim and deposited the remains across three states. Who in their right mind would do such a thing but someone who is certifiably insane? But such a person, suffering from a personality disorder, may know the difference between right and wrong and choose the latter, fully aware of the consequences – legal and otherwise – of their actions. Personality disorders do not take the afflicted individual off the hook for legal responsibility.

Permitting a serious form of narcissism to join the list signaled that, like the other disorders, narcissism could manifest itself in ways that could disrupt one's life in personal relationships, at work, financially, and even legally. It also suggested that those so afflicted needed treatment by a mental health professional. According to the DSM-IV, individuals suffering from NPD could be diagnosed using the following criteria[14]:

(1) has a grandiose sense of self-importance (e.g., exaggerated achievements and talents, expects to be recognized as superior without commensurate achievements),

(2) is preoccupied with fantasies of unlimited success, power, brilliance, beauty, or ideal love,

(3) believes that he or she is "special" and unique and can only be understood by, or should associate with, other special or high-status people (or institutions),

(4) requires excessive admiration,

(5) has a sense of entitlement, that is, unreasonable expectations of especially favorable treatment or automatic compliance with his or her expectations,

(6) is interpersonally exploitative, that is, takes advantage of others to achieve his or her own ends,

(7) lacks empathy: is unwilling to recognize or identify with the feelings and needs of others,

(8) is often envious of others or believes that others are envious of him or her, and

(9) shows arrogant, haughty behaviors or attitudes.

Some of the NPD traits and behaviors such as arrogance or requiring excessive admiration seem innocuous; they may be off-putting, but they do not necessarily result in personal or social harm. Other traits and behaviors such as sense of entitlement and a lack of empathy portend negative consequences for those with whom the narcissist interacts. This mix of traits suggests a personality style that could exhibit both weaknesses and strengths.

Those suffering from NPD comprise a relatively small percentage of those behaving narcissistically.[15] But the more maladaptive traits such as a sense of entitlement and a tendency to exploit others makes someone with such a diagnosis particularly challenging for those who must interact with them. Such individuals can wreak a lot of interpersonal and social havoc.

Psychiatrists, like clinical psychologists and other licensed therapists, not only diagnose and treat disorders, but they also charge for their professional services. To justify billing patients' insurers for the services rendered, the treated malady must be listed in the International Classification of Diseases (ICD), the official compilation of diseases and injuries that can afflict humankind.[16] Once NPD qualified for inclusion in the ICD, psychiatrists could professionally treat NPD as they had other mental disorders such as schizophrenia, and they could charge patients for doing so.

Personality disorders, by definition, affect adults. As one might reasonably conclude, however, the traits and behaviors that define NPD and other personality disorders likely present before individuals reach

---

Box 2.2 The Quest to Define Evil

After he completed his medical training, Dr. Michael Stone decided to specialize in forensic psychiatry. He chose as his research subjects offenders who had been charged and convicted of murder, including those who had committed mass, spree, and serial murder. His years of intensive study led to the development of a typology of murder consisting of thirty-four types.[1]

   His unique approach to his subject matter resulted in a TV show, "Most Evil," featuring him and his work. Among his conclusions after years of studying the worst of the worst: The evilest offenders were narcissistic.[2] Psychologists Roy F. Baumeister of Florida State University and W. Keith Campbell of the University of Georgia have reinforced this connection by noting that people who are capable of the worst may attack those who threaten their own favorable self-image.[3]

[1] Roberts, S. (2023). Michael Stone, psychiatrist and scholar who studied evil, dies at 90. *The New York Times*, December 16. www.nytimes.com/2023/12/16/health/michael-stone-dead.html Accessed 5-27-2024.
[2] Carey, B. (2005). For the worst of us, the diagnosis may be "evil." *The New York Times*, February 8. www.nytimes.com/2005/02/08/health/psychology/for-the-worst-of-us-the-diagnosis-may-be-evil.html Accessed 8-28-2024.
[3] Baumeister, R. F. & Campbell, W. K. (1999). The intrinsic appeal of evil: Sadism, sensational thrills, and threatened egotism. *Personality and Social Psychology Review*, 3, 210–221. https://doi.org/10.1207/s15327957pspr0303_4

---

adulthood. This realization prompted both clinicians and researchers to explore NPD in children. Conduct disorder, for example, a condition in children, generally is diagnosed as antisocial personality disorder when the individual reaches adulthood.[17] And so before children reach the point at which they can be said to suffer from NPD, they exhibit narcissistic traits and engage in narcissistic behaviors.

Narcissism, in common parlance, implies pathology. Something is wrong with these people who seek attention, feel entitled, and take advantage of others. But if viewed as lying on a broad spectrum ranging from unhealthy to healthy, the implication is that some of these people might function well in society. Those who exhibit the traits and behaviors, but who fail to meet the criteria for NPD, are said to have milder or subclinical narcissism.[18] This catchall category arguably includes the bulk of those exhibiting narcissistic traits.

2.2.1   DSM Revision and the NPD

Periodically, the DSM undergoes a major revision. Presumably this does not happen often because it represents a tremendous undertaking involving hundreds of mental health experts and years of effort. When the time does come to tackle this job, the American Psychiatric Association convenes esteemed groups of mental health experts including psychiatrists, neurologists, psychologists, academic researchers, clinicians, and others whose insights can inform the new version. Throughout its several iterations, the DSM has added new disorders and dropped some of the old ones.

When in the 2000s the time came for the DSM-IV-TR to undergo a major revision, the experts discussed numerous changes, one of which was dropping NPD from the list of personality disorders.[19] Some influential experts argued that given its overlap with other DSM disorders such as antisocial personality disorder and borderline personality disorder, NPD could and should be omitted from the fifth edition.[20]

The announcement that the editors were considering such a radical change incited immediate blowback. Defenders of NPD argued that the long, rich history of the diagnosis and treatment of NPD warranted keeping it among the array of personality disorders.[21] In the end, the editors chose to retain NPD for the DSM-5.[22] But the controversy is indicative of widespread professional disagreement in the field.

Whether NPD stays on the official roster of mental disorders remains to be seen. If eventually discarded, mental health professionals will have to confront the question of what to do with individuals who present with what once were the symptoms of NPD. Regardless, the traits and behaviors associated with NPD once prompted psychiatrists, psychologists, and other mental health professionals to argue for its existence and importance. Such questions do not disappear even if the formal designation does. This suggests that narcissism, including its more severe manifestations, represents not just a diagnosable condition but a constellation of traits and behaviors that are present in the general population and that are recognizable by professionals and laypersons alike.

The controversy over whether to include NPD in the DSM-V has implications not only for mental health practice; it says something important about psychology and psychiatry as sciences. If professional opinion could so easily question the validity of a condition like NPD, just how scientific was the foundation upon which the designation rested? Clearly, clinicians have long recognized – and continue to recognize – a collection of largely maladaptive traits and associated behaviors that brought individuals to therapy. But the controversy over whether to include NPD in the DSM should shake the confidence of those who insist on the scientific certitude of psychological science.

The professional disagreement on NPD notwithstanding, the work of psychiatrists and psychologists clearly homed in on a construct that, individually and collectively, they agreed existed in the population, was different from other personality styles with which patients presented, and whose habits and behavior posed a personal, interpersonal, and perhaps even social risk. NPD's inclusion in the DSM did lead to a history-making body of research by social-personality psychologists.

2.3 The NPI and the Empirical Measurement of Narcissism

Just as medical specialties such as psychiatry were evolving in the early twentieth century, so were the social and behavioral sciences. With the development of increasingly sophisticated psychometric tools to measure personality traits, the focus on narcissism expanded from the clinician's couch to university labs in which legions of undergraduate students would participate in psychology experiments. The twentieth century saw advancements in research methodology and statistics, and the field of psychology was both a catalyst and beneficiary of these innovations. L. L. Thurstone, an English statistician, devised methods for the scaling of rank-ordered responses.[23] Another psychologist and statistician, Charles Spearman, developed factor analysis, a data reduction technique that would prove indispensable in psychological measurement.[24] Armed with these and other new tools, research psychologists and other behavioral scientists were able to devise data collection instruments with ranked response choices for research subjects. Psychologists subsequently applied these methods to a wide variety of phenomena including personality.

In time personality psychologists took a greater interest in narcissism, adding an important empirical element missing from what largely had been a clinical, psychoanalytic approach. In the late 1970s, University of California at Berkeley psychologist Robert Raskin and his colleagues developed and later refined the Narcissistic Personality Inventory (NPI), which would become the most widely used psychometric measure of narcissism. Raskin and colleagues took the DSM-III description of NPD and developed a large pool of statements, each of which represented an aspect of narcissism.[25] They then used factor analysis to identify the various traits represented by their initial pool of fifty-four items, and their analyses yielded seven subscales, which they labeled arrogance, grandiosity, superiority, vanity, entitlement, exhibitionism, and exploitativeness. Inasmuch as the items had been grounded in the DSM-III's description of traits and behaviors, it was unsurprising that the resulting subscales reflected the NPD traits. The developers continued to refine the NPI, eventually reducing the fifty-four-item version to forty items. The NPI was first announced in 1981, but it would be several years later that Raskin and his team would settle on the instrument which consisted of forty pairs of statements, each one assessing a facet of narcissism.[26]

Not long after its appearance in the psychology literature, personality researchers began using the new measure to assess its relationship with a variety of traits and behaviors. It is doubtful that Raskin and his colleagues could have anticipated how influential their measure of narcissism would become. Several teams of research psychologists seized the opportunity afforded by the NPI and pursued studies of the instrument itself, as well as how it correlated with other constructs. The development of the NPI set in motion a decades-long commitment to the empirical assessment of narcissism. Indeed, it could be argued that, without the NPI, much of what social-personality psychology knows about this personality style would have remained undiscovered.

Raskin and his colleagues interpreted seven factors, but not all researchers felt bound by this interpretation. Emmons and colleagues, for example, analyzed the same forty items and, using principal components analysis, another data reduction technique, interpreted four dimensions, which they labeled leadership/authority, self-admiration/self-absorption, superiority/arrogance, and exploitativeness/entitlement.[27]

But while the NPI must be given its due, it has limitations and shortcomings. One criticism centers around precisely what the NPI measures. As noted, Raskin and his colleagues developed the NPI by converting the DSM description of NPD into statements. So one obvious argument against such an approach is that a personality disorder – an extreme, severe form of a personality type – should not form the basis for assessing the subclinical manifestation. The criticism is valid, but social-personality psychologists interested in researching narcissism needed a starting point, and the NPI provided that.

Another criticism of the NPI focused on the extent to which traits are adequately represented by their subscales. W. Keith Campbell of the University of Georgia and his colleagues, for example, developed the Psychological Entitlement Scale as an improved, more sophisticated measure of one's sense of entitlement.[28] The NPI's exploitativeness scale ostensibly measures the willingness of individuals to take advantage of others. Amy Brunell of The Ohio State University at Mansfield and her colleagues, however, argued that while the exploitativeness scale measures something, and most likely a maladaptive trait, its items do not address the tendency of an individual to take unfair advantage of others. In response, they developed the Interpersonal Exploitativeness Scale.[29] Its limitations notwithstanding, the NPI was serving as a catalyst for a great deal of research.

The principle of parsimony has a long tradition in the social and behavioral sciences.[30] It expresses itself as a commitment to empirical brevity. If a construct such as narcissism can be measured with 40 items such as those in the NPI, the reasoning goes, fewer items are better. It should have come as no surprise, then, that social-personality psychologists took on the task of reducing the NPI to even shorter versions. Parsimony was taken to what is perhaps its logical extreme when Sara Konrath and her colleagues proposed a one-item measure of narcissism.[31] Clearly such a tack obviates teasing out subtraits like entitlement and exploitativeness. But for investigators who have limited space in their data collection instrument, a single-item measure of narcissism may serve their purposes.

It may not be an overstatement to assert that the development of the NPI revolutionized research on narcissism. Armed with what was considered a valid and reliable psychometric instrument, social-personality researchers were able to build an impressive body of knowledge about narcissism and its correlates over several decades. The NPI made possible hundreds of studies on narcissism as well as the careers of the social-personality researchers behind them.

Many studies employing the NPI offered an unexpected bonus: They permitted a look at narcissism over time. Longitudinal studies typically follow a cohort of individuals over time, periodically calling on them to update information through surveys or interviews. The NPI studies, in contrast, offered snapshots of data made available through experiments conducted over time, none of which used identical groups of participants, but all of which had employed the NPI. Since the same psychometric instrument had been used across the span of more than a generation, researchers could look at change and stability over time. The results would not be as strong as a well-thought-out, prospective, longitudinal study. But the availability of the data, despite its limitations, was just too good to ignore.

Jean Twenge of San Diego State University and a team of seasoned narcissism scholars capitalized on the opportunity. Using several decades of data from studies in which college students had completed the NPI as research subjects, they illustrated how narcissism had increased over time.[32] The study confirmed what many already suspected: narcissism, a personality style many consider problematic, was getting worse in America.

Not everyone, however, agreed with their approach. One criticism from fellow academics centered on the fact that the authors' data derived from university studies in which undergraduate students served as the experimental subjects. And thus the data would not be as representative as those gathered, say, in the General Social Survey, which surveys a statistically representative sample of the US population.[33] Given the fact that many people in the US do not have college educations, just how representative can these results based on college students be? Such a criticism is not new. Indeed, much psychological research rests on a similar foundation.

In time, however, social-personality psychology recognized the NPI's limitations and began to develop improved and more precise measures for the various forms of narcissism and their traits. These refinements, however, owe a debt of gratitude to the NPI, which permitted researchers interested in narcissism to explore its connection to a wide range of traits and behaviors. Beginning in the 1980s and extending to the present, the number of studies has burgeoned, as has the interest of the social-personality community in narcissism. As a result, a great deal is known about certain domains. Later, other measures such as the Grandiose Narcissism Scale[34] and the Narcissistic Vulnerability Scale[35] would gradually begin to take the NPI's place as more precise measures. But it is perhaps no exaggeration to state that the NPI transformed the study of narcissism. Once the social-personality field had a valid and reliable measure of narcissism, researchers were able to pursue questions that had arisen from psychodynamic work. How do narcissists behave in romantic relationships? What is the connection between narcissism and self-esteem? Which narcissistic traits are more adaptive and maladaptive? The possibilities were now endless.

2.4 Some Correlates of Narcissism

Social-personality psychologists took full advantage of the NPI to conduct research on narcissism. For the next couple of decades, the NPI reigned as the main measure of grandiose narcissism, resulting in literally hundreds of published studies. This literature is too voluminous to cover, and it is not the purpose of this analysis to provide an exhaustive overview of this body of work. Such coverage has been provided by edited collections, and the reader interested in the panorama of narcissism research should consult these more comprehensive books.[36]

Inasmuch as both researchers and laypersons have had a longstanding interest in narcissism, particularly how it comes about, researchers explored the influence of parenting. Those scoring higher on narcissism and interviewed about the parenting they experienced as children have reported being treated as exceptional by their parents[37] who in some cases were overly permissive.[38] Consistent with insights revealed by clinicians who treated patients who presented with narcissistic disorders, research shows parental warmth was negatively associated with narcissism.[39]

As individuals with the reputation of having an inflated sense of self-worth, it should not be surprising that as romantic partners, they have a problem with fidelity, and research bears this out. Those who score higher on narcissism are more likely to have other sexual partners, including those who are in relationships. Narcissists are also more apt to poach the mates of others.[40]

As a personality style with a largely pejorative reputation, it is under-standable to focus on narcissism's more troublesome aspects. Narcissists are more apt to experience anger and aggression toward others.[41] This aggression can take many forms including bullying,[42] delinquency,[43] sexual assault,[44] and child abuse.[45] Among the array of personality types associated with criminal behavior, such as borderline personality disorder and antisocial personality disorder, narcissism surely must be a contender.

2.5 Pop Goes Narcissism

Narcissism may be the defining malady of modern times, but its pop-ularity has been decades in the making. Christopher Lasch's 1979 best-seller, *The Culture of Narcissism: American Life in an Age of Diminishing Expectations*, took what was a rather obscure psychoanalytic construct and turned it into an everyday word by showing how an entire society, dismis-sive of history and its many lessons, falls victim to materialism, shallowness, and egocentrism. The culture Lasch described was one of "… competitive individualism, which in its decadence has carried the logic of individual-ism to the extreme of a war of all against all, the pursuit of happiness to the dead end of a narcissistic preoccupation with the self."[46] Lasch noted that [the narcissist] "… extols cooperation and teamwork while harboring deeply antisocial impulses. He praises respect for rules and regulations in the secret belief that they do not apply to himself."[47]

Lasch's book not only introduced a broader audience to narcissism, but it also touched off an explosion of academic and popular works on the subject. Since the appearance of Lasch's book in the late 1970s, journalists, psychologists, psychiatrists, and social critics have pushed narcissism to center stage, arguably where the concept belongs. The

Enneagram expert, Don Richard Riso, noted in his 1987 book, *Personality Types: Using the Enneagram for Self-Discovery*: "Exhibitionism and self-promotion are becoming acceptable as people do whatever it takes to be noticed in an increasingly competitive marketplace. The ideal is to be a winner – to be successful, famous, and celebrated."[48] Daniel Boorstin, historian and Librarian of Congress, went even further: "As individuals and as a nation, we now suffer from social narcissism. We have fallen in love with our own image, with images of our making, which turn out to be images of ourselves."[49]

Lasch and these other commentators were clearly onto something: narcissism does express itself in myriad ways in Western society, and perhaps in some ways they did not anticipate. In the 1980s and 90s, it became trendy to try to boost the self-esteem of youth through programming in which participants were told they were special, unique, and therefore deserving of love and attention.[50] Every player on a losing team was still given a participation trophy. Experts have since warned that such a well-meaning tack may be misguided, for it encourages an inflated sense of one's self.[51] TV viewers in the twenty-first century tune into reality shows such as the various iterations of *The Real Housewives of* – in which glamorous people living in palatial homes meet at fashionable boutiques and restaurants where they exchange petty grievances, all of which rivets a large audience for an entire hour. Evidence indicates that those who watch these shows score significantly higher on measures of narcissism.[52] Between programs viewers find themselves bombarded with messages that call on them to look better, dress better, vacation better, and drive a better car, and research supports a link between narcissism and materialism.[53] As one luxury automobile dealership advised prospective customers: "Don't just drive ... Arrive!"[54]

Social media has become a virtual nirvana for narcissists. In a phenomenon that mirrors reality shows, the mundane activities of one's everyday life have become so noteworthy that "friends" relish and comment on up-to-the-minute personal details. Facebook has given narcissists a unique forum, and research suggests they have taken full advantage of it.[55] One popular form of post, selfies, seems to have a special appeal to narcissists.[56] In their study of selfies and narcissism, psychologist Dan Halpern and his colleagues concluded that those who post selfies "... probably feel rewarded by sharing their own images with other users, augmenting their levels of narcissism and consequently their use of [social networking sites] for selfie production."[57] And how telling is it that the extension rod used to facilitate the taking of selfies is referred to as a "narcissistick?"[58]

But as much as society treats narcissism as a social disease, its actions imply broad acceptance. As Christopher Lasch put it, "In his emptiness and insignificance, the man of ordinary abilities tries to warm himself in the stars' reflected glow."[59] The fascination with narcissists, however, cannot be blamed solely on poorly educated members of the working class. Despite the exploitative behavior of Bear Stearns and Lehman Brothers in the 2008 financial collapse, none of their representatives went to jail. In the music world, Justin Bieber's alcohol-fueled antics and arrests for assault and vandalism did not keep his record released the following year from debuting at No. 1.[60] America seems to have a love-hate relationship with narcissism, and love may be winning out.

One need not be a trained therapist to recognize narcissism, particularly subclinical narcissism, which does not rise to the level of pathology. Professionals rightly should attend to the extreme version of narcissism, NPD, the psychiatric condition in which traits including entitlement and exploitativeness create problems for the individual in relationships, at work, in finances, and sometimes even in legal involvement. But according to best estimates, those afflicted with NPD make up a small percentage of the population.[61] Operating under the radar of the DSM are countless individuals who feel superior and entitled, who take advantage of others to one degree or another, and who lash out at those who dare to challenge their claims of superiority. These narcissistic traits and behaviors are evident in the workplace, the neighborhood, the businesses people patronize, politics at all levels, and among families and friends. One does not need to be trained in psychology to recognize narcissism. Much like rudeness or bad manners, people know it when they see it, and they see it just about everywhere.

And compelling evidence exists that narcissism is on the rise. As noted, after analyzing nearly three decades of studies employing the NPI, Jean Twenge and her colleagues found a "systematic increase in scores."[62] Some experts recommend caution in jumping to these conclusions,[63] but Janet Rovenpor and her colleagues, using an altogether different measure – narcissism as expressed in bestsellers – agreed that there is more narcissism now than there used to be.[64] The authors did not mention specific book titles in their sample, but one can imagine the likes of *Gone Girl* and *White Oleander* making the list.

2.6   Broadening the Concept of Narcissism

The interest in narcissism prompted scholars to push conceptual boundaries and demonstrate that this personality style applied not only to individuals but also to organizations and entire societies. This movement did not imply that all or even most of the individuals or organizations suffered from NPD; it did mean, however, that narcissistic traits and behaviors expressed themselves at different levels of explanation. And it suggested that narcissism held explanatory power greater than the insights of a psychoanalyst with a single patient.

2.6.1 Vulnerable Narcissism

The term narcissist conjures up an image of an individual who loves the limelight and is outgoing and gregarious. They not only steal the show; they often are the show. These bigger-than-life personalities dominate social events with their good looks, their talent, and their overwhelming presence. They gravitate to leadership positions and frequently achieve great success in their lives. There is, however, a less well-known side of narcissism, one characterized not by standing in the limelight, but by withdrawing from social interaction. When criticized by others, instead of lashing out with characteristic narcissistic rage, they internalize the criticism by withdrawing further, becoming not an attacker, but a victim.[65] Such individuals are said to suffer from vulnerable narcissism.

Vulnerable narcissism represents a very different form of this personality style. Contrary to common conceptions undoubtedly grounded in grandiose narcissism, the vulnerable narcissist is more socially withdrawn, preferring to remain offstage and behind the scenes.[66] But the less complimentary traits of narcissism – a sense of entitlement and a tendency to exploit others – are present, though they take more subtle forms.

2.6.2 Communal Narcissism

By traditional definitions, narcissism affects individuals and it is self-serving. For example, a person might think they are particularly attractive or intelligent, and their behavior reinforces this picture. But to some people, it is important to project an image, not solely of inherent specialness, but specialness in the eyes of others. This form of narcissism is known as communal narcissism.[67]

Communal narcissism can express itself in a variety of ways. The individual might engage in volunteer activities in their spare time. It would be important to the volunteer that others recognize the sacrifices and contributions. Likewise, whereas one person who helps rescue children from a burning house might play their heroics down, a communal narcissist will want the community to know and recognize the brave act. Communal narcissism demands validation from important reference groups, be they based in social media, peers at work, or elsewhere.

2.6.3   Organizational Narcissism

Industrial and organizational psychologists had long been interested not only in how individuals behaved within complex organizations but also in how the organization itself engaged in various forms of adaptive and maladaptive behavior. Likewise, criminologists who studied white-collar crime began to write not just about individual CEOs and mid-level managers whose behavior violated criminal law and administrative codes but also about the organizations – juristic persons – which were responsible for a measurable degree of social harm.

Once organizations became a topic for study, it would be a small step to the concept of organizational personality. Early sociologist Max Weber identified unique features of organizations that were distinct from the humans upon which psychoanalysts and psychologists focused their attention. Organizations promulgated rules. They produced a body of written work for both internal and external consumers. They presided over their own unique forms of social control, meting out punishments and other consequences for violations of the organization's rules. And they engaged in behaviors that were unique to them and similar organizations. In essence, these complex organizations had a distinct personality, and that personality engaged in various behaviors, both adaptive and maladaptive.

Organizational narcissism, according to Dennis Duchon and Michael Burns, occurs when organizations "… become self-absorbed and focus on protecting an identity that has taken on narcissistic qualities."[68] They go on to delineate two types of narcissistic organizations: those with high self-esteem and those with low self-esteem. The organizations with low self-esteem, much like individuals, are at greater risk of engaging in unethical and illegal behavior. If Duchon and Burns are correct, organizations possessing narcissistic characteristics can do much more harm than individual narcissists.

2.6.4   Collective Narcissism

Christopher Lasch took what had been an individual personality style and applied it to an entire society. In doing so he removed the professional blinders that had kept some psychiatrists, psychologists, and others from seeing a broader applicability of this important construct. His work gave rise to the question, if entire societies could fall victim to this malady, how exactly does this occur?

Collective narcissism represents an exaggeration of the importance and superiority of the group to which one belongs. Over the past century it has been discussed by Sigmund Freud, Jerrold Post, and others to describe a more prevalent form of narcissism in the population. Agnieszka Golec de Zavala of the University of London, however, brought collective narcissism to the fore with the development of the Collective Narcissism Scale.[69] She and her colleagues enabled social-personality psychologists to better understand this form of narcissism and its correlates.

Collective narcissism takes the notions of superiority and entitlement beyond the individual to other like-minded individuals. When large numbers of people share the belief in their specialness, that belief takes on the characteristics of a virus, one that can spread throughout a given population. Once this occurs, a narcissistic posture theoretically poses a far greater threat than any one individual diagnosed with NPD.

2.7 Conclusions

The concept of narcissism is as old as the field of psychology. Sigmund Freud traded on the Greek myth of Narcissus to describe individuals who, like the myth's namesake, appear to have fallen in love with their own image. Freud's protégés used this foundation to build a more elaborate structure. Through sessions with patients whose internal and interpersonal struggles had brought them to therapy, Heinz Kohut, Karen Horney, Otto Kernberg, and others painstakingly documented a psychological construct in which arrogant, often attractive exhibitionists used others to maintain the fragile façade behind which they stood and which they would angrily defend.

Social and personality psychologists, equipped with an increasingly sophisticated set of methodological and statistical tools, took the psychoanalysts' insights and developed a raft of psychometric instruments to measure different forms of narcissism and its various traits including exhibitionism, arrogance, entitlement, grandiosity, and exploitativeness. This in turn permitted them to correlate individual narcissism with romantic behavior, sexual and physical aggression, relationship infidelity, and a host of other behaviors of interest.

Even those who might not score high on standard measures of narcissism can engage in narcissistic behavior. The health-conscious liberal who, having gotten vaccinated against COVID-19, looks down on the less-educated anti-vaxxer arguably engages in narcissistic condescension. Worse yet is the person who feels the anti-vaxxer deserves to be on a ventilator in the ICU. Likewise, the individual who, upon being insulted by a sibling, strikes back by homing in on a raw vulnerability has arguably behaved narcissistically. Such examples illustrate just how easily ordinary people can fall victim to a narcissistic posture.

Narcissism, much like other personality styles, lies along a continuum that ranges from normal and healthy to abnormal and unhealthy. At the normal, healthy end of the spectrum are individuals who exhibit narcissistic traits like leadership, but these cause few or no disruptions in their personal lives. Indeed, it may well be that some normal narcissists realize they possess these traits and behaviors and consciously work to contain them.

Psychologists, psychiatrists, social critics, and journalists, on the other hand, have pushed narcissism onto the public almost to the point of saturation. Romantic partners are narcissists, as are siblings, coworkers, and neighbors. One cannot go anywhere without encountering these vain individuals who feel entitled to wreck lives with their self-centered behavior. Narcissists and narcissism have gotten so much attention that some people have become skeptical of, or even inured to, the voluminous media. If society finds narcissists in all these places, is not everyone a narcissist? How special or threatening can such a set of traits be if they indeed are everywhere?

These observations, as empirically grounded and accurate as they may be, miss what may be a larger, more important point. Narcissism's reach extends well beyond the personality of individuals. Rather, it consists of a mindset, a way of thinking, that positions certain social actors – whether individuals or organizations or nation-states – above others. This superordinate position entitles the actor to mistreat those assigned to lower status. And should these subordinate entities object to their lower status or otherwise challenge the authority of those above, the former can expect to encounter narcissistic rage and retaliation.

The importance of expanding the concept of narcissism beyond the individual should not be underestimated or underappreciated. Analysts saw that the reach of this set of traits and associated behaviors infected organizations and, indeed, entire societies. So, as important as the body of research on individual narcissism was, it merely formed the foundation for something that held far greater implications for social relations.

So, rather than solely a personality disorder that affects individual members of society, narcissism represents a style that announces itself as superior to others. By virtue of this belief, the narcissistic entity feels free to disregard the rules and norms that guide behavior in a civil society. The entitled can exploit inferior others for whatever the former need to get psychologically or materially ahead. When challenged, narcissistic entities ignore their critics, defending or rationalizing their behavior. They may even strike back, and when they do, the retaliation may well be out of proportion to the perceived transgression.

The picture of narcissism that has emerged since the 1970s is that of a malady that moves through the population like a contagious virus. Some actors are immune, but all are susceptible to this psychic disease spread by politicians and other powerful voices, amplified through social and mass media, exacerbated by crass materialism, and given space to grow, with the decline of civility and empathy the result.

Of the various behaviors that characterize narcissism, exploitativeness and the tendency to retaliate seem the most personally and socially harmful. These behaviors are maladaptive since neither typically ends well. But social actors are capable of a wide range of behavioral options. How do exploitation and retaliation fit into this overall picture?

CHAPTER 3

A Matter of Fairness

Israeli education researcher Orit Hod-Shemer and her colleagues set up a study to see how preschool-aged children would respond when presented with fairness dilemmas. They interviewed the children, aged three-and-a-half to six, to investigate three aspects of fairness: behavioral, emotional, and cognitive.

The children were presented with hypothetical scenarios and asked to respond to them. Events described by the researcher concerned four situations in which fairness could occur: sharing; considering the other; following the rules; and accepting the other. The research team analyzed the responses both quantitatively and qualitatively.

The researchers found that the older the children were, the more likely they were to propose a fairer solution, use a rule or norm to explain the event in question, and, interestingly, express more empathy.[1] Evidence such as that provided by the study demonstrates that fairness concerns begin very early.

* * *

Perceptions of fairness such as those experienced by the children in the Israeli study preoccupy people throughout life.[2] Those participating in or watching athletic contests such as football games or soccer matches expect the officiating to be done fairly. When an official misses a rule infraction or calls one wrong, spectators express their displeasure, sometimes in angry and even violent ways.[3] Give customers less product or product of less value than they have come to expect, and they will be quick to let the merchant or manufacturer know.[4] Brothers and sisters are aware of when they receive less or more from parents than do their siblings.[5] Participants in the criminal justice system realize when they are treated unfairly, and it causes them distress.[6] Fairness matters a great deal to people in virtually every aspect of their lives.

Fairness concerns also express themselves in offending behavior. Some of the mass shootings highlighted in Chapter 1 represented efforts by the perpetrators to get even with a segment of the population they blamed for some alleged transgression such as illegal immigration or crimes against whites. The sex offenses and the crimes of deceit were attempts by the perpetrators to take something to which they were not entitled. A close examination of these crimes reveals two predominant behavioral responses: exploitation and retaliation. Both are considered maladaptive in that they often lead to personally and socially detrimental outcomes. They are also closely associated with narcissism. But these are only two of several common responses in social exchanges.[7] An understanding of the broader range of common behavioral options will put the two most closely associated with narcissism in a more meaningful context.

3.1 Behavioral Options in Social Exchange

In his book, *Fairness and Crime: A Theory*, the author discusses behavioral options employed in social exchanges:[8] cooperation, reciprocity, exploitation, retaliation, withdrawal, acquiescence, spite, reconciliation, and altruism. There may be other options, but these nine are frequently encountered in everyday exchanges.

3.1.1 Cooperation

Social actors can engage in *cooperation* with one another, that is, to approach the exchange as though both parties will give and take in like measure. Cooperation suggests a situation wherein two or more social actors get along with one another. They do each other favors. They share opportunities and resources. And in doing so, they cooperate.

A neighborhood block party illustrates cooperation among residents. Someone seeks permission from local authorities to cordon off the street for the day of the party. Others donate tables for the food and games such as cornhole and volleyball. Most participants bring prepared dishes to share with their neighbors. And when the festivities end, participants pitch in to clean everything up. The entire block party represents an exercise in cooperation.

Cooperation is not, of course, limited to exchanges between individuals. It is also important in business and the economy.[9] Organizations have opportunities to cooperate with various social actors including other organizations.[10] The concept of strategic partnerships, wherein corporations collaborate with others and share resources, can lead to accessing new markets.[11]

Likewise, nation-states must decide whether to cooperate with one another in trade and defense relationships. Early in the Gaza conflict of the 2020s, where millions of Palestinian civilians suffered loss of housing and shortages of food, water, medical supplies and other necessities, the World Food Programme, the governments of the US and Israel, and even the Hamas leadership engaged in a form of cooperation to make possible the construction of a floating pier on which donated goods could be delivered.[12] All of this occurred during a military conflict in which thousands were being killed and injured. Cooperation suggests that social actors, for whatever motivations, can work together to achieve a benefit.

Cooperation represents a challenge for those who behave narcissistically, and available research confirms this picture. Clinical psychologist Marion F. Ehrenberg and her colleagues found that among divorced couples, those who were more narcissistic were more likely to disagree about parenting arrangements.[13] In a study designed to assess cooperation involving narcissists, University of Georgia psychologist W. Keith Campbell and his colleagues set up a tragedy-of-the-commons game in which participants had the opportunity to either conserve or exhaust common resources. Such studies are common in economic research.[14] Campbell and his team found that narcissists took care of themselves at the expense of competitors and social resources.[15] Using a different form of economic game, the prisoner's dilemma, Marta Malesza of Heidelberg University found that those scoring higher in grandiose narcissism were less likely to cooperate over time.[16] These studies lend support to the notion that narcissistic actors have difficulty cooperating, irrespective of the consequences to themselves and others.

A sense of superiority and entitlement permits them to bend or break rules, particularly in exchanges with those they deem inferior. They willingly take from others without any intention of giving back, the antithesis of cooperation. Cooperation, from a narcissistic point of view, offers them little and therefore represents a chump's behavioral choice. The narcissistic actors position themselves above others, exempting themselves from the written or unwritten rules governing how social actors should interact, including norms governing cooperation.

3.1.2   Reciprocity

Reciprocity involves returning a behavioral gesture, such as a gift.[17] Responding to an overture with reciprocity characterizes not only modern societies but also many primitive cultures of the past.[18] The history of reciprocity is as old as humankind.

A dignitary visiting a foreign country takes with her special items produced in her homeland. When she presents one of the gifts to a high government official, he in turn bestows upon her a special object from his country.[19] These two officials have engaged in reciprocity as have the two friends who meet for lunch and take turns picking up the check.

Narcissistic actors do not appreciate the importance of reciprocity. The narcissistic sense of entitlement implies that receiving without the expectation of giving back is not only acceptable, it is a benefit of being superior.[20] Reciprocity, then, may not yield the benefits narcissistic actors believe they deserve. They do, however, appreciate what some analysts have termed "negative reciprocity,"[21] which will be covered in the section on retaliation.

3.1.3 Exploitation

Sometimes one party in a dyad will take from the other, resulting in *exploitation*. Exploitation represents the taking of something from another "for one's own advantage."[22] In everyday social exchanges between individuals, this can be something as simple as borrowing money from a relative or friend without any intention of paying it back. Or it can, as put forth by the German political economist Karl Marx more than a century ago, consist of taking advantage of proletariat workers by an elite ruling class.[23]

The tragedy-of-the-commons game discussed earlier not only tests the cooperation on the part of some participants, but it also mirrors the real-life exploitation of natural resources. Lumber companies, which in the past have harvested timber on thousands of acres of land without regard to the collateral consequences, engage in a form of environmental exploitation.[24] Not only are future generations deprived of the beauty of the depleted forests but the loss of timber may create other problems such as erosion and deadly landslides. Likewise, companies that strip-mine for coal, scarring the landscape and rendering it unusable for most other purposes, arguably exploit the environment and those who otherwise might enjoy it.

In the 1970s, residents of Love Canal, a neighborhood of Niagara Falls, New York, discovered that they were getting sick from chemicals in the local water. An investigation revealed that Hooker Chemical Company, a manufacturer of dyes and perfumes that had purchased the land in the 1940s, dumped chemicals over a span of several decades.[25] The chemicals made their way into the groundwater and eventually to community water supplies. Hooker exploited not only the canal and surrounding land but also several generations of residents who relied on clean water for drinking, bathing, and overall good health. Profits, it seems, were more important than the health and welfare of locals, a business decision enabled by a shortage of empathy.

Exploitativeness is not simply a hallmark attribute of narcissism, it is considered maladaptive.[26] Whereas some narcissistic traits such as grandiosity and exhibitionism may simply be off-putting to others, exploitativeness exacts personal and social costs, some of which were illustrated in Chapter 1. Indeed, as discussed in Chapter 2, the DSM description of NPD includes interpersonal exploitativeness as one of the defining traits. So prominent is this trait in grandiose narcissism that a specific measure has been developed to assess it.[27]

Some forms of exploitative behavior are clearly criminal. Property crimes such as burglary and theft represent exploitation in that they are attempts to acquire material goods without making the appropriate inputs. Likewise, offenses such as fraud and embezzlement constitute efforts to take advantage of others by trickery or deceit. In between exploitative acts that merely offend propriety and those that clearly violate criminal laws lie others that breach ethical or moral standards. The research misconduct discussed in Chapter 1 is an example.

Exploitation, criminal or otherwise harmful, extends beyond the individual. Chapter 2 discussed how psychologists have developed the concept of narcissistic organizations. If organizations can adopt traits and behaviors like those of narcissistic individuals, then they too can behave exploitatively. The petroleum corporation whose lax standards and irresponsible practices result in a major oil spill, such as that created when the tanker Exxon Valdez ran aground in 1989, arguably exploits the environment and the larger society that depends on clean water and beaches.[28] Contractors that charge government agencies such as the Pentagon more than fair market value for their products and services likewise are guilty of exploitative behavior.[29] The lending institutions that in the early 2000s extended home loans to borrowers who were, by all reasonable measures, poor financial risks, exploited these customers as well as the government agencies that were eventually forced to bail the lenders out.[30]

Nonprofit organizations, many of which are founded to respond to a social need such as poverty or mental illness, are not immune from taking unfair advantage. The private foundation whose officers receive exorbitant salaries arguably violates the spirit, if not the letter, of a charitable organization. When a nonprofit hospital pressures staff to order and perform medically unnecessary procedures, it takes advantage of patients and the companies that insure them. The Trump Foundation, established as a charitable organization, not only failed to act beneficently, but it also allocated its funds to questionable expenditures such as a portrait of Donald J. Trump.[31] In doing so, it took unfair advantage of the donors who in good faith had supported it.

Exploitation can and does extend beyond individuals and organizations. The attempt by Donald Trump and his supporters to overturn the 2020 presidential election results involved thousands of Americans. So widespread was the support for the allegations of election fraud that something else must have been at work. Regardless, they collectively tried to obtain an outcome – the US Presidency – without having made the appropriate inputs, which, in this case, was enough popular and electoral votes for Donald J. Trump.

Exploitation results in a gain for one party at the expense of another. One form, theft, violates common conceptions of fairness, not to mention the Biblical commandment, "Thou shalt not steal." The other forms of exploitation also result in various kinds of personal and social harm. For these reasons, it represents a maladaptive behavioral option, an option inextricably associated with narcissism.

3.1.4   Retaliation

Those who experience exploitation may engage in *retaliation* to restore a sense of fairness. Retaliation represents an effort "to get revenge."[32] It consists of getting even for some real or perceived transgression or slight. Experimental research has shown that retaliation is a normal, if often socially disapproved, reaction to distributive injustice.[33] Some analysts refer to retaliation as negative reciprocity.[34]

Retaliation, as understandable as the impulse may be, frequently makes more problems than it solves. In some cases, the retaliatory act affects a party that had nothing to do with the original transgression, such as students who had nothing to do with the bullying that prompted a mass shooting. In other cases, the retaliation may be out of proportion to the original wrong to which it purportedly responds, thereby creating its own form of unfairness.

Several forms of narcissistic retaliation are criminal. Some of the mass murders discussed in Chapter 1 represent retaliatory attacks against individuals or groups perceived by the perpetrator as having committed transgressions warranting a violent response. The infamous nineteenth-century

---

Box 3.1 Cruel Retaliation

The 2022 invasion of Ukraine by Russia gave rise to numerous confirmed atrocities, many of which were directed at citizen noncombatants, the most horrific taking place in Bucha, where hundreds of citizen noncombatants were summarily executed.[1] So egregious was this and other unwarranted attacks on the civilian population that the International Criminal Court in The Hague initiated an investigation.[2] Ukrainian officials collected their own evidence in the belief that those responsible would one day have to face justice. Reports from Russia revealed that some of these attacks on citizen targets were in retaliation for Ukrainian resistance.[3]

[1] Gall, C., Kramer, A. E. & Kitroeff, N. (2022). Russia-Ukraine War: What happened on Day 39 of the war in Ukraine. *The New York Times*, April 3. www.nytimes.com/live/2022/04/03/world/ukraine-russia-war Accessed 8-28-2024.
[2] Vinograd, C. & Kramer, A. E. (2022). Ukraine accuses Russian forces of executing civilians in the town of Bucha. *The New York Times*, April 2. www.nytimes.com/live/2022/04/03/ukraine-russia-war Accessed 9-4-2024.
[3] Gall, C. (2022). Bucha's month of terror. *The New York Times*, April 11. www.nytimes.com/interactive/2022/04/11/world/europe/bucha-terror.html Accessed 9-4-2024.

Appalachian feud between the Hatfield and McCoy families, which involved deadly exchanges that spanned several decades, was driven largely by retaliation.[35] On a far less serious level, the 2017 assault on US Senator Rand Paul, by his neighbor during a dispute over their yards, appeared to be an instance of retaliation.[36]

As noted in Chapter 2, retaliation is a maladaptive behavioral response closely associated with narcissism. When narcissistic actors perceive a threat to their ego, status, or power, they strike back. Students who participated in a study conducted by Amy B. Brunell and this author reacted to scenarios depicting unfair behavior. Those scoring higher on narcissism were more likely to retaliate.[37] Based on the results of a meta-analysis, Canadian social scientist Kyler Rasmussen found narcissism to be positively associated with provoked aggression,[38] that is, aggression in response to a perceived transgression or threat.

3.1.5   Withdrawal

Sometimes a social actor chooses not to participate in an exchange. They instead remove themselves for some reason. To avoid exploitation. To avoid retaliation. The dictionary defines *withdrawal* as "a retreatment or retirement especially into a more secluded or less exposed place or position."[39] This behavioral option has been described elsewhere as retreat.[40]

Withdrawal can take several forms. An individual can withdraw from an unsatisfactory relationship by ending a friendship. As Columbia University sociologist Robert K. Merton theorized in his famous 1938 essay on anomie, an individual who rejects the pursuit of socially desirable goals and joins a cult engages in a form of withdrawal.[41] A person dissatisfied with society can withdraw to a less-populated region like the Alaskan wilderness. The homeless, who lack employment and who often grapple with mental health or substance abuse issues, engage in their own form of social withdrawal. Suicide, of course, represents withdrawal in the extreme.[42]

Less is known about narcissism and social withdrawal than some of the other behavioral responses. Common sense suggests that withdrawal is antithetical to a narcissistic posture. After all, how can one perform and be noticed without an appreciative audience? How can one exploit without potential victims? It may well be that narcissists pull away from those who have little or nothing to offer them. And in the case of vulnerable narcissism, withdrawal from potential criticism or disapproval may constitute a psychological survival technique.

Certain forms of withdrawal can be harmful and, in some circumstances, criminal. The nursing home staff member who neglects the care of a sick person in her care engages in a detrimental type of withdrawal. The Trump administration's failure to take purposive action in the early days of the COVID-19 pandemic could be interpreted as nonfeasance, a harmful form of withdrawal from a president's official duty to "preserve and protect the United States."

3.1.6 Acquiescence

There are dyadic relationships in which one neither withdraws nor retaliates but instead tolerates the other party's behavior. This is known as *acquiescence*.[43] It represents a passive acceptance rather than an active response to the behavioral options of other actors.

Acquiescence can take a variety of forms. The victim of intimate partner violence, who, lacking alternative housing and financial support, may remain in an abusive relationship not because she wants to, but because she has no other options. Likewise, the female member of an urban gang may accede to the sexual demands of male members to avoid what she considers even worse outcomes.

Much like cooperation and reciprocity, acquiescence seems at odds with a narcissistic posture. Rather than accept the maladaptive behavioral responses of others, arrogant, entitled social actors would be more likely to strike back, even perhaps out of proportion to the other party's transgression. Far more likely is that those who want something from a narcissistic actor put up with their behavior to achieve personal goals.

3.1.7   Spite

Of the common behavior options in social interaction, *spite* may be one of those most difficult to understand. It consists of inflicting harm on another, either with no ostensible gain or sometimes even at a personal cost.[44] While spite can easily be confused with exploitation and retaliation, it differs from these in that it yields little or nothing for the actor engaging in it.

Some forms of spite are harmful or even criminal. The vandalism of a cemetery, wherein young people push over or otherwise damage grave markers, appears to be an instance of spite. The vandals in such cases do not derive any obvious material gain from such an offense. This and other forms of vandalism such as applying graffiti may result in some form of psychological gratification, but rarely does it yield a tangible benefit for the perpetrator.

Researchers have not explored the connection between narcissism and spite to the extent they have exploitation and retaliation. This may in part be because social and behavioral researchers for a long time

---

Box 3.2   Native American Sentencing Circles

From its founding, the United States has prided itself on its system of criminal justice. Over time, more rights were extended to the accused, such as the right against self-incrimination, the right to counsel, and protections against unreasonable searches and seizures. Despite the criminal justice system's strengths, retribution has long served as a rationale for punishment.[1]

As reformers tried to move the system away from a punitive, retributive posture, they discovered that Native Americans embraced sentencing circles, a process whereby offenders and victims come together for a reconciliation and healing.[2] This native tradition helped start an important movement to get away from retribution, the criminal justice system's version of retaliation.

[1] van den Haag, E. (1975). *Punishing Criminals: Concerning a Very Old and Painful Question.* New York: Basic Books.
[2] Smith, C. (2017). Peacemaking circles: Justice in tribal communities. *Out West Student Blog,* October 17. https://west.stanford.edu/news/peacemaking-circles-justice-tribal-communities Accessed 8-29-2024.

neglected spite.[45] A study by psychology professor David Marcus of Washington State University and his colleagues did, however, reveal a positive association between narcissism and their new measure of spitefulness.[46] This suggests that at least at the individual level, those scoring higher on narcissism are more likely to engage in spiteful behavior.

3.1.8 Reconciliation

There are circumstances wherein an aggrieved party forgives another's transgression and publicly makes the forgiveness known. *Reconciliation* represents the behavioral manifestation of forgiveness.[47] It consists of a cancellation of the debt created by a transgression, such as instances of exploitation or retaliation.

Reconciliation undergirds restorative justice, a decades-long movement within criminal justice.[48] Recognizing the limits of a retributive criminal justice system, some advocates have argued that attempts to achieve an understanding between offender and victim, particularly in cases of violent offenses, promise a better resolution of a criminal case. Consequently, victim-offender reconciliation programs strive to move beyond a retributive stance toward healing.[49]

A behavioral response such as reconciliation constitutes a particular challenge for narcissistic actors. Psychologist Ryan Brown of the University of Oklahoma found that those scoring higher on narcissism are less likely to forgive transgressions.[50] These findings were echoed by those of Amy B. Brunell and this author who found that those scoring higher on grandiose narcissism were less likely to forgive in response to unfair treatment.[51]

3.1.9 Altruism

When one party gives to another without getting anything tangible in return, the exchange is characterized by *altruism*. The dictionary defines altruism as "unselfish regard for or devotion to the welfare of others."[52] Examples range from the individual who hands a few dollars to a homeless person to the billionaire who establishes charitable foundations that distribute millions each year to certain worthwhile causes.

Many corporations engage in what is known as corporate social responsibility (CSR), that is, corporations profiting in a moral and ethical manner.[53] This is an area in which the narcissism of the CEO can compromise the corporation's reputation. Marwan Al-Shammari and his colleagues explored this very issue, hypothesizing that the narcissism of CEOs, as otherwise beneficial as it can be, moderated CSR.[54] They found that CEO narcissism is positively related to external CSR, suggesting that CEOs prefer to portray a beneficent face to the public.

Narcissistic actors might engage in altruistic behavior to make them look better in the eyes of others. It can be argued that either way, the recipients benefit. Narcissism has been associated with extreme altruism, that is, altruism that violates social norms or the law[55] and what has been referred to as pathological altruism, that is, altruism that leads to unanticipated harm.[56] Terrorists who sacrifice their lives in a suicide bombing are behaving altruistically, but in a way as to be glorified.[57]

Clearly some of the common behavioral responses carry not only pejorative connotations, but they also often result in various kinds of personal or social harm. Exploitation benefits one party in a social exchange at the expense of another. It is not uncommon for real or perceived exploitation to lead to retaliation, which constitutes another less-than-desirable response to social exchanges. Retaliation expresses the intent to get even for some wrong. And spite, the willingness to inflict harm without any ostensible benefit, may be among the most difficult of the common behavioral responses to understand.

Because these behavioral responses are maladaptive, they are more likely to be prohibited by criminal laws.[58] Examples of exploitative offenses include theft, burglary, robbery, and various sex offenses. Many violent crimes including some murders and assaults are retaliatory in nature in that they are an attempt by the offender to get even for some real or perceived transgression.

But for the majority, outcome fairness matters, and this is one major reason people are put off by narcissistic behavior. In engaging in exploitative behavior, narcissistic social actors violate norms of fairness. Such exploitation may consist of nothing more than an unreciprocated favor, but in other circumstances, the cost to the other party could be far greater.

3.1.10   Fairness in Other Contexts

In the 1970s, social psychologists John Thibault and Laurens Walker published a book, *Procedural Justice: A Psychological Analysis*, in which they asserted that people care not just about outcomes such as those associated with distributive justice, they are also concerned with how decisions are made.[59] They prefer to have a voice in the decision-making process. And they pay attention to the fairness of the rules that govern that decision-making process. Thibault and Walker argued that this comprises a special form of fairness known as procedural justice. Their little book would be responsible for a major movement in social psychology.

Social psychologists and I/O psychologists built on Thibaut's and Walker's work, one of the most prominent and active being Tom Tyler of Yale Law School. In what has become a seminal book on procedural fairness, *Why People Obey the Law*, Tyler made the case that citizens develop respect for laws and for law enforcement when they are treated in a procedurally fair manner.[60] He and his collaborators have since built an impressive body of research reinforcing the importance of procedural fairness.[61]

Tom Tyler has taken the additional step of translating the basic research on procedural justice and legitimacy into information that criminal justice professionals such as police officers can use to improve the public's perceptions of their performance. Through the Justice Collaboratory at Yale University, Tyler and his colleagues have undertaken initiatives designed to improve police-community relations.[62]

Social and organizational psychologists eventually discovered that the nature of interactions between social actors also matters. Interactional justice speaks to these concerns.[63] The ways in which people communicate with one another matter. Do they express civility and common courtesy? Or, like Donald Trump, are they used to belittle the other party, as when he assigned a pejorative nickname like Crooked Hillary Clinton or Sleepy Joe Biden? Together with outcome fairness and procedural fairness, interactional justice provides a more comprehensive picture of the ways fairness – or the lack of it – shapes exchanges between social actors.

Less is known about how narcissism relates to procedural and interactional justice. In a study designed to examine how narcissists respond to abusive treatment by a supervisor, James P. Burton and Jenny M. Hoobler found that such treatment caused those scoring higher on narcissism to respond aggressively.[64] So although narcissistic actors may not always treat others courteously, they clearly do not like it when they receive abusive treatment.

The more maladaptive traits associated with narcissism suggest that social actors would feel entitled to do what serves their interests, regardless of how fairly it was perceived by other parties. The work of social psychologists demonstrates that individuals care greatly about fairness. But what happens when dozens or hundreds or even thousands of individuals experience the same kind of unfairness repeatedly?

3.2 Social Movements as Collective Responses to Profound Unfairness

When enough individuals experience profound, ongoing unfairness, they sometimes band together to voice their common concerns. In the past, people in various occupations, such as miners, factory workers, and farmhands have organized to improve working conditions, salaries, and benefits, which they considered to be unfair. In doing so, they collectively transform their individual concerns over unfairness into a movement intended to bring about widespread, meaningful change. The first two decades of the twenty-first century witnessed the rise of new social movements, which appear to be responses to profound unfairness, forms of which violate not only civil or criminal laws but basic human rights.

3.2.1 *Black Lives Matter*

On February 26, 2012, Trayvon Martin, a black teenager, was walking in a residential Florida neighborhood at night. One of the residents of the area, George Zimmerman, a self-appointed neighborhood guardian, grabbed a handgun and went to investigate what he considered suspicious activity. The two had a brief exchange in which Zimmerman claimed his life was in danger. Zimmerman fatally shot Martin, who was unarmed.[65]

Mr. Zimmerman subsequently invoked Florida's "stand your ground" law, based on the premise that individuals threatened by another have the right to defend themselves, even with lethal force.[66] In public remarks after the incident, then president Barack Obama said, "If I had a son, he would look like Trayvon Martin."[67] The implication was clear: what happened to Trayvon Martin's family could happen to any black family in America.

A lot of concerned citizens, particularly members of the black community who had experienced discriminatory behavior at the hands of whites, saw the Trayvon Martin incident as unjustified and simply another instance wherein a black life seemed to have had little value in modern American society. Consequently, there were widespread and growing public assertions that "Black Lives Matter." (BLM)[68]

Trayvon Martin's death, unfortunately, was not an aberration. The twenty-first century saw a spate of police killings, many of which were captured by witnesses wielding smartphones, by police body cameras, or both. Two years later, the shooting death of Michael Brown in Ferguson, Missouri, may have served as a turning point for activism opposing the questionable killing of minorities by police. Brown had a confrontation with Ferguson police officer Darren Wilson, who at first was seated in his cruiser. After Brown allegedly tried to grab Wilson's gun, the officer fired two initial shots. He then exited his cruiser and fired additional rounds at Brown. Michael Brown was unarmed.[69]

The protests that followed closed I-270, the outer belt freeway north of St. Louis that passes through Ferguson. Members of the clergy, academics, and various levels of government weighed in on what happened and why. Their concerns suggested that protests over Michael Brown's seemingly senseless death could grow into something much more volatile, even violent.

The subsequent killing of George Floyd in Minneapolis in the early days of the COVID-19 pandemic could simply have been another death of a black suspect at the hands of police. Certain features, however, set it apart. In May 2020, many Americans found themselves "sheltering in place" at home, unable to move about freely without fear of contracting a highly contagious, potentially deadly disease. Consequently, a lot of Americans were stuck at home with little to do but watch TV.

Minneapolis police officers responded to the alleged use of a counterfeit bill at a neighborhood store. They soon zeroed in on George Floyd, a black man who waited in a car near the store. Police approached Mr. Floyd and took him into custody. At one point one of the officers placed his knee on the suspect's neck. The pressure made it difficult for Floyd to breathe, and he told the officers that. When it became evident Mr. Floyd was in distress, the officer removed his knee, but Floyd died of his injuries.[70] Almost immediately, the incident ignited international protests.[71]

Box 3.3 White Lives Matter

The Black Lives Matter movement gained momentum in large part due to the all-too-frequent killing of unarmed blacks. White nationalists countered that white lives matter.[1] Perhaps predictably, still others argued that all lives matter,[2] regardless of color or race.

What many failed to acknowledge is that whites did not have a centuries-long history of oppression by those who considered themselves superior. The racial or ethnic group to which they belong could not identify with those who had suffered discrimination or worse at the hands of others.

[1] No Author. (no date). White Lives Matter. www.splcenter.org/fighting-hate/extremist-files/group/white-lives-matter Accessed 8-30-2024.
[2] For an opinion piece on the problems with All Lives Matter, see Victor, D. (2016). Why "All Lives Matter" is such a perilous phrase. *The New York Times*, July 15. www.nytimes.com/2016/07/16/us/all-lives-matter-black-lives-matter.html Accessed 9-19-2024.

The BLM protests were not limited to US cities; London and Paris experienced large throngs of protesters who saw the killing of George Floyd and others as the last straw of senseless, extrajudicial killings of blacks. These cities, too, had significant black populations, and thus they could envision something similar taking place in their communities. Arm-in-arm they marched remotely with their American brothers and sisters.

People of color, blacks in particular, view these dynamics through a very different lens. They know that even the most law-abiding members of their race stand a better than even chance of having an encounter with police, an encounter that could easily end with their death. So prevalent is this belief within black communities that parents would have "the talk" with their sons.[72] This talk, which even former President Barack Obama has acknowledged forms an essential part of black life in America,[73] relates to the son and how he should conduct himself in the presence of law enforcement. The talk speaks to keeping one's hands where the police officer can see them. It advises that one should speak as articulately as possible, not in cultural black vernacular that might be offensive or threatening to the officer. No sudden movements that could be misinterpreted. One should be courteous even if the officer is not. For black families, the talk is less about navigating these encounters than it is about surviving them.

The United States has experienced numerous instances wherein law enforcement officers, generally white, kill a black suspect. Most of these involve shooting the individual, but some victims have died as the result of chokeholds or other means of bringing about asphyxia. A public outcry for justice and accountability soon follows such an event. Officially, the law enforcement agency conducts an internal investigation. Sometimes the local prosecuting attorney is asked to investigate and, if appropriate, take the case to a grand jury. In many cases the officers involved are exonerated, having been found to have acted not only within departmental guidelines for use of force, but also within the laws of the jurisdiction.

With most young people carrying smartphones, the owners could now quickly capture special moments. Routine encounters between police and citizens could now be recorded and shared immediately through social media. Bystanders thus became not only eyewitnesses but also activists whose phone videos now served as important parts of the historical record.

Technological advances had also made their way into law enforcement agencies. Dashboard cameras had long been standard equipment in police cruisers, and they captured a great many police-citizen encounters, particularly when an officer pulled over a motorist. But to capture the encounter, the event had to unfold with the camera's view. Many encounters do

---

Box 3.4 Missing: Fairness in Coverage

Gabby Petito was a twenty-two-year-old white woman who had traveled out west with her fiancé, Brian Laundrie, to go hiking. Laundrie returned to his parents' home in Florida alone. Several days later, Petito's parents told authorities that their daughter was missing.[1] Eventually, Petito's remains were found in Wyoming. Autopsy results later revealed her death was by manual strangulation and was thus classified a homicide.[2] Mr. Laundrie, the obvious suspect in the case, was later found dead in a Florida swamp.[3]

During the search for Ms. Petito, members of the black community noted publicly that hundreds of people of color go missing each year, but none get the attention from authorities or from the media that Gabby Petito's case drew. Why, they wondered, does society not treat all missing persons with the same sense of urgency?[4] As with the killing of unarmed blacks by police, the system did not seem fair.

[1] Larkin, A. (2021). 22-year-old reported missing after boyfriend returns home from cross-country trip without her. *CBS News*, September 15 https://cbbnews.com/news/gabby-petito-missing-incident-brian-laundrie/ Accessed 8-13-2023.
[2] Jimenez, J. (2021). Gabby Petito's death ruled a homicide, F.B.I. confirms. *The New York Times*, September 21. www.nytimes.com/2021/09/21/us/gabby-petito-homicide.htlm Accessed 1-11-2022.
[3] Levenson, M. & Grullon Paz, I. (2021). Human remains found in Florida park were Brian Laundrie's, F.B.I. says. *The New York Times*, October 20. https://nytimes.com/2021/10/20/us/brian-laundrie-body-found-florida-park.html Accessed 1-11-2022.
[4] Robertson, K. (2021). News media can't shake "missing white woman syndrome," critics say. *The New York Times*, September 22. www.nytimes.com/2021/09/22/business/media/gabby-petito-missing-white-woman-syndrome.html Accessed 1-11-2022.

---

not, limiting the dash cam's effectiveness. Law enforcement agencies subsequently moved toward small cameras worn by the officers, which, at least in theory, would record all interactions in front of the officer.

Official reactions to BLM may have been as revealing about racism in America as the many instances of excessive force by police. Once blacks began marching through the streets, local government made it clear that they were preparing not for peaceful protests, but for violent, destructive riots. The implication is that blacks cannot come together without engaging in violent or destructive behavior.

Unfortunately, the BLM protests in response to excessive force by police did include socially unacceptable, even illegal, behavior. During the protests, some participants engaged in a range of crimes, including vandalism, arson, and looting. Whether these acts were perpetrated by protesters pushed to the brink or by outside agitators, or a combination of the two, these crimes tainted what otherwise would have been peaceful demonstrations.

These crimes occurring in conjunction with BLM protests did hurt the movement. Right-wing critics quickly latched onto these incidents as evidence of dangerous, left-wing extremism. Multiple conservative voices, including both pundits and politicians, blamed "Antifa" for fanning the flames of illegal, even violent, civil unrest. This, in turn, prompted many concerned citizens to express an interest in purchasing firearms, possibly for the racial conflagration they saw as imminent.[74]

Washington, DC, was among the many cities in which BLM protests took place. As a result of the protests and attendant vandalism, St. John's Church sustained damage on the night of May 31. The following day, President Trump decided to walk over to the church accompanied by prominent government officials, including Attorney General William Barr and General Mark A. Milley, who was an unwilling participant.[75] Just prior to this show of strength by the President, the park police cleared all protesters from the park using horse-mounted officers, tear gas, rubber bullets, and, at one point, a low-flying helicopter whose propeller created a loud, powerful downdraft, which seemingly was intended to help intimidate and disperse the crowd.

Critics of the police tactics blamed the president's Bible-wielding publicity stunt in front of the church for their decision. An inspector general report later determined that the park police needed to clear the crowd to install fencing to protect the Church.[76] Regardless, the optics translated into yet another heavy-handed effort to suppress the protesters, many of whom were minorities.

Only a month after the death of George Floyd, Atlanta police responded to an incident at a Wendy's restaurant where a black man, Rayshard Brooks, suspected of being intoxicated, was found sitting in a car. He explained to the responding officers that he had had some drinks. The officers made the decision to take him into custody. When they attempted to put handcuffs on him, he resisted, prompting the officers to use a taser. It was then that he attempted to flee at which time he was shot twice in the back.[77]

Many of the incidents have several factors in common. A black man is suspected of a crime, often one that is not violent. Law enforcement responds and instead of issuing a citation or deescalating the situation, they choose to make an arrest, using force, and killing the black suspect in the process. Apologists for the police might argue that they are doing exactly what they have been trained to do.

The movement's name, Black Lives Matter, implies that to certain segments of the population, law enforcement agencies in particular, black

---

Box 3.5 The Wrong Way to Address Perceived Unfairness

On July 7, 2016, an organization called the Next Generation Action Network held a protest in Dallas, Texas. Two black men, Alton Sterling and Philando Castile, had recently been killed by white law enforcement officers in Louisiana and Minnesota, respectively.[1]

During the protest, police officers assigned to the event began taking fire from an unknown sniper. They finally managed to corner the shooter and kill him with explosives attached to a robot, but not before he had shot and killed five officers and wounded nine others, including two civilians.[2]

The assailant, Michal Xavier Johnson, was a black Army Reservist and Afghanistan War veteran who was upset about the killing of blacks by police. He used an AK-47-style semi-automatic rifle and wore ballistic body armor with metal plates, making it harder for Dallas officers to neutralize him.

Micah Johnson had every right to be upset about the unjustified killings of blacks by law enforcement. He was not alone; protesters around the country voiced their concerns. But these deaths, as tragic as they were, did not entitle him to a retaliatory shooting spree.

[1] Fernandez, M., Perez-Pena, R. & Bromwich, J. E. (2016). Five Dallas officers were killed as payback, police chief says. *The New York Times*, July 8. https://nytimes.com/2016/07/09/us/dallas-police-shooting.html Accessed 12-21-2021.
[2] Ibid.

---

lives have little or no value, or at least they matter less than white lives. Police facing such criticism might counter that their own ranks include officers of color. They might argue that most of their encounters with black residents do not end in physical injury or death. But to many persons of color, particularly those who are older and have years of experience with law enforcement encounters, police in general do not value black lives the same as their white counterparts. This superior position enables police officers to treat inferior blacks differently from the way they treat whites. The counterargument from some quarters, including conservative commentators, that indeed "All Lives Matter" proved unconvincing in the face of the mounting evidence of racialized policing. The voices of BLM, which included not only critics like the Rev. Al Sharpton and civil rights attorney Ben Crump but also some enlightened whites, dictated aloud a new chapter in American history.

The BLM movement sends several messages to the broader society. The first, spelled out in the movement's name, states unequivocally that people of color, blacks in particular, have just as much value as white people. BLM implies that the subordinate position to which blacks have traditionally been assigned in society is unacceptable and will no longer be tolerated. Also implicit in BLM is the notion that the social narcissism that supports blacks' inferior status harms not only people of color but an entire American culture, which has long promoted itself to the world as ideal.[78]

The overview of contemporary crime in Chapter 1 included examples of sexual assault and sexual harassment. Much like the unwarranted violence toward blacks by law enforcement, the sexual exploitation of vulnerable individuals eventually gives rise to a unique form of organized rebellion against unfairness.

3.2.2   The #MeToo Movement

The image of the Hollywood casting couch – the piece of furniture purportedly used by producers and directors for the seduction of young actresses – goes back to the beginnings of the film industry.[79] So embedded is this cliché in American culture that it has served as the basis for research on mock jurors' perceptions of rape and sexual assault.[80] But behind the time-worn image lies a raft of stories, true-to-life accounts of young women who found themselves faced with a horrendous choice: succumb to the lascivious overtures of powerful male gatekeepers or be prepared to surrender one's dreams of an acting career. These stories often lacked specifics, but their enduring nature suggested that somewhere beneath the smoke of Hollywood gossip smoldered some embers of truth. The perpetuation of this trope implies a degree of acceptance.

Harvey Weinstein was one such Hollywood producer, responsible for a string of box office hits including *Sex, Lies, and Videotape*, *Pulp Fiction*, and *Shakespeare in Love*.[81] He rose from relatively humble beginnings to become one of the most influential figures in the film industry. In 1997, he was named as one of TIME Magazine's twenty-five most influential Americans.[82] As a film producer, Weinstein occupied an extremely powerful position, one that enabled him to make or break the careers of aspiring actresses.

Rumors had long circulated throughout show business about Weinstein's sexual proclivities. He had garnered a reputation as a sexually aggressive man who arranged meetings to discuss upcoming roles at luxury hotel rooms rather than well-populated public venues. Female ingenues who put themselves in such situations often discovered through word-of-mouth that the encounter likely would culminate in a sexual overture. So considerable was his power within the movie industry that for many years, few had been willing to level formal accusations.

In 2018, the successful Hollywood mogul found himself charged with multiple counts of forcible rape, his accusers were celebrated actresses, including Salma Hayak[83] and Annabella Sciorra.[84] Such cases draw national attention not only because of the participants' fame, but also because his sexually predatory behavior bore the label of rape, qualitatively different from a starlet's voluntary submission on a casting couch and, perhaps more importantly, a serious crime. Soon other prominent actresses emerged from the shadows and pointed their fingers directly at Harvey Weinstein.[85]

Throughout history women have made their voices heard. The suffrage movement broadcast women's collective demand for the right to vote.[86] Various attempts to pass the Equal Rights Amendment to the US Constitution signaled to men that women had grown sick and tired of their second-class, subordinate position within American society.[87] While the magnifying glass of #MeToo may have been trained initially, primarily on Harvey Weinstein and his alleged predations, the movement announced that women had reached the point where they not only signaled their disapproval of men's sexual misbehavior in general, but they now stood ready, willing, and able to name specific predators who had violated them. #MeToo is an example of what happens when entitlement and exploitation go unchecked for too long. As despicable as Harvey Weinstein's actions may have been, they were emblematic of what countless women and girls had suffered at the hands of powerful men for decades and longer.

Indeed, Weinstein did not stand alone in the twenty-first century in his sexual exploitation of women and girls. Matt Lauer, the one-time cohost of *Today*, lost his job over allegations of inappropriate sexual advances toward women in his workplace.[88] Charlie Rose, a CBS staple for many years on such popular programs as *60 Minutes*, was forced to step down from his role when women revealed that he entertained them at his home, clothed in a bathrobe, which, in some instances, did not remain closed.[89] These men behaved as though they were entitled to take sexual advantage of their female victims.

#MeToo illustrates the importance of fairness norms in several ways. It shows that the exploitation of victims by powerful men will continue only so long before the former revolt against the profound unfairness. One was that these women, some of whom were highly successful, were no longer willing to permit themselves to be sexually exploited by powerful men. #MeToo said that these exploited women would go public with their allegations despite their exploiters' threats of retaliation. The signal communicated that the victims were ready to risk anonymity, reputations, and careers to achieve justice and prevent future instances of predation. The sheer numbers of those coming forward gave strength to the movement, sufficient to end the reign of some very powerful men.

3.3   Conclusions

Fairness norms rank among the most important of all social norms. They pervade every aspect of social life including family, work, friends, and neighbors. From the time children begin to communicate and interact with others, they express a preference for fairness and a revulsion for unfairness. Thereafter, these norms guide the behavior of individuals, organizations, and nation-states.

Of the range of behavioral options social actors have at their disposal, exploitation and retaliation are among the unfair and most harmful. Exploitation results in a loss to one party, often something they do not want to give. Often something that cannot be restored. Retaliation, the striking back at a perceived transgression, often results in more personal and social harm. When people violate fairness norms through instances of exploitation or retaliation, they do damage to the social fabric.

Procedural justice, another form of fairness, also matters to social actors. The processes by which decisions are made, including the degree to which people have a voice in those decisions, create additional opportunities for unfairness. Research reveals that narcissism has a negative relationship with procedural justice.

A narcissistic posture violates social norms governing fairness. Narcissistic entitlement announces that as a superior actor, they deserve what they want and therefore have the right to take it, regardless of the costs to others. When these actors perceive threats to ego, such as when criticized or attacked, they strike back, often in far greater measure than the wrong they have experienced. Narcissistic actors, feeling superior to others, can ignore those on the lower, less powerful, or less fortunate rungs of society. And they are also quite capable of spite, that is, intentionally inflicting harmful behavior on others for which there is little or no personal gain. All these forms of unfair behavior are normal fare for maladaptively narcissistic social actors.

The Black Lives Matter and #MeToo social movements share several important characteristics. They emerged in large part in reaction to the harmful narcissistic behavior of powerful white men. In the case of #MeToo, many men clearly considered themselves entitled to sex from vulnerable, often young women and girls. To engage in such behavior, the offenders have placed their targets in a subordinate position. Likewise, the white police officers who use excessive, sometimes lethal force against minority suspects are retaliating against not only a single suspect but also a class of people they deem responsible for a disproportionate amount of crime. In both cases, white men with power victimize the vulnerable in society.

Some shootings of suspects by police officers are fully justifiable. Shooting to protect oneself or others. Shooting a fleeing felon who poses a danger to the community. Shooting to neutralize a mass shooter. Such shootings are a necessary but tragic part of police work. Many of the shootings by police, however, do not have such justification.

Narcissism does not underlie all exploitative and retaliatory crimes. The individual who steals to feed herself or her family does so to meet basic human needs. She need not have a sense of superiority toward the victim or feel entitled to taking whatever she wants. Likewise, the individual who gets even with a dishonest contractor by posting negative online reviews need not be motivated by a fragile, threatened ego. The negative review may be one of the few acceptable ways to show disapproval and to try to prevent others from falling victim to an unscrupulous service provider.

Violations of fairness norms lie on a spectrum ranging from mildly annoying on one end to horribly devastating on the other. Those possessing the characteristics described in Chapter 2 commit these norm violations, some of which are unethical while others clearly violate criminal laws. An examination of some of these individuals and their unfair, offensive behavior will illustrate the harm they do to society.

CHAPTER 4

Narcissistic Crimes of Individuals

On June 15, 2013, sixteen-year-old Ethan Couch drove a pickup truck in Burleson, Texas accompanied by two friends. All were intoxicated. At one point in their drive, Couch went left of center, hitting another vehicle head-on. The four individuals in the other vehicle were killed. Couch's two friends sustained serious injuries.[1]

Evidence suggests that Ethan Couch was indulged by his parents. When he was only thirteen years old – too young for a driver's license – his parents permitted him to drive to his private school. When the school principal complained about the practice, Couch's father threatened to buy the school.[2]

After his arrest, Couch had to abide by several conditions including not drinking alcohol. He was subsequently captured on video partying with friends, clearly intoxicated.[3] To avoid further prosecution, Couch and his mother fled to Mexico. The Mexican authorities took them into custody and turned them over to American law enforcement.[4]

Ethan Couch's attorney employed the "affluenza defense," which argues that because his wealthy parents had failed to set appropriate limits on his behavior, he acted as though there were none.[5] This defense goes back at least as far as the infamous Leopold and Loeb case of the 1920s in which the two precocious, college-age men from well-off Chicago families tried to pull off the perfect murder of an innocent boy.[6] Couch's case was quite different; regardless, the judge accepted the defense.[7]

Whether Ethan Couch would be diagnosed with NPD is beside the point. His inferable sense of entitlement defines him as narcissistic, as do his irresponsible actions and his apparent lack of empathy or remorse. His actions were also criminal.

* * *

The present analysis conceives of narcissistic crime as the result of a sense of superiority and entitlement and a shortage of empathy that frees a social actor to engage in harmful exploitative or retaliatory offenses. It is a narcissism recognizable by professionals and laypersons alike. This view, while informed by the work of mental health professionals and behavioral scientists, goes beyond clinical distinctions and laboratory studies, broadening the concept to include offenders who might never qualify as having NPD or those who might not score high on subclinical narcissism. Their words and deeds demonstrate their narcissism.

Some of the crimes highlighted in Chapter 1, such as sex offenses and forms of deceit, took advantage of unsuspecting, vulnerable victims. Violent crimes including mass murder often represent attempts to get even with individuals or groups the perpetrators consider responsible for real or perceived transgressions. Chapter 2 discussed some of the traits and behaviors associated with narcissism, including exploitativeness and a tendency to retaliate. Chapter 3 discussed that of the array of available behavioral options, these two are particularly maladaptive and harmful. This chapter takes a deeper dive into some of the ways in which individuals who assume a narcissistic posture involve themselves in criminal and unethical acts.

4.1 Some Narcissistic Crimes of Individuals

Exploitative offenses, as discussed in Chapter 3, involve a social actor obtaining outcomes to which they are not entitled. These include garden-variety thefts such as shoplifting and burglary. Some offenders use deception to get what they want. They can also commit sex offenses through the violation of trust such as the crimes of Larry Nassar and Boy Scout leaders discussed in Chapter 1. In all such cases, the exploitative behavior and the sense of entitlement behind it link the actor to narcissism.

4.1.1 *Stephen Breuning, Eric Poehlman, and Their Research Fraud*

"Science," Nobel laureate Linus Pauling once reminded a politically driven world, "is the search for the truth."[8] To pursue specific truths, researchers collect and analyze data and then report their findings, generally in scientific or scholarly journals. Those working in the same field rely on these new findings as building blocks of knowledge placed upon the foundation laid by others in the past. In this way, contemporary scientists are said to stand on the shoulders of giants.[9]

Conducting publishable research has also become one way by which professors and researchers are evaluated in their jobs. Success in obtaining competitive grants to support their research is another metric.[10] Those who seek tenure and promotion know they must publish a threshold number of papers or books to earn a permanent position. Should they fail to publish the required amount of original work or work of sufficient quality, they may find themselves back on the job market. This structural requirement in academia, commonly referred to as "publish-or-perish," places untenured faculty members under pressure and thus may serve as a stressor.[11] The degree to which it does is a subject of ongoing debate.[12]

Most scholars and scientists respond to this pressure by producing publishable work. They allocate a portion of their work time to collecting and analyzing data and submitting their results for publication in refereed journals or other acceptable outlets. The editors of these journals enlist the assistance of referees,[13] scholars who volunteer their time to read and assess the scientific merit of the submitted work. If the work is sufficiently well-done, it will be recommended for publication. When the researcher has enough of these published papers to their credit, they qualify for tenure and promotion. Obtaining tenure should alleviate the anxiety associated with job insecurity.

As in many other occupations, it is possible for researchers to take ethical shortcuts in the pursuit of their goals. They can simply change values of the data that do not support their hypotheses.[14] Or, in more extreme cases, they can simply make up data from whole cloth. Others may deviate from accepted scientific practice by misappropriating the ideas or written work of others. All these constitute forms of research misconduct.[15]

Most of those who have been formally accused of research misconduct have made their way through graduate or professional school, earning a PhD, an MD, or some other advanced degree. Occasionally, research assistants or technicians engage in unethical practices, but most respondents, as those accused of research misconduct are called, hold advanced degrees or are on their way to earning them. Like Eric Noji, who was discussed in Chapter 1, they have demonstrated they can perform scientific and academic work. There should be no need to engage in dishonest behavior like plagiarizing or faking data.

For a long time, the scientific community played down the amount of research misconduct. Some analysts asserted that instances of research misconduct were the work of a few bad apples, whereas others feared that the known cases were just the tip of the iceberg.[16] In time, the number of cases proved to be greater than many observers thought. The blog *Retraction Watch* has followed retractions of published papers, many of which are flagged due to various irregularities including forms of research misconduct.[17] *Retraction Watch* maintains a database of such retractions, which number in the thousands.[18] So rather than just a few bad apples,[19] it seems as though this misconduct disease has infested much of the orchard.

As noted in Chapter 1, research misconduct can be charged as a crime, but relatively few cases have been prosecuted under federal or state law. When a scientist, working with the support of a federal grant, passes off bogus or plagiarized work through a scholarly publication or grant application, they have in essence made a false statement, prosecutable under federal law in the US. Whereas errant scientists once only had to worry about dismissal or debarment – the prohibition against engaging in federally funded research for a specified period of time[20] – they now know that a criminal conviction involving jail or prison time is a real, even if remote, possibility.

Whether charged as a crime or not, research misconduct results in real harm. If the research in question was supported by grants, some or all of that money is wasted. Those whose work is plagiarized or otherwise misappropriated may feel violated.[21] And the reputations of mentors and colleagues of the respondents may suffer collateral, reputational damage due to the scandal.

The research institutions in which scientific misconduct occurs bear a certain degree of responsibility for the wrongdoing of individuals in their employ. They set the standards that must be met for tenure, promotion, and other goals such as merit pay raises. While they place a great deal of emphasis on the goals successful researchers must attain, they traditionally have not put as much effort into supporting those researchers in attaining those goals. Some institutions, however, have developed mentoring programs for junior faculty to help them successfully navigate the first few years as an assistant professor.[22] Faculty and staff must undergo online training in the responsible conduct of research, but this requirement usually results from conditions placed on the institutions by federal funding agencies.[23]

Publish-or-perish may serve as a partial explanation for the research misdeeds of junior scholars. With family and the associated financial obligations, a young scientist lacking job security might cut certain ethical corners, rationalizing such behavior as a one-time departure from accepted practice that results in no real harm. Far less excusable is the fabrication of data or plagiarism by a well-trained or more senior scholar who has already successfully undergone the academic rites of passage to earn an advanced degree and an academic position. For such researchers, something else must explain their criminal behavior.

4.1.2   Stephen Breuning

Stephen E. Breuning was a thirty-four-year-old psychologist who conducted research on the psychotherapeutic effects of various drugs on developmentally disabled children, referred to in the 1980s as "mentally retarded."[24] Breuning held a faculty position at the University of Pittsburgh, and he served as assistant facility director at the Polk Center, then Pennsylvania's largest institution for the developmentally disabled. His research garnered a great deal of attention because it offered hope for thousands of afflicted children in the US and elsewhere.

Breuning's former mentor at the University of Illinois, Robert Sprague, became suspicious of his former student's research.[25] When the two were discussing the rate of agreement between two nurses collecting data, Breuning told Sprague that he achieved 100 percent, which is a virtual impossibility.[26] That boast prompted his former supervisor to dig deeper into Breuning's work. This confirmed his worst suspicions, and he reported them to the National Institute of Mental Health (NIMH), the federal sponsor of Breuning's research.

Once allegations were leveled, Breuning argued that he had in fact conducted the research in question. During a telephone interview, he said, "We vehemently deny the allegations and think they're patently untrue."[27] The evidence against him, however, was incontrovertible. The NIMH appointed a distinguished panel of experts to conduct an in-depth analysis of Breuning's work. As a result, the University repaid the grant money to the NIMH.

Of the many cases of research misconduct that have been brought against researchers, Stephen Breuning's is among the most egregious. His work involved the treatment of mentally disabled children, a particularly vulnerable subset of young people. His fictitious findings may have influenced their treatment.[28] Thus the potential harm reaches far beyond cluttering the scientific literature with meaningless research or the retraction of one or more papers; Breuning's bogus results very well could have hurt young, vulnerable patients.

The seriousness of Breuning's case resulted in federal prosecution. He eventually pleaded guilty and was sentenced to serve sixty days in a halfway house and was ordered to make restitution in the amount of $11,352. He also had to perform 250 hours of community service. Further, he had to agree to refrain from conducting scientific research for ten years. He was the first scientist known to have been convicted criminally for research misconduct.[29] At his sentencing, the judge said, "Fraud eats at the very guts of society."[30] The same could be said of the narcissism underlying the fraud.

Stephen Breuning, like the young Ethan Couch, may not have suffered from NPD. But Breuning's arrogance in thinking he could reap science's rewards without doing the appropriate work qualifies his behavior as narcissistic, as does his failure to take responsibility for his actions once he was formally accused. Breuning, much like Eric Noji, seemingly possessed both the native ability and the necessary academic training to do scientific research the way it should be done. He quite simply positioned himself above the rules and concluded he was entitled to engage in fraud to achieve his own professional ends. Further, his failure to consider the negative ramifications for the mentally disabled children who could be harmed by his criminal behavior bespeaks a complete lack of empathy.

4.1.3 Eric Poehlman

A few respondents have faked data or plagiarized over a period of months or years, wasting vast sums of money, causing reputational damage to numerous colleagues, and cluttering the scientific literature with meaningless papers. One such case is that of Eric T. Poehlman of the University of Vermont's College of Medicine, a full professor who was found to be involved in a long-term pattern of misconduct. In addition to the fabrication and falsification of which he was accused, Poehlman destroyed evidence of his misdeeds, failed to fully cooperate with investigators, gave false testimony, and even solicited others to provide false documents.[31] So, not only did Poehlman engage in research misconduct, but he also committed traditional offenses to cover his tracks and evade responsibility for his actions.

The seriousness of Poehlman's aggravating circumstances was matched by the Office of Research Integrity's formal response. Poehlman's was the first case of research misconduct in the US in which the respondent was banned from receiving federal funds for life.[32] Such a ban for a scientist signals the end of their career in research. "Preserving the integrity of the grant process administered by the Public Health Service is a priority of the Department of Justice," the US Attorney David V. Kirby was quoted as saying. "This prosecution demonstrates that academic researchers will be held fully accountable for fraud and scientific misconduct."[33]

Research misconduct is an offense of individuals. While structural features of academic science such as publish-or-perish pressure may in some cases play a contributing role, particularly in cases of early-career investigators with concerns about job security, individuals who position themselves above the norms of science and scholarship and the laws of relevant jurisdictions bear responsibility. Unlike organized crime wherein the illegal behavior of individual underbosses, caporegimes, and soldiers serves the goals of the larger enterprise, organized science gains nothing from individual acts of fraud and plagiarism. To the contrary, misconduct is antithetical to the search for the truth. And it frequently costs the institution dearly, as in the misconduct case involving Duke University, which was forced to pay the federal government $112.5 million.[34] The individual's behavior says, "I do not have to abide by rules or laws; I am above that." The person engaging in such entitled, exploitative acts behaves narcissistically, regardless of whether that label would have clinical support.

Box 4.1 Jonah and His Big Fish Stories

Between off-putting narcissistic behavior such as condescension and actual violations of the law lay a range of behaviors that, while not illegal, offend ordinary standards of honesty, fairness, and decency. The case of journalist Jonah Lehrer illustrates the relationship among narcissism, unfairness, and these objectionable behaviors. In 2011, it was discovered that Lehrer plagiarized writings in his blog posts and fabricated quotes by Bob Dylan in his book *Imagine*, which the publisher pulled from store shelves. Lehrer's narcissism was evident in his behavior as well as in the text of his post-fall-from-grace lecture. He told his audience, "My mistakes have caused deep pain to those I care about," and he suggested that a newly adopted system of organization should prevent future misdeeds.[1] The facts show that Lehrer did far more than make "mistakes." He violated not only journalistic ethics but also fairness norms by intentionally taking these shortcuts, exploiting, and betraying the trust of his readers, his publisher, and others by garnering outcomes he had not earned. His contrition was unconvincing.[2] Prior to his career in journalism, Lehrer worked in neuroscience at Columbia University where he earned his undergraduate degree. Had he committed these very same acts – plagiarism and fabrication – while doing scientific work under the support of a federal grant, he could have been charged with the crime of making false statements. In both scenarios the narcissistic behavior is the same; only the context differs.

---

[1] Schuessler, J. (2013). Plagiarism pays: Jonah Lehrer gets $20,000 for speech. *The New York Times*, February 12. http://artsbeat.blogs.nytimes.com/2013/02/12/plagiarism-pays-jonah-lehrer-gets-20000-for-speech/ Accessed 8-15-16.

[2] Bercovici, J. (2013). Jonah Lehrer thinks he can humblebrag his way back into journalism. *Forbes*, February 12.

Much of the literature on research misconduct and other questionable research practices implies that ignorance of, or inadequate socialization in, the practice and ethics of science and scholarship is partially to blame. Consequently, one way to remedy the problem consists of more training and education. Rehabilitative programs have even been developed to retrain errant researchers who have been referred by their respective institutions.[35] Eric Noji, Stephen Breuning, and Eric Poehlman, however, were well-trained in the conduct of scientific work. They knew the right way and the wrong way to do research. That they knowingly and willfully chose the latter suggests that they put themselves above the rules and norms governing science and scholarship. They attempted to exploit the system in which so many others follow the rules. Simply put, their attitude toward their professional obligations was narcissistic as was their behavior.

Research on research misconduct supports this role of a narcissistic posture. Allison Antes and her team found that narcissism was negatively associated with ethical decision-making in research.[36] In a study of Dutch scientists, Joeri K. Tijdink of Vrije Universiteit Amsterdam and his colleagues conducted a study in which they looked at personality in research misconduct involvement. They found that among senior researchers, narcissism was indeed associated with research misconduct.[37] Other research lends support to this connection. The author and his collaborators Kelly L. Wester and Bridget King conducted a survey of counseling academicians and discovered that narcissism and entitlement were related to irresponsible research behavior.[38] These findings strengthen the argument that some individual scholars and scientists who cut ethical corners do so because they feel entitled to science's rewards without doing the requisite work. Consequently, they exploit other individuals, their sponsors, and indeed the entire scientific community to achieve their ends.

The problem of research misconduct illustrates how structural factors can encourage individual narcissistic crimes. The world of scholarship offers an array of tempting rewards well beyond tenure and promotion. Endowed professorships with high salaries. Opportunities to consult and give speeches. Membership and officer positions in scientific or scholarly societies. Prestigious honors and awards. And for those willing to do the requisite work, they serve as motivators to do well. But for those who crave these rewards, and who feel superior and entitled, they may take ethical or legal shortcuts.

Box 4.2 The Curious Case of George Santos

The 2022 election in the US brought some new faces to the fore, one of whom was George Santos, who ran for a seat in the US. House of Representatives. Originally from Brazil, Santos moved to New York where he became involved in politics. Despite the fact little was known about him, he charmed Republican officials who advanced his candidacy for the 3rd Congressional District of New York. Before the election, but more aggressively after, journalists delved a bit more deeply into Santos's background. Among their discoveries was that his educational and work histories were fictitious. Officials in Brazil reopened an old fraud case against him. Federal and local prosecutors initiated separate investigations. Katty Kay, a BBC reporter and regular commentator on MSNBC's *Morning Joe*, said, "Last I looked up what it was to be a serial liar on this scale, it says you have to have a narcissistic personality disorder, which may be what Mr. Santos has, but it does look like he's going to get into office."[1] Santos was elected, and he ignored repeated requests to resign his new Congressional seat.[2]

As more revelations surfaced about his falsified background, many of his Congressional colleagues remained conspicuously silent. Speaker of the House Kevin McCarthy said that the matter should be left up to the voters in Santos's district. George Santos finally resigned and was later convicted and sentenced.[3] When it came time to report to prison, Santos announced in true narcissistic form: "I may be leaving the stage (for now), but trust me legends never truly exit."[4]

---

[1] Sheth, A. (2022). 'Morning Joe' blames George Santos' lies on 'Narcissistic Personality Disorder': 'That is a guy exhibiting some instability' *Y!Entertainment*, December 28. www.yahoo.com/entertainment/morning-joe-blames-george-santos-151346348.html Accessed 12-8-2024.

[2] Price, M. L. (2023). George Santos refuses to resign despite political pressure. *APNews*, January 11. https://apnews.com/article/politics-george-santos-b2bdca89d67a68343073048b 922cb4aa Accessed 6-1-2023.

[3] Katersky, A., Deliso, M. & Charalambous, P. (2025). George Santos sentenced to over 7 years in federal fraud case. ABC News, April 25. https://abcnews.go.com/US/george-santos-sentencing-federal-fraud-case/story?id=121126792 Accessed 6-1-2025.

[4] www.usatoday.com/story/news/politics/2025/07/25/george-santos-prison/8537035007/ Accessed 7-29-2025.

4.1.4   Lori Loughlin, Felicity Huffman, and the Varsity Blues Scandal

College has long been regarded as a ticket to a better job and a better future. Those with a college degree earn salaries nearly double those with only a high school education.[39] And so it is understandable why so many people work so hard to obtain a college education.

Among a subset of college-bound students, there has always been intense competition to gain entrance to elite universities. Harvard, for example, admits less than 4 percent of those applying.[40] The acceptance rate at the University of Michigan, a highly ranked state university, is only 18 percent.[41] Students who aspire to such selective schools know that they must have first-rate credentials to get serious consideration. High grade-point averages. AP courses. Strong ACT or SAT scores. Extracurricular activities. And, if an interview is required, a stellar one.

In 2019, a news story broke about a college admissions scheme in which affluent West Coast parents paid exorbitant sums of money to get their children into elite universities. The accused included actress Lori Loughlin, best known for her role in the successful sitcom, *Full House*, and her husband, fashion designer Mossimo Giannulli. They also included Felicity Huffman, another American actress well-known for her roles in *Desperate Housewives* and *American Crime*. This collection of frauds would become known as the Varsity Blues scandal.[42]

A subsequent investigation revealed that the scheme worked in two ways. One, which did not involve college officials, consisted of methods of generating ACT scores sufficiently high to meet the admission standards of the college in question. This could involve a confederate to sit in and take the entrance exam for the student, thereby guaranteeing a high score.[43] According to Mary Trump, Donald Trump's niece, her uncle enlisted a smart friend to take the admission test for him, which resulted in his ability to transfer from Fordham University to the University of Pennsylvania's prestigious Wharton School.[44] Such schemes have been used for decades.[45]

A second method relied on a university athletic department official who was positioned to recommend admission of an unqualified candidate, one with no athletic ability or experience. Thus the affluent offenders did not act alone. Facilitating the illegal admissions were co-conspirators who were willing to accept sums of money up to $450,000. This scheme involved falsifying photographic or video evidence of the applicant's alleged athletic abilities. In exchange for such a falsified, recommended admission, the college official accepted money under the table.[46]

When authorities caught wind of these schemes, they secured the cooperation of a co-conspirator who himself was facing federal charges. He agreed to wear a wire that would record a proposed criminal transaction. Those subsequently indicted for mail fraud and other crimes included thirty-three parents, as well as Yale University's women's soccer coach.

Lori Loughlin and her husband both received prison sentences.[47] The prominence they enjoyed as celebrities was insufficient to shield them from the legal consequences of their criminal behavior. Two others involved in the scheme, Gamal Abdelaziz and John Wilson, later met the same fate.[48] Felicity Huffman had to spend fourteen days in jail, serve one year on probation, pay a fine of $30,000, and perform 250 hours of community service.[49]

The Varsity Blues scandal contains several elements associated with individual narcissistic behavior. The parents all were very wealthy, some worth tens of millions of dollars or more. In the case of Lori Loughlin, part of her wealth derived from a career in show business in which she had enjoyed a great deal of attention for her looks and performances. As affluent, popular celebrities, these people had grown accustomed to getting what they wanted. In this case, they wanted their children to attend highly selective colleges. Admission, however, was not attainable through legitimate means such as strong high school grades and college admission test scores. The parents' behavior suggested that they felt entitled to obtain an outcome they and their children had not earned and did not deserve.[50] They engaged in exploitative, illegal behavior.

Box 4.3 "Predator in a White Coat"

Dr. Robert Hadden had long served as a gynecologist with Columbia University's Irving Medical Center and New York Presbyterian Hospital. Over more than thirty years, Dr. Hadden sexually assaulted hundreds of women and girl patients. His criminal behavior included groping breasts, digital penetration, and performing oral sex. One of his victims was Evelyn Yang, wife of 2020 presidential candidate Andrew Yang.[1]

In the words of US Attorney Damian Williams, "Under the guise of medical treatment, Robert Hadden sexually abused and assaulted numerous patients for approximately twenty-five years, exploiting them in vulnerable moments for his own sexual gratification."[2] He further labeled the defendant as "a predator in a white coat."[3] Hadden, who was sentenced to twenty years in prison, said, "I just want to say I am very sorry for all the pain I caused."[4] He also faced a lifetime of supervised release once he gets out. Like Larry Nassar, he behaved as though he was entitled to sexually exploit trusting female patients who existed to satisfy his perverse pleasures.

[1] Kennedy, M. (2020). Ex-Columbia University gynecologist accused of abusing dozens of patients is indicted. NPR, September 9. www.npr.org/2020/09/09/011122701/ex-columbia-university-gynecologist-indicted-for-allegedly-abusing-dozens-of-pat Accessed 12-11-2024.
[2] Meko, H. (2023). Doctor who abused women sentenced to 20 years imprisonment. The New York Times, July 25. www.nytimes.com/2023/07/25/nyregion/manhattan-gynecologist-sexual-abuse-hadden.html Accessed 12-11-2024.
[3] del Valle, L. (2023). Ex-Columbia University gynecologist sentenced to 20 years in prison on federal sex abuse charges. CNN, July 25. www.cnn.com/2023/07/25/us/robert-hadden-gynecologist-sentencing Accessed 7-19-2025.
[4] www.cnn.com/2023/07/25/us/robert-hadden-gynecologist-sentencing Accessed 7-22-2025.

Because of the number of actors involved, including those who played different but critical roles in the scam, it could be argued that the college admissions scandal constituted the work of a group, and not just solely an individual, crime. But the original intent – to gain admission to an elite school outside the regular, legitimate process – could have been accomplished with a far less elaborate scheme. Indeed, they used a proxy to take the required, standardized college admission test. Or one set of parents or a parent acting alone could have bribed an admissions official at the college of choice. The success of the scheme did not depend on a complex organizational structure.

College admissions fraud, much like research misconduct, does not drive the crime rate in the US. If a handful of unqualified wealthy kids gains entrance to elite colleges, Western civilization will not collapse. But if young people, enabled by entitled parents, use deceit to get into college, what might they do next? Cheat and plagiarize to get good grades while in college? Commit tax fraud or lie to consummate a business deal? Abuse power if elected to political office?

4.1.5   Jeffrey Epstein and Ghislaine Maxwell

Children, by definition, are vulnerable and incapable of making major life decisions by themselves. Consequently, parents and other caregivers often go to great lengths to protect them from the world. Sex offenses involving children, therefore, rank among the most reprehensible of crimes. One measure of their seriousness is how they are regarded even by hardened prison inmates.[51] Sexual crimes traumatize the victims physically, psychologically, and emotionally, so much so that some may never fully recover.

Jeffrey Epstein was a prominent financier who in 2005 was investigated for having sexually abused a fourteen-year-old girl. He subsequently was charged with and convicted of procuring a child for prostitution and soliciting a prostitute. His sentence included time in jail with work release.[52] To many, his lenient treatment for such a serious crime constituted a sweetheart deal. The criminal justice system's slap on the wrist arguably allowed him to continue his predatory behavior toward vulnerable girls.

Epstein took an interesting if unconventional path to success. Born in New York, he had an aptitude for mathematics. He attended, but did not graduate from, New York University. When he dropped out of NYU, he took a position in the banking industry. He would eventually start his own investment firm. In time, he attracted some very prominent clients, one of whom was Leslie Wexner, billionaire founder of The Limited and other successful clothing chains.[53] It is unclear exactly how, but Jeffrey Epstein became a wealthy man. His numerous money transfers, however, which passed through J. P. Morgan Chase, raised financial red flags.[54]

Throughout the years Jeffrey Epstein surrounded himself with other prominent friends and acquaintances, including not only Les Wexner but also former President Bill Clinton, future President Donald J. Trump, and Prince Andrew of the British Royal Family. His lavish parties frequently featured beautiful young women, some of whom were reportedly under the age of consent. Donald Trump was once quoted as saying about Epstein: "He's a lot of fun to be with. It is even said that he likes beautiful women as much as I do, and many of them are on the younger side."[55] And for Epstein's birthday, Donald Trump included a cryptic note inside the hand-drawn form of a woman's body, complete with breasts.[56] Whether Epstein's prominent guests knew about, or took part in, his trafficking and sexual abuse of girls may never be known.[57]

Epstein owned a mansion in Manhattan, which he purchased from his one-time friend and client, Les Wexner. He also owned Little St. James, a private island in the Caribbean where he and certain guests would travel to by way of his private jet. Both properties became crime scenes where he molested and raped dozens of underaged female victims who had been trafficked from the US and abroad. After Epstein faced charges in the early 2000s, Wexner disassociated himself from his former financial adviser.

Epstein had a collaborator in his sexual abuse of girls. Ghislaine Maxwell, his one-time girlfriend and close companion, would frequent locations where teenage girls would hang out. There she befriended the girls, many of whom were impressed by Maxwell's clothes, car, and polished demeanor. Some of the girls had vulnerabilities such as the recent loss of a parent or family financial stress. Maxwell played on these weaknesses, and once she had garnered the girls' trust, Maxwell would let them know that they could make good, easy money simply by massaging a male friend of hers.[58] Some were not interested, but others apparently thought the promised rewards were worth the type of work involved.

Once at Epstein's mansion, the girls would be asked to massage the middle-aged millionaire or his friends, who often would be clothed in little more than a towel or bathrobe. From there it was a short step to taking liberties with the girls by fondling their breasts or asking them to do more than a massage.[59] Epstein's and Maxwell's number of female victims has been estimated at over 1,000.

In 2019, Epstein once again faced criminal charges involving sexual activity with minors.[60] He was subsequently held in Manhattan's jail where he was found hanging in his cell.[61] His death was ruled a suicide despite widespread, conspiratorial rumors that he had been the victim of foul play to silence him. For her role in the trafficking of underage females for sexual purposes, as well as participation in their sexual assault, Ghislaine Maxwell was sentenced to serve twenty years.[62]

Jeffrey Epstein's and Ghislane Maxwell's narcissism told them that they were important enough to be entitled to whatever they wanted, including involuntary sex with adolescent girls. Even more tragically, one of their victims eventually took her own life,[63] and two others died from drug overdoses. Had Jeffrey Epstein lived, would he have been diagnosed with NPD? Perhaps, but his despicable behavior tells the story.

4.1.6 Donald J. Trump

Donald John Trump was born in the New York borough of the Bronx in 1946. His father, Frederick Trump, was a successful real estate developer. According to Donald's niece, Mary Trump, Donald's mother suffered from mental illness.[64] As a result, she could not play the nurturing role mothers typically play. This left a vacuum, which was filled largely by Donald's father, who by most accounts was a ruthless businessman who hated losing more than anything else. He would do whatever was required to succeed, regardless of the consequences to others. Fred Trump, Sr., thus became his son Donald's primary role model.[65]

Mary Trump further asserts that Donald was a bully as a child. He would pick on other kids and when one would stand up to him, he would run home in frustration.[66] Donald Trump arguably never grew out of the petulant, self-centered behavior that characterized him as a child.

Donald's father had made a great deal of money after World War II, which permitted the family to enjoy a lavish lifestyle. They lived in a comfortable home in Queens. Donald attended private schools and, upon graduation, entered Fordham University. After two years he transferred to the University of Pennsylvania, graduating from the prestigious Wharton School.

Upon graduation, Donald went to work for his father in the family real estate company. His father paid him a high salary, one that permitted him to live the life of a millionaire playboy. He made appearances at high-visibility venues such as New York's infamous Studio 54 and participated in numerous interviews with reporters during which he reinforced the growing public perception of him as a highly successful entrepreneur. His ghostwritten books, which included *Trump: The Art of the Deal*, became bestsellers and put him on talk shows. His persona and lifestyle projected the image of a confident, successful man.

Donald Trump undertook numerous business ventures, some of which straddled the line between unethical and illegal. One of these was Trump University, an unaccredited entity that offered workshops that, according to the hype, would impart Donald Trump's alleged business acumen to the students. Dissatisfied students lodged formal complaints about the program, and a lawsuit resulted in an award to bilked students.[67]

For several decades *Forbes* magazine annually published a list of the wealthiest Americans. According to a story published in *Fortune*, Donald Trump called *Forbes* and, disguising his voice, argued that his wealth was several billion dollars, which would guarantee him a prominent place on the list.[68] His ruse worked and *Forbes* put him on the list. The incident begs the question: What kind of person would want to be on the *Forbes* list under these circumstances?

Well before declaring his candidacy for the US presidency in 2015, Trump spent his lifetime in the public eye, first as a young business entrepreneur who as a member of New York's jet set dated beautiful

---

Box 4.4 Donald Trump and the Central Park Five

In 1989, a twenty-eight-year-old investment broker, Trisha Meili, was beaten and raped in Central Park. A group of five black and Hispanic teenaged boys were accused of the crimes. Donald Trump took out a full-page ad in *The New York Times* calling for their execution.[1]

After the boys had spent several years in prison, DNA evidence exonerated them. Despite this, Donald Trump never apologized for his error in judgment. In 2024, the five, now men, sued Trump for his disparaging remarks.[2]

Trump's behavior is consistent with insights from social-personality research: narcissistic individuals are less likely to apologize, even when they are wrong.[3] This narcissistic lack of empathy and contempt for people of color would manifest years later as President of the United States.

[1] Diaz, J. (2024). The Central Park 5 are suing Trump over Philly debate comments. *NPR*, October 21. www.npr.org/09/11/nx-s1-5108632/central-park-five-trump-debate Accessed 7-22-2025.
[2] Ibid.
[3] Leunissen, J. M., Sedikides, C., Wildschut, T. & Back, M. (2017). Why narcissists are unwilling to apologize: The lack of empathy and guilt. *European Journal of Personality, 31,* 385–403. https://doi.org/10.1002/per.2110

women, spent lavishly and garishly, and projected the image of success, all promoted in best-selling books. On his popular TV show, *The Apprentice*, Donald Trump gave hopeful entrepreneurs a chance to show off their business savvy by making strategic moves. Once they failed, Trump, the chief executive, ceremoniously told them, "You're fired," humiliating them in front of their *Apprentice* peers and a large TV audience. It was through *The Apprentice* and other public appearances that the future president garnered the admiration of countless fans. Trump looked successful. He boasted about his own success. Why would he not make a successful president?[69]

Before, during, and after Trump's appearances on his reality show, the public had opportunities for exposure to his personality. Ample evidence exists that the façade Donald Trump presented to the public was just that, a façade. The gambling casino he built in Atlantic City, New Jersey, was plagued with substantial cost overruns and scheduling delays. Trump may have subscribed to the old saw, "Build it and they will come." Well, they did not come. Trump's casino was a bust.[70] He was eventually forced to sell it at a significant loss even though he personally made millions.[71] The so-called successful entrepreneur Donald Trump had to declare bankruptcy six times.[72] His ex post facto rationalizations cast these decisions as savvy business strategies, that is, using available legal

---

Box 4.5 Where there's smoke…

When Donald Trump was running for president in 2016, The *Washington Post* published a video of Mr. Trump and TV host Billy Bush talking about women. During the now-infamous tape, Trump told Billy Bush, TV personality and nephew of the 41st President, that "…when you're a star, they [women] let you do it. You can do anything … grab 'em by the p***y. You can do anything."[1] Apologists for Donald Trump dismissed the remarks as nothing more than locker room talk,[2] suggesting that it is common for men to use such language among themselves.

As damning and disqualifying as many considered the video, Trump went on to win the election. The incident suggests that in the twenty-first century, certain powerful, narcissistic, white men in America can demean and exploit women without consequence. And they can even go on to become president.

[1] New York Times (2016). Transcript: Donald Trump's taped comments about women. *The New York Times*, October 8. www.nytimes.com
[2] CBS News (2016). I've never said I'm a perfect person, Trump says about lewd comments. *CBS News*, October 8. www.cbsnews.com/news/donald-trump-defends-lewd-2005-conversation-about-women-as-locker-room-banter/ Accessed 7-25-2025.

devices such as bankruptcy to minimize losses. But the truth suggests that the famous Wharton School grad had not inherited his father's business acumen, nor had it rubbed off during their years of working together.

Donald Trump's liabilities were not limited to business. Just before the presidential election of 2016, Trump's attorney, Michael Cohen, arranged for the payment of $130,000 to Stormy Daniels, a one-time adult film star who claimed to have had a sexual liaison with Trump. According to media reporting, Trump had slept with Daniels right after his wife, Melania, had given birth to their son, Barron.[73] Trump, of course, denied the affair.[74] His alleged behavior at the time was not criminal, but it spoke loudly about his character, or lack thereof. Trump's ardent supporters apparently considered their candidate's assets more important than his liabilities, and they voted him into the White House.

4.1.7   The Sexual Assault of E. Jean Carroll

Donald Trump's alleged sexual misadventures were much more serious than male locker-room talk. In November 2019, E. Jean Carroll, a former magazine editor, claimed in her memoir, *What Do We Need Men For?: A Modest Proposal*, that she had been sexually assaulted by Donald Trump. In 1995 or 1996, she had run into him at Bergdorf Goodman in New York. She further claimed that Trump asked her to accompany him to the lingerie department to help him pick out a gift for a woman. It was then, according to Carroll, that Donald Trump cornered her in a dressing room and sexually assaulted her.[75] According to Ms. Carroll, the assault did not involve sexual intercourse, but it did involve digital penetration. Carroll did not report the incident to the police, but she claims that at the time she did confide in a close friend.

In true Trump style, he denied knowing Ms. Carroll, despite the existence of a photo showing him and his former wife Ivana together with Ms. Carroll and John Johnson at a social gathering.[76] Also in Trump style, he told a reporter that "She's not my type."[77] Such a comment begs the question: Would Donald Trump have made a similar overture toward a woman who was his type?

The criminal statute of limitations had long passed, but Ms. Carroll was able to sue Trump in civil court under New York law. Donald Trump was ordered to pay Ms. Carroll $5 million.[78] When he failed to restrain himself and defamed her again, she took further legal action, and he was ordered to pay her an additional $83.3 million.[79] Trump appealed the verdict and in 2025, it was upheld.[80]

By both professional and lay assessments, Donald Trump possesses narcissistic traits, and he engages in narcissistic behavior.[81] As discussed in Chapters 2 and 4, many mental health professionals and laypersons alike consider Donald J. Trump the poster boy for maladaptive narcissism. He is arrogant and exhibitionistic. If criticized or insulted, instead of ignoring it or laughing it off, he openly seethes and plots his revenge. He constantly needs affirmations of his worth, and when they are not forthcoming, he supplies them himself, telling his audience that he is competent, the best dealmaker, and so on. He thus epitomizes the narcissistic leader.

Trump's narcissism, however, does not consist solely of harmless exhibitionism. Compelling evidence suggests he has engaged in sexual harassment and perhaps even sexual assault. He was found guilty of thirty-four felony counts of falsifying business records.[82] Trump's prominence, particularly since declaring his candidacy for president in 2015, spawned a cottage industry of dozens of nonfiction books by former colleagues, journalists, pundits, and academics, many of which include details of his alleged unethical and criminal behavior. If nothing else, these reinforce the connection between Trump's narcissism and his alleged wrongdoing.[83]

4.2 Conclusions

The literature on narcissism suggests that factors such as parenting style play a significant role in setting the stage for subclinical grandiose narcissism. Such studies confirm the common-sense conclusion that permissive parents fail to provide the necessary structure and discipline during the so-called formative years of a young person's life, thus setting the stage for entitled behavior once they grow up. Such is the case of Ethan Couch. It arguably occurred years earlier in the life of Donald Trump. This analysis, however, does not ground its arguments in either the clinical form of narcissistic personality disorder or the subclinical narcissism measured by the NPI and other psychometric instruments. The maladaptive narcissism connected to various forms of crime such as sexual assault and harassment and research misconduct shows itself in these harmful behaviors. And so it matters little if these offending individuals would score high on such measures; their narcissistic words and behavior tell the world that they pose a threat to civil society.

Some individuals who exhibit narcissistic traits and behaviors engage in acts defined in the law as criminal. They commit violent crimes such as sexual assault, physical assault, and murder, including mass murder, often to get even for real or imagined transgressions. And they also perpetrate crimes using various forms of deceit to take something to which they have no legal, ethical, or moral right.

The profile that emerges from the analysis is that of an individual possessing a sense of superiority and entitlement, permitting them to not only look down on certain others but also to feel entitled to ignore the rules and laws by which most people abide. Such an individual can take advantage of the inferiors, whether the goal is material goods, sex, or something else. Should the inferiors offend the narcissistic offenders, the latter will strike back with a vengeance.

Crimes highlighted in various media mirror the maladaptive narcissism. Whether a mass shooter bent on revenge or a Hollywood mogul determined to molest young actresses, these offenders express the worst that narcissism represents. It is through the analysis of high-profile crimes that the role of narcissism and narcissistic traits becomes clear. The influence of individuals assuming a narcissistic posture, unfortunately, does not confine itself to the infected individual. Others, including their victims and those who suffer collateral injury, sometimes transmit the virus. Witness the bullied boy who himself turns into a bully. Salvador Ramos, discussed in Chapter 1, was ridiculed by cruel classmates lacking empathy. In response, he struck back and joined the school shooters' hall of infamy.

History, including recent history, offers numerous examples of harmful individual narcissism. Robert Haddon, the New York gynecologist who molested dozens of female patients who had placed themselves in his care, betrayed not only his patients' trust but also his Hippocratic Oath to "first do no harm." And in the political arena, Donald J. Trump engaged in selfish, exploitative behavior in multiple ways, and when challenged, vented his narcissistic rage in verbal tirades, threatening social media posts, and retaliatory behavior. Narcissistic individuals operating on their own clearly can wreak a tremendous amount of personal and social damage. Some of the narcissists discussed in this chapter benefitted from the support of enablers who either proactively assisted the narcissist in their schemes or, knowing full well what was going on, sat by and did nothing. And sometimes organizations begin to take on narcissistic traits and behaviors. This different, higher level of narcissism and the crimes associated with it are the subject of Chapter 5.

Narcissistic Crimes of Organizations

Stone Foltz was a sophomore at Bowling Green State University (BGSU) in northwestern Ohio. As a Pi Kappa Alpha pledge, he knew that humiliation and degradation were part of the hazing process. On the night of March 4, 2021, the young man spoke with his parents on the phone and told them he was expected to drink alcohol. He was not looking forward to it.[1]

Foltz and other pledges were each ordered to drink what was later described as "a copious amount of alcohol." It was 750 mL. He did as he was told and then passed out. He was then taken to his apartment. A roommate later noticed that Foltz was unresponsive and a call was placed to 9-1-1. The operator asked about his condition and color, which the caller described as blue.[2]

Stone Foltz was rushed to the hospital, but he never regained consciousness. The Wood County coroner determined that Foltz's blood-alcohol content was .394, almost five times the legal limit to drive in the State of Ohio.[3] When Stone died, his parents honored his wishes and donated his organs so that others might live.[4]

As a result of Foltz's death, BGSU banned Pi Kappa Alpha from the campus.[5] The following month, the Wood County prosecuting attorney charged eight members of the fraternity with a variety of crimes including involuntary manslaughter.[6] A stupid fraternity prank had needlessly taken a life and ruined many others.

Officials held specific individuals responsible for the actions that led to the death of Stone Foltz. Even the fraternity was punished for its role. But behind preventable tragedies like this lies a history and organizational culture that has long supported dangerous traditions like hazing.

* * *

The traits and behaviors that define an individual personality can and do manifest in organizations. Because the term "personality" has for so long been associated with individuals, it is understandably difficult to picture an organization, whether large and multinational or modest and parochial, exhibiting characteristics like those associated with people. But the accumulating evidence suggests that not only do organizations possess personalities, they also engage in harmful acts. This chapter analyzes some of these organizations and the harm they have done.

5.1   Organizational Narcissistic Crimes

As they take on a narcissistic posture, organizations become increasingly capable of promoting or engaging in exploitative and retaliatory behavior. Some act with little or no empathy. This includes not only private corporations but also government agencies and nonprofit organizations. Perhaps surprisingly, it can include organizations that purportedly exist for the public good.

5.1.1   Fraternities

Near many colleges and universities in the US, visitors may encounter "fraternity row," one or more streets lined with imposing, mansion-like structures bearing oversized Greek letters. These stand apart from other off-campus housing. Frequently they have a stone or brick facade. Some have two- or three-story porticos supported by massive white columns. Most are well-maintained, and they often occupy higher ground. Their very countenance suggests they represent something special. Something exclusive.

Fraternities offer an alternative undergraduate lifestyle to male students who want it and whose families can afford it. They spare members the experience of living in drab, claustrophobic dorm rooms or seedy, campus-area apartments. During the college years they provide members with friends and an active social calendar.[7] More senior members serve as mentors and role models for younger members, helping them to navigate both academic and social life. Membership provides access to a variety of resources and activities unavailable to nonmembers. After graduation, these extended networks continue to serve members as they begin their careers and face future opportunities and challenges.

Most fraternities exist as nonprofit organizations. The official federal designation requires that the organization serve a fraternal function.[8] And to be sure, in addition to serving their members, many chapters of fraternities engage in fundraising for charities such as hunger, childhood diseases, and other worthy causes. The fraternity Kappa Alpha Psi, for example, committed to raising $2 million for the St. Jude Children's Research Hospital in Memphis, Tennessee.[9] Members of Pi Kappa Alpha raise nearly $2 million annually for philanthropic causes, and they donate more than 100,000 hours of community service.[10] In this way, the fraternities serve not only the members, but also the larger communities in which they are located.

Fraternities, however, exemplify organizations at risk of taking on a narcissistic posture. By their very nature, they convey the message that only a select few deserve membership and others do not. This exclusivity – their prerogative – projects an air of superiority. Highly selective fraternities occupy a position higher in the hierarchy than less-selective fraternities, which in turn sit above those not in fraternities. They are fundamentally narcissistic by design and function, admitting only a fraction of students who participate in "rush."

For Greek letter organizations, rush comprises the interview process. During rush week aspiring members visit the fraternities they would consider joining. Fraternity brothers meet the prospective members, chat with them, ask them questions, observe their appearance and behavior, and in other ways size them up. Would this young man be a good fit in our fraternity? Students who participate in rush face a brief period of uncertainty and anxiety until they learn their favored fraternities' decisions. It is then up to them to decide if they want to pledge.

For those who make the cut and accept the invitation, the next step in the process of initiation is hazing, a time-honored set of rituals associated with Greek life. The practice of hazing places pledges in a subordinate, even subservient, position to established fraternity members. Whether spoken or implied, this says, "We are up here, and you are down there, and therefore you have little demonstrated worth." To reinforce this stratification, hazing includes rites of passage intended to remind the pledges of their lowly position among their new brethren. Indeed, much of hazing is reminiscent of servitude or worse.[11] Scrubbing floors or toilets with a toothbrush. Carrying books or running errands for senior members. Tasks designed to demean and humiliate.[12] And frequently hazing involves drinking alcohol, large amounts of alcohol.

Drinking has long been associated with college fraternities and with college life in general.[13] Parties at which beer and other alcohol are available – commonly referred to as keggers – promote binge drinking.[14] The 1978 movie, *National Lampoon's Animal House*, which depicted a fictional fraternity in which partying had run amok, may not, for some fraternities, have been too much of an exaggeration.

Alcohol, as psychopharmacologists have long known, suppresses the inhibitory function of the human brain.[15] This increases the chances that the drinker will engage in risky and otherwise inappropriate behavior. Excessive amounts of alcohol, particularly higher-proof liquor, can also slow respiration to dangerously low levels.[16]

Such was the case of BGSU freshman Stone Foltz. His story, unfortunately, is only one of many in which hazing rituals resulted in the tragic death of a pledge. In just the 2010s, there were sixty-three hazing deaths in the US.[17] It is as though hazing, as potentially dangerous as it has been shown to be, is too time-honored and too important to rethink its place in Greek life.

The hazing deaths making the news reveal another narcissistic trait: a shortage of empathy. When Stone Foltz slipped into unconsciousness after downing an entire bottle of liquor, more than one "brother" walked by him without checking to see if he needed medical help. Some of this indifference could be chalked up to their own intoxication and inability to think clearly. This excuse cannot extend to everyone, and the failure to attend to Foltz and others similarly impaired bespeaks a lack of caring within the hazing process.

Once hazed and accepted as a full-fledged brother and awarded the fraternity's official imprimatur, members have access to the house's resources. These can include old term papers, past exams, and other study aids collected and archived by local members throughout the previous years.[18] The questionable fairness of such practices is likely rationalized; students outside Greek organizations could do the same if they so desired. The maintenance of exam and term paper files represents a deviant, exploitative, and arguably dishonest means of meeting college course requirements.

Just as drinking occupies a special place in college fraternities, so does sexual conquest. Young college women exist for one principal reason: sexual partners. Attending classes and studying may occupy much of the week, Monday through Friday, but the weekends are for fun, and fun includes hookups – casual sex without the formalities of dating.[19] The sense of entitlement implicit in the use of ethically questionable academic aids extends to sexual behavior. Members of fraternities, whether narcissistic before their indoctrination or not, gain exposure to the mindset that college women are there for their sexual pleasure.[20] Sexual conquest may not be a stated expectation in any fraternity handbook, but much like hazing, it is accepted and reinforced.

In an ideal world, the target voluntarily complies with the fraternity brother's advances. And there undoubtedly are many encounters where

---

Box 5.1 Collin's Law

In 2018, Collin Wiant, an Ohio University freshman, collapsed and died from drinking too much alcohol during a hazing ritual.[1] He had also inhaled nitrous oxide from a Whip-it cannister. Before the hazing, he texted his girlfriend: "I'm gonna rush the hardest frat. They have the hardest hazing but imma gonna do it."[2] His decision led to an unnecessary, tragic event that unfortunately has played out at numerous college campuses around the US.

In response to Collin's death, as well as that of Bowling Green State University student Stone Foltz, the Ohio General Assembly passed Collin's Law: The Ohio Anti-Hazing Act, a law designed to deter and punish instances of hazing on campus. It provides criminal penalties for those who engage in these practices on campus.[3]

Collin's Law may prevent future deaths due to hazing. At a minimum it will serve as a warning to those who engage in or support hazing in its most dangerous forms. Whether it does anything to improve the overall narcissistic culture of Greek letter organizations in Ohio seems less certain.

[1] Wagner, M., Sullivan, L. & Hendrix, S. (2019). Broken pledge: The fraternity hazing and death of Ohio University freshman Collin Wiant. *USA Today*, December 2. www.usatoday.com/in-depth/news/education/2019/12/02/ohio-university-frat-hazing-death-fraternity-sigma-pi-collin-wiant/4328634002/ Accessed 8-10-2025.
[2] Ibid.
[3] Wagner, M. & Hendrix, S. (2021). Collin's Law: aimed to deter hazing in Ohio, signed by Gov. Mike DeWine. Here's what to know. *Columbus Dispatch*, July 6. www.dispatch.com/story/news/2021/07/05/collins-what-know-ohios-anti-hazing-act/7842126002/ Accessed 11-06-2024.

---

this occurs. But should there be any possible resistance, the use of alcohol, drugs, or coercion may be permissible, particularly if the brother is impaired. The ends seem to justify the means. A California woman described one of her experiences as a college student: "In dark and beer-drenched rooms, the predatory culture was palpable. Men ogled and appraised us. They cornered women who stumbled in drunkenness. With lucid sneers, they groped and grinded on women who were half-responsive. Some had to be rescued from molesters by their friends."[21]

In the late summer of 2021, perhaps inspired in part by the #MeToo movement, several universities including Auburn University, the University of Kansas, the University of Nebraska-Lincoln, and the University of Massachusetts-Amherst experienced protests against the sexual assault of women and girls by members of Greek fraternities.[22] At Amherst College, one young woman claimed to have been "roofied," that is, had a drug slipped into her drink at a frat party. Fortunately, she was not sexually assaulted.[23] But too often sexually exploitative behavior by members of fraternities ends up costing the victims dearly.

Most universities have codes of conduct to which all students are supposed to adhere. Ohio State University, for example, has a written code
that not only covers general student expectations such as attending class
but also prohibited behavior including various forms of academic misconduct, acts that endanger others, and hazing.[24] On top of that, the federal
Title IX law, which "prohibits discrimination based on sex in education
programs and activities that receive federal financial assistance," ostensibly
offers another layer of protection for women in college.[25] Rules and laws,
however, may not be enough. The narcissistic culture that permits these
harmful behaviors may have to change.

Despite existing safeguards, colleges and universities have inadvertently
aided and abetted the sexual abuse of campus women. Universities, like
other organizations, have multiple reasons to protect their reputations
against ugly incidents and the bad press they bring. As might be expected,
university officials prefer not to have the negative publicity associated with
an alleged sexual assault, especially one involving a prominent fraternity.
The history of sexual assault by members of fraternities tells victims that
seeking justice involves a costly, uphill battle. Some victims who choose to
speak out soon learn that the sexual assault itself is just the beginning of
their victimization.

One of the keys to understanding the connection between narcissism
and sexual aggression lies in the sense of entitlement. Individuals in dyadic
relationships in which there exists the potential for sexual activity typically
negotiate such exchanges. Each partner may wonder if or when a sexual
liaison will take place between them, but it is not necessarily automatic or
expected. The topic is broached and both parties come to an agreement.
Individuals behaving narcissistically, in contrast, enter such a relationship
with the expectation that the other partner will accede to their sexual overtures. Entitlement, by its very nature, preempts the relevance of the other
party's input. It permits the aggressor to treat sex much like other goals
that will enhance the status of the narcissist. A starring role in a play.
Sexual conquests. Both present opportunities for the narcissist to reinforce
to others their specialness. And research confirms the connection between
entitlement and sexual aggression.[26]

Fraternities illustrate the slippery slope created by being part of an
exclusive group. It sets the stage for feelings of superiority and entitlement.
In the case of fraternities, entitlement to good grades is easily obtained.
Entitlement to drunken partying. Entitlement to sex, even if not given
voluntarily. And entitlement to exemption from the administrative and
legal consequences others would likely face for the same harmful conduct.

Social dominance orientation (SDO), a concept popular in psychological research, may help explain the thinking and behavior of fraternity members. SDO conveys the belief of individuals that their in-group is superior to other groups.[27] It has been applied to various social groups and issues including fraternities. Members of fraternities score higher on SDO than those who are not members.[28] This suggests that fraternity members do indeed consider their social group superior to others, a finding that undoubtedly confirms the suspicions of many.

Greek organizations have a long and storied history in the US. Some chapters go back almost as far as the institutions themselves. Some of the most accomplished American men had fraternity membership as part of their undergraduate college experience including Warren Buffett, Michael Jordan, Robert Kraft, and Mike Pence.[29] Multiple generations of college students have enjoyed the camaraderie and fellowship these organizations offer. These young men form bonds with their fraternity brothers that can last lifetimes. Surveys of fraternity members suggest they benefit from the experience.[30] And research shows that membership translates into greater career earnings,[31] providing an additional incentive for male students to participate. They also have a long history of service.

Their history, unfortunately, has permitted an insidious change to take place. Among the benefits that fraternities offered were academic aids that straddled lines between ethical and unethical conduct. Rather than simply innocent weekend dates, sorority members and other campus women became viewed as sexual partners to which fraternity brothers are entitled. And hazing, a ritual that has long enjoyed support, has gone from demeaning to dangerous to deadly.

Individual fraternity members participate in hazing rituals, encouraging and coercing pledges to engage in humiliating and risky behavior. Individual members also take sexual advantage of defenseless, sometimes impaired young women. And sometimes individual members must face the legal and other consequences of their behavior. But over time these Greek letter organizations inadvertently reinforced these behaviors by permitting such traditions to be handed down to successive generations of members and by giving them tacit approval. In playing this role, the organization itself becomes a narcissistic offender that engages in behavior designed to protect its image. Leadership knows these practices occur, and the failure to take purposive action to prevent future occurrences makes them complicit in the narcissistic crimes of their members.

The individual chapters at various colleges and universities do not operate in total isolation. Virtually all have a national organization to which they are connected and beholden. Communication and money flow bidirectionally. This relationship reinforces the organizational nature of fraternities as well as their size and reach. When an incident occurs, such as a hazing that turns deadly or an instance of alleged sexual assault, it necessarily involves both the chapter to which the specific incident is linked and the national organization whose reputation and financial health might depend on the disposition of, and publicity about, the incident. Consequently, the national organization has more than a vested interest in safeguarding both its reputation and its financial future.

If the organization denies the allegation, maintaining instead that the victim's irresponsible choices led to their involvement in the incident, its behavior suggests narcissism. Any accusation leveled against the organization or its members represents a form of narcissistic injury. How dare someone accuse such a staid, storied institution with a history of service and a long list of accomplished members? Given the litigiousness in modern society, the allegations of sexual assault by a college woman must be an attempt to make a quick buck from an organization perceived to have deep pockets. The victim of alleged sexual assault is transformed into being the instigator, if not the offender. And thus what began as a crime by a member of a local chapter morphs into a gross miscarriage of justice against an organization with an unblemished reputation.

5.1.2   White Supremacists

White supremacists, also referred to as white nationalists,[32] can trace their history back more than 150 years. The Ku Klux Klan and other similar groups opposed freedom for black slaves and thus targeted blacks for discrimination, threats, and violence. Over time the groups they hated expanded to include other people of color, Jews, and members of the LGBTQ+ community. Their identity and activities announced that whites and whites only deserved privileged status in America. In the 1960s, after the senseless, brutal murders of three civil rights workers in Mississippi, the federal government was finally forced to investigate and prosecute Klan activities.[33] These efforts led to several convictions, but white supremacy and the underlying sentiments that motivated them remained alive and relatively well, even if forced into the shadows.

The period between President Lincoln's Emancipation Proclamation and the passage of the Civil Rights Act of 1964 – an entire century – gave white supremacists in America the time and freedom to organize and terrorize with relative impunity. That it took so long for federal and state governments to finally push for meaningful legislation speaks loudly about the national posture toward blacks and other non-white, non-Christian populations. In the intervening 100 years, white supremacists committed an almost incalculable number of crimes of racial violence against their so-called enemies and faced little reckoning for most of it.

By the late twentieth century, the crimes of white supremacists were deemed so vile that they helped spawn a new category of crime: hate crime. Ordinarily, crimes require *actus reus*, that is, the actual act of committing a crime.[34] Legislators typically do not add a motivation such as "revenge murder," "spiteful vandalism," or "lust rape." It is only necessary that the charged individual committed the prohibited act. Why, then, should legislators add "hate" crimes?

The arguments for the addition of hate crimes, however, require a different kind of reasoning. In cases involving the murder, assault, or intimidation of certain classes of people such as racial, ethnic, or religious minorities, or those of sexual identities, the offense is not solely against the individual victim but against the class of individuals of which the victim is a member. And whereas the robbery of a convenience store clerk victimizes primarily just one person, the perpetration of a so-called hate crime targets not only the victims but also the entire class of people they represent. When the members of an entire class of victims become the target, it takes on greater seriousness. In fact, given the damage they do to the social fabric, hate crimes are arguably offenses against all citizens.

To hate the members of a class of people so much as to commit crimes of vandalism and violence against them implies that they are somehow inferior to those carrying out the crimes. The white supremacist who paints a swastika on the house of a Jewish family is saying that not only is the family unwelcome in the community, but it is also somehow inferior to Christians and therefore deserves a fate such as that suffered by Jews at the hands of Nazis. Such crimes are not instrumental; there is no material yield. They involve physical or psychological harm or property damage, and they send a message of narcissistic superiority by way of retaliation.

Hate crimes have been around long enough for officials to track trends in statistics. The data indicate that in the twenty-first century, hate crimes are on the increase.[35] What remains unknown is whether individuals with a sense of superiority are committing more offenses or whether there is greater awareness of such crimes. Regardless, the number of incidents has been on the rise, and a democratic nation should take notice.

Many white supremacists find their motivation to hate in the great replacement theory, the conspiratorial belief that Jews are orchestrating an attempt to replace whites in America with people of color.[36] This in turn will enable the Jews to assume power through sympathetic voters. As a result, white Christians will become a powerless minority.

As expected, some white supremacists become involved in criminal behavior, and thus prisons have become heavily populated with them. Some have been convicted for hate crimes, but most often they have been sentenced to prison for other felonies such as robbery, aggravated assault, or the sale of drugs. In fact, prisons became one of the safe havens for white nationalists and for good reasons.[37] Inasmuch as American correctional institutions house black inmates out of proportion to their representation in the general population due to mass incarceration, the white supremacists behind bars had convenient captive enemies to hate. White inmates banding together under the aegis of white supremacists, neo-Nazis, or some similar banner also offered members some measure of protection against violence by inmates of color. And so correctional facilities have played an unintended role in stoking the flames of white supremacy.[38]

Several hundred white supremacists went to prison as the result of their participation in the events of January 6. When they converged on Washington, DC, on January 6, 2021, they may have come across to TV viewers as a cross-section of conservative Republicans who genuinely believed the election had been stolen from their president. But as the FBI and other law enforcement agencies began to collect intelligence and evidence, aided by citizens who helped identify the accused in photos, the picture that came into focus was one of a well-organized, coordinated attack by established groups of white nationalists.

In Donald Trump, white supremacists seemed to find a sympathetic president. He implicitly denigrated certain segments of the population. He did not aim his remarks at Jews. After all, his son-in-law, Jared Kushner, was Jewish, as was the Trump Organization's longtime, trusted chief financial officer, Allen Weisselberg. And he showed support for Israel and its controversial prime minister, Benjamin Netanyahu.[39] But Donald Trump's apparent courting of white nationalists had the unintended, though predictable, consequence of fanning the flames of antisemitism in America. Did Donald Trump think he could give white nationalists a megaphone and they would somehow set aside their enmity for Jews? Perhaps his thinking about such matters did not run that deep? Or did he not care? Regardless, antisemitic sentiments among white supremacists grew during Trump's terms in office and some of that can be laid at his doorstep.

Donald Trump did not create the Proud Boys, the Oath Keepers, and other white nationalist groups. These organizations existed well before he descended the gold escalator in Trump Tower to announce his candidacy in 2015. But when asked to disavow white nationalists, Trump famously told them to "Stand back and stand by."[40] In doing so, these and similar right-wing organizations may have thought they were being given tacit permission to come out of hiding and make public their hatred of Jews, minorities, immigrants, and the LGBTQ+ community. With the president's official blessing, such groups became emboldened to the point of attending public events en masse and intimidating peaceful demonstrators and other citizens.[41]

Groups like the Proud Boys and the Oath Keepers are both nationalistic and narcissistic. Their members consider themselves superior to those who are non-white and non-Christian. As a result, they look down on blacks, Latinx and other non-white immigrants, Jews, and others. Their verbal and physical attacks are retaliatory as they represent attempts to get even for the damage the undesirables have done to what they consider mainstream, white American culture, a culture that belongs to them. Their attack on the US Capitol has an exploitative element, that is, an attempt to take what they wanted – a Republican presidential win – without having garnered the necessary votes.

The SDO, used to explain the mindset and behavior of fraternity brothers, has applicability to white supremacists. Those who consider themselves superior to people of color, non-Christians, immigrants, and the LGBTQ+ community have concerns that their preferred way of life is slipping away.[42] It is only by speaking out against these undesirables and, if necessary, engaging in violence that those to whom America rightly belongs can preserve their society. Research reveals that those holding white supremacist views score significantly higher on SDO.[43]

White supremacists have been in America well before the Civil War, and events of the early twenty-first century suggest they have only grown in number and sophistication. They have also been responsible, individually and collectively, for various forms of criminal activity. What Donald Trump did through his pronouncements and tweets was to send them a signal that he empathized with their disgust over the browning of America and, that as their president, he would work on their behalf to change it.

5.1.3 Police

Not long after the May 2020 killing of George Floyd in Minneapolis, the Atlanta police responded to a Wendy's restaurant where a patron at a drive-through appeared to have passed out. While he was still in his vehicle, officers approached him. Rayshard Brooks informed them that he had consumed a couple drinks but was not bothering anyone. The officers decided to take him into custody. After removing Brooks from his car, they attempted to place him in handcuffs. He resisted, which prompted one of the officers to draw his taser to subdue him. Brooks wrested the taser from the officer and tried to use it on him instead. This action prompted the officer to draw his handgun. Brooks freed himself and attempted to flee at which time he was shot in the back. He died from his wounds.[44] His original offense appears to be that he was intoxicated at a Wendy's restaurant. Rayshard Brooks was black.

In December 2020, Columbus, Ohio, police officers received a report of a suspicious person. When they arrived at the scene, the officers went to the front door of the house to speak with the occupant. About the same time, a black man made himself visible in the open garage. When he saw the officers, he held up his cellphone. Officer Adam Coy fired several shots at the man who collapsed just outside the garage. Despite the man's serious wounds, several minutes elapsed before anyone at the scene attempted lifesaving measures. Andre Hill, who was simply leaving a friend's house, died from his wounds.[45]

These instances, like the many others that helped inspire the Black Lives Matter movement, represent an all-too-frequent outcome of police encounters with black citizens, and they appear to have several elements in common. White police officers respond to an alleged crime or suspicious activity involving a black person, most often a male. In most cases, the individual is unarmed. The suspect often takes no action that should be interpreted as threatening to life or limb. Nevertheless, the police use force, which results in the individual's death.

Police departments exist to "protect and serve" the public, much like fire departments and emergency medical services[46] They respond to calls for service such as reports of crimes and accidents. In between these calls, officers stay on the lookout for violations of laws, and they interact with and assist local citizens. And in the process, they frequently face life-threatening danger. In 2024, 102 law enforcement officers in the US died in the line of duty.[47] When Trump supporters marched on the Capitol on January 6, dozens of Capitol Police tried valiantly to hold them back.[48] Many of these officers sustained serious injuries, and several lost their lives. This example and countless others illustrate the many ways in which law enforcement officers dedicate their lives to keeping American communities safe.

So given this mission to protect and serve, why does there seem to be so many instances of minorities being killed or injured by police for what appears to be little or no justification? Why have so many of these incidents taken place that it gave rise to a major social movement? A reasonable conclusion after analyzing individual incidents would be that law enforcement agencies have among their ranks officers who hold racially prejudiced attitudes. After all, if racist individuals are normally distributed in the population – as they are found in many families, in neighborhoods, in the workplace – it would be unsurprising to find them among the ranks of police officers.

Many of these minorities in the community seem to be disproportionately involved in criminal activity, particularly in socially disadvantaged areas of big cities. It is a reality to which police are exposed every day. Blacks are arrested disproportionately to their representation in the population. The possible logic of police has a certain transitivity to it. "In my job I interact with a lot of black people. Most of the black people I interact with are involved in criminal activity. Most black people, therefore, are criminals. After all, prisons are full of black criminals."[49] Such a conclusion, while simplistic, would only reinforce the belief that blacks are not only dangerous, they are inferior. And inferiors do not deserve the respectful treatment given to law-abiding whites.

Police in the US also have unique protections that may reinforce narcissistic superiority and entitlement. Qualified immunity gives officers some legal protection from being sued for actions they take in the performance of their duties.[50] Ordinarily, civil suits would be one mechanism by which victims of inappropriate police use of force could achieve some measure of justice. Qualified immunity, in the eyes of critics, puts police officers above the law, signaling to them that they can use excessive force without facing legal consequences.

Police unions serve as another layer of protection for officers accused of using excessive force. They began with organizing their members for the purpose of increasing wages and benefits and improving work conditions, much like unions associated with truckers, pipefitters, teachers, and other occupations. And for a long time, police unions functioned in this way. Over time, however, police unions moved into realms traditionally the province of police management, such as weighing in on whether officers' behavior warrants discipline.

In the aftermath of an officer-involved shooting (OIS), the local police union represents the officer involved. They often take the part of the accused officer, stating publicly that the killing, while an unfortunate event, was both reasonable and within departmental guidelines and therefore justifiable.[51] They accompany the officer during department interviews. The union's lawyers advise the officer on what to say and what not to say. Officers in the US are socialized to have their union representative present throughout the OIS investigative process. As law enforcement has come under increased scrutiny for its sometimes-questionable interactions with the public, the police unions work hard to defend their members against accusations, even those that appear to be well-founded. In Philadelphia, the police union president called those protesting an OIS "rabid animals," perhaps because they were outside the officer's home.[52] Whether intentional or inadvertent, police unions may frustrate accountability by treating OISs as though they are, prima facie, justified. This may come across to those who accuse their members of inappropriate behavior as a counterattack in response to a narcissistic injury.

Certain other features of the local criminal justice system sometimes shield police from accountability. Local law enforcement works closely with prosecutors, handing off felony cases after arrest and investigation. This relationship, if not an outright conflict of interest, gives the appearance of one.[53] The local prosecuting attorney investigates the incident. In some cases, the officer or officers involved lose their jobs, but rarely do they face prosecution. One cannot help but wonder if the close relationship police officers enjoy with prosecutors compromises the objectivity of the latter in cases of OIS.

Social dominance orientation, which offers insights into the thinking and behavior of fraternities and white nationalists, has applicability to why police seem to be involved in so many incidents in which minorities are killed or otherwise brutalized. SDO conveys that some people belong to groups that consider themselves superior to certain others in society, such as immigrants and people of color. Since the development of the SDO measure, researchers have explored its connection with police officers and have found that they score significantly higher than other criminal justice actors.[54] This suggests that among police there may be officers who consider themselves superior to those they police, minorities in particular.

The implication is that those of inferior status deserve fewer rights and privileges than those of higher status, particularly those who are white. Once the inferior status of a minority group has been conferred, it becomes easier to rationalize their mistreatment. "These inferior black criminals should obey my commands. If they refuse or resist, I have the right to retaliate with force, including lethal force, if I consider it necessary."

An incident or two of this kind might suggest that the law enforcement officers, thinking their lives are legitimately in danger, acted appropriately and without prejudice. But the weight of dozens of such cases points to a systemic problem, one reinforced by structural racism in American society.

The police killings of unarmed blacks send several unmistakable messages. One is that many working in law enforcement seem to relegate people of color to a position below their white counterparts. Having successfully done so, they can justify using force – even excessive or lethal force – to prevail in an encounter. Police culture is largely supportive of this approach, vigorously defending accused officers in most cases. It is only when such cases become public, through available video footage, that there is some reckoning for the harm done. Otherwise, such instances go down as justified or as "mistakes," which happen sometimes while maintaining public safety. And the police culture that tacitly supports the extrajudicial killing of blacks merely reflects the widespread racism that permeates contemporary society.

Law enforcement officers play an indispensable role in maintaining order and ensuring public safety. The job involves inherent risks, and

---

Box 5.2 The Ordeal of Tyre Nichols

On January 7, 2023, Tyre Nichols, a twenty-nine-year-old black man, was pulled over in his car by Memphis police. Video from the officers' body cameras and from a security camera affixed to a pole captured several officers from the Memphis Police Department pulling Mr. Nichols from his vehicle and wrestling him to the pavement. Officers yelled for him to get on the ground, even though he was clearly there. Nichols briefly got away from the officers who eventually recaptured him. It was then that they began beating him, kicking him, and spraying him with teargas. At one point in the video, Nichols could be calling for his "Mom." The officers were all black men.[1]

Paramedics arrived on the scene, but it was some time before they rendered any medical care. Mr. Nichols was transported to the hospital where he lingered for three days before he died.

The five officers, who were members of a Scorpion unit developed to address violent crime, were fired. All five were also charged with several crimes including second-degree murder and kidnapping.

Inasmuch as the officers were also black, something other than simple racism by white officers underlies all cases of police killing minorities. Could narcissism influence not just white officers, but the entire culture of law enforcement agencies? If so, could this culture cause black officers, like their white counterparts, to consider themselves superior to those they police?

[1] Rojas, R. & Jaglois, J. (2023). Memphis police kept clubbing as Nichols screamed, "Mom, Mom, Mom." Here's the latest. *The New York Times*, January 27. www.nytimes.com/live/2023/01/27/tyre-nichols-memphis Accessed 12-12-2024.

Box 5.3 The Triangle Shirtwaist Factory Fire of 1911

In the early 1900s, factories that produced clothing employed hundreds of mostly young women who worked in large buildings. One such business was the Triangle Shirtwaist Factory located in New York's Greenwich Village. The owners of the factory, aware that employees would sneak out and take breaks, locked the doors to prevent this practice. In 1911, a fire started in a bin of discarded fabric, quickly spreading throughout the multi-storied building. Unable to escape the smoke and flames, many employees made it to windows and jumped to avoid burning to death. The fire department responded and eventually extinguished the fire, but many employees perished.[1]

The victims of the Triangle Shirtwaist Factory fire deserve mention for several reasons. Most were women who worked under harsh conditions at low wages. They labored long hours with few breaks for food or comfort. Women, particularly immigrant women, had few options at the time. In the wake of the tragedy, their surviving families received paltry payouts. These facts reinforce that the work and lives of women had little worth at the time. It seems as though they were, in the eyes of narcissistic business owners who felt little empathy, inferior human beings who could be exploited and were expendable.

[1] No author (1911). The calamity. *The New York Times*, March 26. https://timesmachine.nytimes.com/timesmachine/1911/03/26/104859767.html Accessed 11-20-2024.

---

ordinary citizens should appreciate the many ways police serve their respective communities. That they are valued and respected does not make them immune to scrutiny and criticism. The periodic killing of minorities, many of whom are unarmed, suggests that racial prejudice plays a role in these tragedies. If some officers come to the job already feeling superior to people of color, frequent contact with minorities who break the law likely reinforces such feelings. Once a critical mass of like-minded individuals assumes their duties, a culture can develop in which racially motivated shootings occur, are rationalized, and are defended.

5.1.4   *The Trump Organization*

Frederick Trump started what would be the Trump Organization in the 1930s. He built houses in the borough of Queens and later benefited when the Federal Housing Administration permitted him to build more homes in Brooklyn.[55] During World War II, he built housing for naval personnel and after the war built numerous apartment buildings in Brooklyn.

Fred had two sons, Fred, Jr., and Donald, as well as two daughters. Fred Jr. had no interest in his father's real estate business; he instead wanted to become a pilot. This, of course, was a huge disappointment to his father, who, once aware of his namesake's aspirations, basically wrote him off.[56] It would thus be up to Donald to carry on the Trump real estate dynasty.

Fred Trump had amassed a considerable fortune in real estate holdings, and Donald, who joined the company in 1968, intended to build on the foundation created by his father by acquiring, developing, managing, and selling commercial properties. In time, Donald would branch out into other endeavors, but real estate would remain the core of the Trump Organization.

The Trump Organization, like other companies in the real estate business, entered into contracts with a variety of service providers. Builders. Electricians. Plumbers. Concrete specialists. Arrangements with such providers imply good faith, and they legally require both parties to do what was agreed. At various points during his tenure as head of the Trump Organization, Donald reportedly reneged on multiple contracts.[57] Rather than sue the Trump Organization, many such contractors simply wrote off the losses, knowing that a protracted legal battle could cost them even more. This behavior, if true, represents exploitative behavior that does real harm to others.

Once Donald Trump became the 45th president, he handed the reins of the Trump Organization to his children, specifically Donald Jr. and Eric. President Trump claimed that he no longer had any role in the family business. Given the myriad ways he has trampled on norms, it strains credulity to believe that he truly let go of those reins. In fact, as president, Trump engaged in several practices that suggested he used his new role to generate additional income streams for the Trump Organization. Secret Service agents, as one example, stayed in Trump properties.[58] Thus each of his many trips to his various properties became income-generating opportunities for the company he claimed he had stepped away from.

Well before he became the 46th US President, Donald Trump had the reputation, deserved or not, of disliking minorities. He had openly condemned the Central Park Five. The Trump Organization allegedly engaged in various kinds of discriminatory housing practices.[59] It is a theme that would rear its head again and again.

As discussed in Chapter 2, management experts Dennis Duchon and Michael Burns delineate two kinds of narcissistic corporations: those with high self-esteem and those with low self-esteem.[60] The former, much like the individual possessing narcissistic traits, exudes confidence born of competence. The latter, on the other hand, know they are not among the best, and thus their thin skin is easily penetrated by criticism and other narcissistic injuries. The Trump Organization had all the hallmarks of a narcissistic organization with low self-esteem. Such traits also make them more vulnerable to unethical business practices.

It is difficult, if not impossible, to separate Donald J. Trump from the Trump Organization. For one, the Trump Organization has never been a large, multi-layered conglomerate. Most of its officers are family members, and the rest of the table of organization consists of a very few trusted staff.

Social dominance theory, useful in explaining the narcissistic behavior of fraternities, white supremacists, and the police, likely has little to offer in understanding the maladaptive behavior of the Trump Organization. A group of researchers at Stanford University and the University of California at Berkeley have studied the effects of narcissistic leadership on the organizations they lead.[61] They make a convincing case that narcissistic leaders can lead organizations down a dark path toward legal vulnerability and worse. Donald Trump is such a leader.

5.2   Conclusions

There appear to be two paths an organization can take toward involvement in narcissistic crime. The first, elucidated by organizational psychologists, places primary responsibility on a narcissistic leader. This individual creates the organization in their image, infecting all layers in the hierarchy with narcissistic traits and behaviors that express themselves in what the organization does, some of which may be harmful. And organizations, by virtue of their extended reach, generally can do more harm than any one individual.

Law enforcement organizations illustrate the transformation of a government organization whose mission includes serving and protecting to one comprised of a critical mass of individuals who have as part of their personality baggage a sense of superiority toward people of color, a shortage of empathy, and a willingness to retaliate toward those who challenge their power and authority.

The mounting evidence points to leadership. Business schools, the training centers for tomorrow's corporate leaders, have an understandable interest in exploring ways in which corporations start, how they grow, how they behave, and even how they die. This natural analogue to the life course of a human raises several questions: Do complex organizations such as private corporations possess personalities like people? If so, how do these personalities express themselves? What role does the CEO play in shaping the personality of the corporation they lead?

Just as orchestras need conductors to guide the strings and the woodwinds and the percussion through a complex piece of music, large organizations need their conductors to coordinate the work of various divisions in meeting organizational goals. The thought of CEOs conjures up luminaries of the past such as Lee Iacocca of Ford and John DeLorean. Leaders who were well-educated, seasoned, and who led their respective corporations to attain record-breaking profits. Silicon Valley entrepreneurs such as Steve Jobs, Mark Zuckerberg, and Elon Musk have melded intellect and creativity with business acumen to become billionaires whose influence would be felt around the globe.

Business researchers who have studied corporations and their respective leaders have noticed that some of them, just like people outside the world of business, show evidence of narcissistic traits and behaviors. They reveal that they enjoy being in the limelight. They boast about themselves and their accomplishments. They exhibit arrogance and a sense of superiority. Their words and actions suggest a sense of entitlement. These and other indicators paint a portrait of a narcissist.

The concept of an organization having a distinct personality may be difficult to grasp, but when one looks closely at their structure and actions, these parallel the traits and behaviors of individuals. But the analysis of corporations, government agencies, and nonprofits points to features that can be used to set apart those that abide by laws, administrative rules, and ethical standards from organizations that flaunt such conventions.

The arrogance and sense of superiority people associate with narcissistic individuals manifests in organizational decisions and public statements. It may also take the form of exploitative or retaliatory behavior toward competitors, customers, or the public. This organizational narcissism can infect not only private corporations seeking profit but also nonprofits and even government agencies. Organizations can show disregard for legal and administrative requirements and their willingness to exploit opportunities at the expense of society. Once called out on their exploitative behavior, these organizations will go to extraordinary lengths to maintain the image they have worked so hard to create. Such efforts range from denial to hiring high-profile attorneys to defend their reputation. They may even viciously attack their accusers, evidencing the retaliatory trait of narcissism. So what was once considered solely individual pathology manifests itself in groups and institutions throughout society.

The behavior of fraternities reveals several noteworthy characteristics. Members assume a position of superiority over others. The maintenance of archives of previous exams and term papers suggests a sense of entitlement to an edge in course requirements. The treatment of campus coeds as objects for sexual gratification reinforces a hierarchical mindset in which women are inferior to men and therefore exist for the latter's pleasure.

Narcissistic organizations do not just emerge out of the blue. Most often CEOs who themselves possess narcissistic traits and exhibit narcissistic behaviors take the helm and eventually transform the organization in their own image. Such leaders do what comes naturally, that is, they behave in ways as to maximize the organization's visibility and status. They extol the organization's superiority of their products and services, even when such claims lack support through objective analysis. And they also work to protect the organization's fragile sense of self. Unfortunately, their sense of entitlement, which over time infects the entire organism, frees the organization to engage in exploitative practices, some of which may result in harm to the very customers whose patronage they need to survive. Removing the CEO, while perhaps necessary for legal and public relations purposes, proves insufficient for ridding the organism of the pernicious condition.

Narcissistic organizations do considerable harm until they are stopped. In some cases, the civil or criminal legal systems bring about their demise. In other cases, legislation aimed at curbing the very harmful abuses becomes necessary. Once organizations contract the narcissism virus, and once these traits spread through family members and friends and through mass communication, the entire society becomes susceptible to infection. This phenomenon is the subject of Chapter 6.

Narcissistic Crimes of Social Movements and Nation-States

The third decade of the third millennium in the United States witnessed the reelection of Donald Trump as forty-seventh president and thus the promise of more of his narcissistic behavior. Prior to the election, some liberals feared that even after having suffered defeat in 2020, Trump might one day return, a revenant who would defy any reasonable odds to once again wreak havoc on the country and on the world.[1] In the words of Trump's niece Mary: "If he is afforded a second term, it would be the end of American democracy."[2] In November 2024, their worst fears became reality.

It could be argued that Trump's reelection and the growing influence of his Make America Great Again (MAGA) supporters were foreseeable stages in the evolution of American narcissism. Was it not a matter of time before a critical mass of white Americans, driven by their belief in superiority and entitlement and crippled by a shortage of human empathy, seized control of the narrative? A similar groundswell of narcissistic support for the enslavement of blacks once led to a civil war. Why did anyone think something of this scale could not happen again?

* * *

Chapters 1 and 4 discussed several forms of narcissistic offenses by individuals. Some of these, like sexual assault and mass murder, fit traditional categories of crime, whereas others, like research misconduct, defy such definitions, yet they can result in substantial physical, psychological, emotional harm, or financial loss. In Chapter 5, the focus turned to organizations, which, while often developed for lawful and even beneficent purposes, experience corruption through narcissistic leadership and the resultant internal rot. For other organizations, the rot begins at the bottom, where a critical mass of individuals with a sense of superiority and entitlement and a shortage of empathy abuse the discretion inherent in their roles. This illustrates that narcissism, rather than solely a set of individual traits, infects private corporations, nonprofits, and government agencies. When this occurs, the organization, and not just its individual employees, becomes a narcissistic offender capable of doing considerable harm.

The virus does not stop there. Maladaptive traits and behaviors evident in narcissistic individuals and in groups and organizations can manifest themselves much more broadly. In his influential book, *The Culture of Narcissism*,[3] historian and social critic Christopher Lasch documented what he observed as a growing self-centeredness in Western society. The book became a bestseller, in part because it struck a familiar, if somewhat discomfiting, chord for many readers at the time. Lasch traced the roots of society's self-obsession to the nineteenth century, but the post-World War II period helped set the stage for what he saw in the 1960s and 1970s. Soldiers returning from service in foreign theaters pursued a new version of the American dream.[4] Some attended college on the G. I. Bill.[5] Others found work in the flourishing postwar industries, including building, automobile manufacturing, oil and gas, and the production of other goods and services American families craved and could now afford.

Many adults of the mid twentieth century as children had suffered the hardships of the Great Depression, as well as the sacrifices of wartime. They knew how it felt to do without. They had participated in scrap drives to support the war effort. And far too many had experienced firsthand the horrors of combat. They did not want their children – those who would become known as the Baby Boom Generation[6] – to be denied opportunities and material things in life as they had. Their children would have toys and bicycles and nice clothes to wear to school. They would enjoy family vacations and summer camps. They would take part in organized sports and scouting. And when the time came, they would be able to attend college because their parents knew that a degree opened doors to an even brighter future.

Many of these young Boomers, however, were spared the sacrifices associated with the twentieth century's economic depressions and wars and, given what their parents could afford, grew up to be self-centered and entitled, preoccupied with the trivial pursuit of their own comforts and pleasures. Some of the young people of the 1970s were unmindful or unappreciative of their parents' sacrifices. They expected things to be handed to them, to be exempt from the responsibilities their forebears had taken for granted, and to do so feeling little compunction over the consequences of their actions.

But to assign historical blame for contemporary societal narcissism to only those who grew up in the late twentieth century or early twenty-first century leaves out important pieces of the puzzle this analysis attempts to solve. Surely forces that predated the Great Depression, the Second World War, and their aftermath played a significant, if not pivotal, role in setting the stage for widespread superiority, entitlement, exploitation, and retaliation. To fully understand this developmental trajectory, it becomes necessary to delve into some earlier US history. The beginnings of America seem like an appropriate place to start.

6.1   America to 1877: A Selective, One-Sided Overview

At an early age, schoolchildren learn about Christopher Columbus's courageous voyage across a vast, uncharted ocean in three wooden sailing ships – the Niña, the Pinta, and the Santa Maria – at the behest of Spain's Queen Isabella.[7] Spaniards, including Ponce de Leon and Coronado, later explored the southeastern and southwestern portions of North America. French trappers and missionaries had made forays into Canada, eventually finding their way down the Mississippi River to establish a settlement at St. Louis.[8] The Dutch sailed to the island of Manhattan, for which they purportedly paid the local Lenape tribe a paltry sum. More recent findings suggest that the Vikings navigated their longboats to North America as early as the eleventh century.[9] It seems that adventurers from different parts of the Old World found themselves irresistibly drawn to this large, strange landmass on the far side of the Atlantic.

The whites who came later in greater numbers from England undertook the perilous transatlantic voyage to find a new place to call home. Many fled religious persecution.[10] Some were relocated criminals.[11] Still others objected to monarchs who ruled their subjects completely and sometimes ruthlessly. For many of these Europeans, life in a far-off land represented a fresh, free beginning.

The new arrivals soon encountered the indigenous tribes that populated the east coast of the North American continent. Elementary school reenactments of the first Thanksgiving portray pilgrims and Native Americans sharing food and fellowship in a tranquil setting. Many of these early encounters were anything but tranquil. The Powhatan, for example, attacked Jamestown in 1622 and killed more than a fourth of that community's 1,200 residents.[12] Some tribes, naturally curious about the white newcomers, did make peaceful overtures. Others, like the Powhatan, met these intrusions with hostility and armed resistance.

Regardless, all the eastern tribes soon discovered that these pale-skinned interlopers took without asking what did not belong to them, including game, timber, and land. These early incivilities by invading whites were but a harbinger of things to come.

6.1.1   The New America and the Enslavement of Blacks

At the same time they were alienating native tribes, the early white settlers began taking shipment of black men, women, and children who had been kidnapped and shackled on the African continent, packed into the holds of wooden ships like sardines in a can, and sailed to North America to be sold as slaves. The first documented arrival of slaves by ship from western Africa to the colonies took place in 1619,[13] a mere dozen years after the founding of Jamestown on the coast of what is now Virginia. The whites, some of whom had fled Europe to escape repression or indenture, apparently saw no hypocrisy in enslaving other human beings in their new homeland.

The early colonists soon found the southern part of the New World well-suited to growing not only corn, beans, rice, and other foodstuffs, but also commercial crops including cotton and tobacco. They needed certain goods from abroad, and that required that they have something of value to sell or trade. Europeans long before had learned that the dark-skinned people of the African continent, accustomed to an equatorial climate, could withstand hard work under hot conditions.[14] Adopting this model, the American colonists imported as many slaves as they could to spare themselves the requisite manual labor and to maximize profits.

The treatment of black slaves by America's early colonists was somewhat better than that of the indigenous people because there was a compelling economic incentive to keep them alive and healthy. Slaves represented a significant financial investment; the average cost of a slave in 1850 was $400, the equivalent of $14,000 in 2020.[15] Natives, by contrast, were deemed heathen, untrustworthy, dangerous, and therefore dispensable. In both cases, implicit in their status and treatment was that they were less than human. Whites, by virtue of color, culture, and divine right, were superior beings entitled to hold dominion over the non-whites.

The slaves were not always willing participants, and so the owners employed brutal methods to maintain order and compliance. Whipping became a common form of punishment, examples of which have been well-documented through archived photographs of survivors' hideous scars.[16] Branding was another form. The severing of tendons was yet

---

Box 6.1 The Dutch in South Africa

The Dutch in the seventeenth century pursued trading in several parts of the known world. In following established routes around Africa, they gained a foothold in what became Cape Town. They soon forced the local Hottentots into slavery. As less-well-educated settlers fanned out from Cape Town, they too kidnapped African natives for slave labor.[1] The experience of the Dutch in South Africa illustrates that white narcissistic exploitation of people of color extended well beyond the North American continent.

[1] Worden, M. (1985). *Slavery in Dutch South Africa*. Cambridge: Cambridge University Press.

---

another. Corporal punishment kept noncompliant slaves in line. As soon as they were physically able, they were forced to resume manual labor. Slaves who did not survive these ordeals served as object lessons to would-be recalcitrants. Disobedience would not be tolerated.

The exploitative, brutal treatment of black slaves went beyond depriving them of their freedom and forcing them to work under threat of corporal punishment or death. The rape of enslaved women and girls became another practice that was not prohibited by law in colonial America.[17] Inasmuch as female slaves were private property, the owners had every right to treat them as the owners wished. Slave owners and certain employees took sexual advantage of female slaves including girls. Most often this occurred simply because it was the will of lascivious white men in charge. In other cases, female slaves found that they could obtain better food, work assignments, living arrangements, or other considerations if they submitted to these overtures.[18] But all instances constituted rape because the women and girls, as enslaved persons without freedom or rights, could not refuse. Female slaves who failed to fend off such advances could not then, and cannot by contemporary standards, be considered voluntary participants; their status as chattel precluded the ability to give free consent. Predictably, many of these sexual encounters between white men and black female slaves resulted in pregnancies, producing children of mixed races. Evidence of the widespread practice of slave rape thus finds confirmation in historical records and in the DNA of the descendants of these involuntary liaisons.[19]

Rape, whether criminal in its historical or cultural context, constitutes a form of exploitation. It takes something from the victims they do not want to give, something they should not be expected to give, and something to which the perpetrator has no moral right to take. But unlike property crimes such as theft or robbery, victims of sexual assault cannot be restored to the state they enjoyed prior to the act through the subsequent use of punishments, apologies, or restitution.[20] They are forever changed, as are those who care about them such as family members and friends.[21]

The institution of slavery in early America involved other abominations. Families suffered separation when doing so met the financial needs of the slave owners. One cannot fathom the heart-wrenching experience of having family members forcibly taken away, not knowing their whereabouts or welfare, and sometimes never hearing from them again. A similar practice of family separation involving immigrants would rear its cruel head centuries later at the southern border of the US during the presidencies of Donald J. Trump.[22]

The widespread acceptance of a practice such as slavery requires the assumption, whether expressed or implied, that the white masters are superior to those they own. Superiors are entitled to treat the inferiors as they wish. They can act beneficently or brutally. As inferior beings, enslaved persons of color do not enjoy the same rights and privileges accorded to whites. Indeed, in early American censuses, slaves were officially counted as three-fifths of a person,[23] affirming their subordinate, undervalued place within society.

Along with this white sense of superiority came a shortage of empathy toward inferiors. Empathy requires one to put oneself in the place of the other. To feel what the other one might feel. To consider the potential consequences of one's actions. Those lacking such a faculty are oblivious to human suffering. The importance of caring and compassion simply does not compute. Slave owners and others supporting the practice lacked the capacity to comprehend the myriad ways slavery inflicted cruelty on individuals and families. If they had, they could not have supported it.

This same sense of superiority and shortage of empathy toward black slaves permitted the early colonists to subordinate the claims of the Native American tribes that populated the eastern regions of the New World. There were, of course, attempts to coexist peacefully, but when the interests of the whites collided with those of the natives, the latter were assigned the status of inferiors without rights. This freed the whites to appropriate their land and, when deemed necessary, to use violence against them to enforce their specious claims.

This sense of superiority and shortage of empathy exhibited themselves at the highest rungs of colonial society. Thomas Jefferson, one of the principal architects of America's Declaration of Independence and the third president of the US, owned slaves who worked in and around Monticello,

---

Box 6.2 The Legacy of Slave Rape

During the Black Lives Matter protests of 2020, many Americans insisted that the remaining vestiges of slavery, including the monuments to Confederate leaders and generals, be removed. After all, not only were these Southerners technically guilty of treason and sedition, but they had also supported one of the most abominable practices in the history of the US.

Caroline Randall Williams is an African-American poet and writer and the recipient of the National Association for the Advancement of Colored People (NAACP) Image Award in Literature. Through the analysis of DNA, she learned that her ancestor, a slave in Alabama, was raped by her owner, Edmund Pettus, a Confederate general and an early, active member of the Ku Klux Klan.[1]

In a piece published in *The New York Times* entitled, "You Want a Confederate Monument? My Body Is a Confederate Monument," Williams argued for a new, honest perspective on the legacy of powerful white men who raped black women they did not love and whose children they refused to claim. Her existence serves as living proof that certain forms of narcissistic exploitation have profound effects felt for generations.

[1] Williams (2020).

---

his sprawling Virginia estate outside Charlottesville. The irony of a slave owner championing a cause like independence notwithstanding, Jefferson is now known to have had sexual relations with at least one of his female slaves, the liaison confirmed through DNA.[24] His inconsistent standard of freedom for humankind was common among his contemporaries;[25] in fact, most signers of the Declaration of Independence were slave owners. This underscores the mindset of powerful white men in early America, a mindset that would long outlive the nation's founding fathers.

6.1.2 Manifest Destiny and Westward Expansion

From the time Europeans first put their feet on North American soil, they enjoyed an uneasy relationship with the indigenous tribes. What at first was a curiosity about people with pale skin who wore strange clothes and spoke unfamiliar tongues soon turned to suspicion and resentment as these newcomers cut down trees, built homes and forts, shot and trapped game, planted crops, and otherwise demonstrated that not only had they come to stay, they were claiming tribal lands as their own. As whites continued to pour into North America from the east, the native tribes resisted as best they could. When they attacked the whites, it frequently followed one or more affronts the former felt they could not overlook. What the indigenous people could not know early on, however, was that their attempts at resistance only forestalled the inevitable destruction of their civilizations.

The native tribes did undertake numerous attempts at organized resistance to the entitled behavior of the whites. In the 1750s, during what became known as the French and Indian War, some of the eastern tribes threw their lot in with the French, thinking that together they could drive the British and the English-speaking colonists back to where they came from. Like other whites, the French, who had already been in North America for many years, had struck cooperative relationships with some of the tribes through the fur trade and the work of their Catholic missionaries. The Native Americans permitted the French to trap for furs in exchange for trade goods such as muskets, tomahawks, and beads. To be sure, the French also considered themselves superior, but they chose to cooperate with the heathens and convert them rather than exploit and exterminate them. After nine years of bloody conflict, the British, together with the colonists and certain sympathetic tribes, defeated the French and their native allies. By this time all native tribes should have realized that the influx of whites could not be stopped, resistance was futile, and the existence they had enjoyed for centuries would soon disappear.

The American Revolution, in which the colonists sought their independence from King George III of Great Britain, unofficially kicked off in 1775 at Lexington and Concord. France chose to fight on the side of the American colonies. The French had long experienced British imperialism on the European continent and elsewhere. Lost in the years of bloody conflict, however, was the hypocrisy of fighting for freedom while at the same time infringing on the rights of natives and slaves. Once the colonists defeated General Cornwallis at Yorktown in 1781 and achieved their independence, there would be little to stop westward expansion.

In 1803, President Thomas Jefferson negotiated the Louisiana Purchase with France, which more than doubled the amount of land owned by the US.[26] The Lewis and Clark expedition, commissioned by Jefferson and financed by the US Congress, set out from St. Louis to explore the newly acquired land between the Mississippi River and the Pacific Ocean. Undertaken before the invention of photography, the expedition relied on detailed drawings and notes about their journey. This expedition has become legendary, but among its achievements was an encyclopedic inventory of all the flora and fauna the explorers discovered during their travels. Some of the natural resources underground such as gold, silver, and copper may have remained a mystery, but the new nation now realized that the vast tract of previously unexplored territory west of the Mississippi held a trove of riches. When the explorers finally made their way home after having reached the Pacific Ocean, people in the east were intrigued by the bravery of the explorers and the wonders that lay out west.[27] All this only further fueled the desire for American expansion.

Predictably, the members of the Lewis and Clark expedition encountered various native tribes including the Blackfeet, the Mandan, and the Lakota. Although some of these exchanges were tense, none turned into armed conflict. Sacajawea, the female Shoshone who served as guide and interpreter, undoubtedly deserves much of the credit for their relatively peaceful journey. Not all western explorers would be as lucky.

In the early 1800s, the phrase "Manifest Destiny" conveyed the divinely ordained obligation of the US to take over the remaining portion of North America.[28] Cast as a noble quest, this philosophy and associated policy motivated the US government and countless individuals to push ever westward. Significant hurdles, however, stood in the way. Those traveling west lacked established trails by which to make the journey. Without roads and bridges, they would be forced to traverse rugged, uncharted terrain, through mountain passes and across deserts, fording rivers and streams. Between the Mississippi River and the Pacific Ocean lived dozens of native tribes, some of them friendly toward whites, but many openly hostile to those trespassing on their lands. The indigenous people in the east may have been forced to submit to white rule, but those living west of the Mississippi had made no such concessions, and most had no intention of doing so. Whites who ventured west during this period did so at their own peril, many falling victim to either natural hazards or native resistance. The US Army had not yet built forts along established trails to protect travelers. Consequently, a trek westward was foolhardy at best and disastrous at its worst.

Native American attacks in both the East and the West did not go unanswered. Indeed, it never took much to prompt a band of organized whites to punish indigenous people for any real or rumored transgression. In the process, whites committed so many atrocities against native tribes that it becomes difficult to single out one or two for special attention. One of the most egregious and consequential was the subjugation and forced relocation of several Eastern and Southeastern tribes. The Indian Removal Act of 1830, signed into law by President Andrew Jackson, set in motion what was to become known as the Trail of Tears. Surviving members of the so-called eastern civilized tribes – Cherokee, Chickasaw, Choctaw, Creek, and Seminole – were forced-marched under military escort hundreds of miles from their homelands to what was then known as Oklahoma Territory.[29]

At least 4,000 Cherokee men, women, and children died along the way from various causes including exposure, starvation, or diseases.[30] The other tribes suffered as well. At the end of the journey, the survivors did get a new homeland, but it was not the land they had roamed, nor under the freedom they had previously enjoyed. What these tribes could not know, but perhaps should have anticipated, was that even their new environs in the West would not be sacrosanct to future whites.

Expansionists faced human obstacles other than Native Americans. The early Spanish explorer Coronado, having traveled north after the conquest of the indigenous people of Mexico in the sixteenth century, had laid claim to much of North America. Mexico controlled what those living in the US felt it was their "destiny" to appropriate. Adventuresome Americans, lured by stories of lush, free land, made the trek down to what is now the State of Texas. The journey and destination proved hard on those who traveled south. Americans choosing to settle there – referred to as Texians – had to live by Mexico's rules, one of which prohibited slavery. This, perhaps predictably, served as a source of growing resentment.

What storytellers often describe as the brave, adventurous spirit of those making their way west and southwest may more properly be labeled arrogance in thinking they could stake claim to lands that had been occupied by native tribes such as the Comanche and by Mexicans. In the case of Texas, the so-called Texians evidently felt they had the right not only to occupy land claimed by Mexico but also to fight for "independence" from the owner. The inevitable clash between the Texians and the Mexican army, which played out at the Alamo and at Goliad – depicted as a valiant stand against a repressive, brutal regime – could just as easily be cast as entitled American whites asserting their superiority and rights over those of brown-skinned foreigners who spoke a different language, a sentiment that has survived to the present day.

The hostilities between the Texians and Mexico in the 1830s had not ended with the siege of the Alamo and Sam Houston's subsequent defeat of General Santa Anna at the Battle of San Jacinto. Ongoing tensions between the two countries created a pretext for another conflict, this one also exacerbated by Manifest Destiny. As whites continued to push westward, they again found themselves in Mexican-controlled territory. Informed by what had happened in Texas, the Mexican government moved against these ever-increasing incursions. A major conflict did ensue and, in the mid 1840s, the US found itself in an all-out war with Mexico. Many of the American officers who would later distinguish themselves in the Civil War less than two decades later made their military bones in this so-called Mexican War. After forays into Mexico to defeat its army, the US netted another sizeable chunk of North American real estate.[31] Might evidently was right.

By this time, the US was less than a hundred years old, yet it was rapidly expanding westward. Having just secured huge tracts of land west of the Mississippi through the Treaty of Guadalupe Hidalgo, there was little to keep the US from gobbling up the rest of the North American continent between Mexico and Canada. Implicit in Manifest Destiny was that the tribes that occupied most of the newly acquired territory stood in the way of progress and therefore, like the Mexicans, must be defeated.

In 1849 gold was discovered near Sutter's Mill in what is now California. The news made its way east, and thousands trekked westward to seek their fortunes. Some traveled by land, whereas others boarded ships at eastern ports, sailed southward around Cape Horn, and then north to Pacific ports including San Francisco. All hoped to become wealthy, regardless of the potential costs to themselves and others. This tsunami of would-be prospectors needed tools, tents, clothing, weapons, and other provisions, spawning an industry of suppliers, most of whom fared better financially than the gold seekers who patronized them.[32] But the gold was there, and papers of the day reported on the returning ships and the amounts of gold they carried back east.[33] These reports only increased the numbers of those who ventured west to strike it rich, guaranteeing an unstoppable wave of whites.

Box 6.3 The Crimes of John Sutter

Many people have heard of Sutter's Mill in California as the place where gold was discovered, kicking off the famous Gold Rush of 1849. Few, however, are familiar with the life and legacy of the locale's namesake.

John Sutter, a Swiss immigrant, traveled to California in the 1830s to seek his fortune. Mexico controlled the territory at that time and required that Sutter become a Mexican citizen if he wanted to own land. Sutter complied and ended up with approximately 38,000 acres, a portion of which forms the present-day San Fernando Valley. Sutter and his men attacked local native villages, pressing the men into slavery and the women into prostitution. He reportedly kept some of the children to satisfy his own perverse sexual proclivities[1]; the Jeffrey Epstein of his era.

When the US took over California after winning the Mexican War, Sutter lost all his land. He returned east, broke, to live out his remaining years in Pennsylvania. But he never answered for the many atrocities he perpetrated against the Native Americans while in California.

[1] Hurtado, A. L. (2006). *John Sutter: A Life on the North American Frontier*. Norman, OK: University of Oklahoma Press.

Manifest Destiny was not without its detractors. In an impassioned speech on the floor of the US Congress, one representative criticized this posture, noting that it conveyed a sense of national vanity.[34] He went on to suggest that such a philosophy could even be used to appropriate South America. But despite some opposition, by the 1850s, Manifest Destiny had more than taken manifest form. The acquisition of more land west of the Mississippi guaranteed a constant flow of settlers and entrepreneurs, given tacit permission by their government to seek their respective fortunes, even though scores of native tribes had called these lands home for hundreds of years.

6.1.3   The Civil War, the Railroads, and Reconstruction

Slavery as an American institution thrived for more than two hundred years. But there were increasing calls from some sectors to put an end to it. Those in the South who had come to rely on slavery for their livelihood resisted this abolition movement. John C. Calhoun, a US senator from South Carolina, expressed the Southern sentiment in a speech:

> A planter, a slaveholder – and none the worse, I believe, for being a slave-holder – I say, for one, I would rather meet any extremity on earth than to give up one inch of what belongs to us as part of this great Confederacy. Sir, the surrender of a right is nothing; but to sit down in acknowledged inferiority; this it is that is galling; this it is that demands resistance.[35]

Irreconcilable differences over this "right" to keep slaves eventually led to formal secession by the southern states. Fort Sumter's bombardment by the Confederacy in April 1861 made war official[36] and thus began four years of bloody conflict that would eventually cost the young America more than 600,000 lives.[37] Narcissism sometimes comes with a high price tag.

Several years before the war, Abraham Lincoln wrote in a letter: "Our progress in degeneracy appears to be pretty rapid. As a nation we began by declaring that 'all men are created equal.' We now practically read it as 'all men are created equal, except Negroes.'"[38] In 1863, roughly midway through the Civil War, President Lincoln issued the Emancipation Proclamation, a document that formally freed all enslaved blacks, including those living in the Confederate states.[39] Inasmuch as the Union had not yet prevailed, Lincoln's Proclamation was neither enforced nor enforceable. It did, however, communicate a powerful message throughout a divided America that the superiority of whites over blacks implicit in the institution of slavery had been met with official governmental condemnation, even though many Northerners cared little about the fate of blacks, enslaved or free, a fact seldom discussed.[40]

The war between the states would grind on for another two years. Over time, the South ran lower and lower on human and material resources. General William Tecumseh Sherman's infamous march to the sea after the fall of Atlanta laid waste to Confederate supply lines, destroyed towns and plantations, and further demoralized Southern resistance.[41] In the final months of the war, some Union troops found themselves fighting Confederate units composed largely of old men and young boys, yet another barometer of the toll the war had taken on the South. Robert E. Lee's surrender at Appomattox Courthouse in April 1865 was perhaps the inevitable conclusion of a war of attrition.

The narcissistic sense of white superiority over blacks that enabled the Southern states to support a four-year secessionist war would not evaporate with their hopes of a separate nation. Generations of whites had grown accustomed to treating blacks as property. As costly as it was in human life and misery, the Civil War would hardly make racism disappear. Such deeply ingrained sentiments would fuel a long and contentious history, one that arguably continues to the present day.

Box 6.4 The Sioux Strike Back

During the Civil War, the Dakota Sioux, starving and angered at broken promises by the US government, rose up and attacked white settlers across the Minnesota frontier, killing hundreds.[1] When the news of these raids reached the rest of the country, it included horrific details such as the slaughter of babies in front of their parents. The US Army, beleaguered by the war between the states, managed to send troops and round up the Dakota they deemed responsible for the atrocities. Ultimately 300 of the alleged participants were convicted and sentenced to death. President Lincoln commuted the sentences of all but thirty-eight Native defendants who were hanged in public on a huge, rectangular gallows specially constructed for the occasion. It would be the largest mass execution in US history.[2] Those not executed were shipped to other states, far away from their homeland, a forced separation reminiscent of those involving immigrants more than a century and a half later during the Trump administrations.[3]

[1] Ramsey, A. (1862). The trouble with the Indians. *The New York Times*, August 27. https://timesmachine.nytimes.com/timesmachine/1862/08/27/78696821.html Accessed 2-28-2022.
[2] No author (1862). The Indian executions. *The New York Times*, December 12. https://timesmachines.nytimes.com/timesmachine/1862/12/12/90524453.html Accessed 2-28-2022.
[3] Shear, M. D. (2021). Trump and aides drove family separation at border, documents say. *The New York Times*, January 14. www.nytimes.com/2021/01/14/us/politics/trump-family-separation.html Accessed 2-28-2022.

At the end of the Civil War, many of those who had managed to survive the four years of bloody fighting chose to make a new start out west. Tens of thousands made the trip on horseback, by wagon, and by stagecoach. They faced an arduous journey marked by both natural and man-driven disasters, and many of those who started out did not reach their intended destinations. America needed a safer, faster, and more reliable means of transportation designed to move large numbers of people. Both the US government and private interests knew that westward expansion would require a railroad, one that would link the civilized east with the distant west.

The planned transcontinental railroad would be a herculean effort by standards of the day. One team started from Missouri and worked westward. The other started in California and worked eastward. They would meet roughly in the middle.[42] Railroads in the 1860s relied on tracks that had to be constructed by manual labor. Heavy wooden ties first had to be laid down on compacted earth. Iron rails then had to be positioned at right angles to the ties. It took many men to lift, carry, and lay in place the heavy iron rails. Crews with special hammers then fastened the rails to the ties with iron spikes. On a good day, the crews could lay only a few miles of railroad track.[43]

The construction of railroads thus required a large, compliant workforce. The low wages and hard labor failed to interest many of the men who had just served in the war. But the project did attract immigrants from foreign countries, including China and Ireland. Consequently, the railroads brought thousands of Chinese to the US to help perform the backbreaking work of clearing the land and laying down track. Naïve Chinese accepted the invitation, believing it would be an opportunity to earn good money and then send for their families, all in the hope of a better life. Some had previously come to the west coast of North America during the California gold rush. Although they were regarded as too small and not strong enough to perform railroad work, they became a suitable substitute when insufficient numbers of whites responded to the call. The Chinese earned wages substantially lower than their white counterparts.[44] In their treatment of the Chinese workers, the white men in charge reinforced the growing American tradition of white dominance over people of color.

Even before its completion at Promontory Point in 1869, the transcontinental railroad opened the floodgates of westward migration, which enabled an intrusion not only on the native tribes on whose lands they were appropriating but also on the environment. Tens of millions of

American bison roamed the great plains in the period 1865–1870.[45] Bison, better known in the day as buffalo, were prized in the east for their hides and tongues. For hunters and sportsmen traveling west, however, the buffalo were little more than a novel form of large game, one that could be brought down from long distances by high-powered Sharps rifles. Photographs taken during the era show gigantic mounds built from hundreds of bison skulls, attesting to the sheer numbers of them cut down for sport.[46] The plains tribes, however, relied on the entire animal for their existence. The tanned hides provided clothing and shelter. Strips of sinew became bowstrings. The dried meat fed the members of the tribe year-round. One cannot overestimate the importance of the buffalo to the plains tribes. The US government knew this better than anyone, and the decimation of the buffalo meant the decimation of the tribes that depended on them.[47]

Box 6.5 Fetterman's Arrogance

Captain William Fetterman was a former Union army officer who, like other Civil War veterans, chose to continue his military career out west. Fetterman considered the plains tribes uncivilized and inept, so much so that he once bragged that with only eighty men, he could march through the entire Sioux nation.[1] In December 1868, Fetterman and his command were assigned to Fort Phil Kearny in Wyoming Territory to protect woodcutting crews. Seasoned soldiers had warned Fetterman not to venture too far from the fort. When he and his contingent of eighty men moved beyond the garrison's line of sight, a small party of Sioux warriors taunted them. The soldiers gave chase and soon found themselves overwhelmed by a much larger band that rained thousands of arrows down on them. When Fetterman realized that all was lost, he and a fellow officer reportedly took each other's lives with their revolvers rather than face torture at the hands of their enemy. A detachment of soldiers later sent from the fort found Fetterman and his entire command scalped and mutilated.[2] Capt. Fetterman's hubris cost him his life and those of his men. One of the Sioux who allegedly took part in this strategic victory was a young Lakota warrior whose name translates as Crazy Horse. Less than eight years later, Crazy Horse would defeat another arrogant army officer near the banks of the Little Bighorn River in Montana Territory.

[1] Ed. Herald. (1866). Reported massacre at Fort Kearny. *The New York Herald*, December 27. See also Smith, S. (2014). New perspectives on the Fetterman fight. www.wyohistory.org/encyclopedia/new-perspectives-fetterman-fight Accessed 2-28-2022.
[2] The New York Times. (1867). The Indian massacres in Dakota – savage mutilation of the dead. *The New York Times*, January 14. https://timesmachine.nytimes.com/timesmachine/1867/01/14/79364719.html Accessed 2-28-2022.

The buffalo was not the only natural resource endangered by western expansion. From the time Europeans first landed on the eastern shores of the North American continent, they viewed timber as inexhaustible. They felled trees to build and warm their homes, cook their food, fashion furniture, and clear land to plant crops. After all, almost everywhere they travelled they encountered nothing but endless forests as far as the eye could see. People moving west needed houses and other buildings, creating a substantial demand for lumber. The military needed to construct large wooden forts capable of housing soldiers and withstanding attacks by hostile native tribes. Railroads required wooden ties. And so settlers and businessmen alike thought nothing about felling all the timber necessary to meet their respective needs.

Throughout this postwar period, the US government struck numerous treaties with western tribes, but often the written promises meant little. If the government itself did not violate the terms of agreements, private citizens did, frequently with catastrophic consequences.[48] From the beginnings of America, most whites had relegated Native Americans to an inferior status. After all, they used primitive tools and weapons, they lived in wigwams and teepees, and they engaged in horrific practices like torture and the killing of children. If the western tribes had any doubt about their status in the eyes of the whites, they had only to take note of what happened to their eastern counterparts who ended up in Oklahoma Territory.

6.1.4   The Post-war Treatment of Blacks

The arrogance and sense of superiority of whites toward blacks did not end with the Emancipation Proclamation or with General Lee's surrender to General Grant at Appomattox Courthouse. No longer facing the master's whip, many former slaves now found themselves forced to work as sharecroppers, living on former slave owners' land and earning a small portion of the plantation's proceeds.[49] Inasmuch as the general stores and other essential businesses were owned by Southern whites, sharecroppers were forced to pay usurious prices for needed goods and services. Gone were the chains and whips, but in just about every other discernible way, these former slaves experienced few of the privileges accorded free white citizens. The Southern whites continued to maintain their sense of superiority over blacks and had simply substituted new forms of exploitation for the older ones. Although the period of Reconstruction may have seen an end to slavery, it did not end institutionalized racism and its worst manifestations. Slave owners had an incentive to keep their invest-ment alive and healthy. After slavery ended, there was no such incentive and indeed many white racists, particularly those in the South, consid-ered it open season on blacks. The horrors that had been visited upon blacks during their enslavement now simply took different forms. Former Confederate officers, no longer in command of soldiers on the battle-field yet still fervently pro-slavery, led nighttime raids against local black residents. Lynchings, castrations, the arson of homes, businesses, and churches and other forms of domestic terrorism were commonplace, as were other means to keep blacks in their place.

It becomes possible to perpetrate such acts against minorities only when those responsible put themselves in a position above those they have targeted. Not only do racists behave as though they consider themselves superior, but also their sense of entitlement frees them to perform acts of exploitation and retaliatory violence. The Civil War ended the formal conflict between the North and the South, and it ended the institution of slavery in America. But the period following the war produced ample evidence that the sentiment of white supremacy over blacks and other non-whites had changed little.

6.1.5　George Armstrong Custer: A Study in Nineteenth-Century Narcissism

The nineteenth century had numerous luminaries, and perhaps few exem-plified arrogance and a lack of empathy more than George Armstrong Custer. A farm boy from eastern Ohio, George Custer managed an appointment to West Point where he graduated at the bottom of his class. In the storied, structured US Military Academy, designed to produce the best of disciplined army officers, the young Custer flouted convention by drinking too much, chasing women, and paying little attention to his studies.[50] His military career might have proven as unremarkable as his Academy experience had he not graduated on the eve of the American Civil War. Both the Union and the Confederacy needed officers to fill leadership positions, and so the West Point Class of 1861 served as a ready-made pool of freshly trained prospects for both sides of the conflict.[51]

In 1861, the twenty-two-year-old George Custer soon proved that he possessed the qualities of a natural leader. A capable horseman since childhood, he led his Michigan "Wolverines" from the front, waving his saber and rushing toward the thick of the fight.[52] His willingness to face danger earned him the admiration and loyalty of his troops,[53] and they participated in many of the war's major battles, including Antietam, Chancellorsville, and Gettysburg. Custer's bravery and battlefield performance resulted in rapid promotion, and his wartime exploits received frequent attention from the newspapers of the day, including *The New York Times*. Custer is said to have been the most photographed Union officer during the Civil War.[54]

When the war ended in 1865, Custer chose to remain a soldier. Western expansion called for an active army presence. The plains tribes including the Sioux, Cheyenne, Kiowa, Arapaho, and others agreed to various treaties, based on promises that their lands would remain theirs. Time and time again the whites failed to live up to the terms of the agreements, angering the Native Americans who often retaliated by raiding homesteads and settlements. Newspapers carried periodic accounts of settlers and travelers killed in these raids.[55] The challenge of subjugating the plains tribes would require intervention of the US Army, a job for which George Armstrong Custer had been preparing his entire adult life.

Custer's western service proved controversial, to say the least. Desertion in the Army was quite common at the time and, on at least one occasion, he had ordered deserters to be summarily shot.[56] At the Battle of the Washita in 1868, the 7th Cavalry under his command attacked a peaceful Cheyenne village consisting mostly of women, children, and old men. In Custer's official report to General Phillip Sheridan, he wrote that after hours of fighting, "… our efforts were crowned with the most complete and gratifying success."[57] Custer and his men gave little quarter, killing many of the helpless villagers including women and children. A contingent of eighteen soldiers led by Major Joel Elliot gave chase to those escaping and became separated from the main force. No one went to find them, and it was later learned they were annihilated by warriors from other camps who had responded to the sounds of the fight. Custer's failure to rescue his own men – a failure of empathy and an unforgivable military sin – would come back to haunt him years later.

It was no secret that Custer held presidential ambitions. American history had demonstrated that victorious generals – including George Washington, Andrew Jackson, and Ulysses S. Grant – had used their wartime success as a springboard to the US presidency. And, like another narcissistic self-promoter who would have presidential ambitions a century and a half later, the General referred to himself in glowing terms, using newspaper articles instead of X (Twitter) and Truth Social.

The year 1876 was to be the year for Custer. President Ulysses S. Grant was in the final year of his second term in office. A new president would be elected in November, and Custer saw himself as a prospective nominee. The Civil War had ended more than a decade earlier, and although Custer had garnered a great deal of positive press by virtue of his battlefield exploits, he needed to put himself back squarely in the public eye. A major victory against the plains tribes could be just the ticket to a nomination. Early that year, some of the Sioux and Cheyenne had refused government orders to report to their reservations. President Grant tapped another Civil War veteran and Custer supporter, General Philip Sheridan, to spearhead a military campaign.[58] According to Sheridan's plan, General Alfred H. Terry would lead his forces toward the Sioux from one direction. General George Crook and his troops would move in from another. Colonel Custer would lead the illustrious 7th Cavalry to form the third leg that would prevent their foe from escaping. Once caught in the Army's vise, the natives would have no choice but to surrender and accept reservation life. If everything worked out as planned, the victorious Custer would be headed to the White House.

Anyone acquainted with nineteenth-century American history knows how the Battle of the Little Bighorn turned out. Custer and the five companies of the 7th Cavalry under his immediate command failed to wait for Generals Terry and Crook. Worried that his enemy would escape, Custer instead charged the large encampment that stretched for several miles along the banks of the Little Bighorn River in what is now the State of Montana. The Sioux, Cheyenne, and members of several other tribes were caught by surprise. Fearing for their women and children, they quickly and efficiently mounted a counterattack. Unbeknownst to the soldiers, the native combatants numbered several thousand, and many of them carried repeating rifles that offered superior firepower to the troopers' single-shot carbines.[59] Captain Frederick Benteen, who could have gone to Custer's rescue, declined and took up a defensive position with Major Marcus Reno, whose troops had suffered heavy casualties early in the battle. Some believe Benteen made this decision because of Custer's failure to save Maj. Elliot and his men at the Battle of the Washita. Regardless, the five companies – more than 200 men – under Custer's immediate command were wiped out.[60] The dead included Custer, his two younger brothers Tom and Boston, his nephew, and his brother-in-law. They also included what was in fact not a phalanx of battle-hardened soldiers but a bunch of ill-prepared, exhausted, mostly young men, many of whom had come to America for a better life. What they found instead was certain and, likely in many instances, agonizing death on a hot Montana hillside. One wonders if Custer had paid more attention to his studies at West Point, would he have avoided such a catastrophic military disaster? Or would his ego still have overridden sound military judgment? Custer's defeat was a devastating narcissistic injury not only to himself but also to the illustrious 7th Cavalry and the US government, one that would not go unavenged.

Reporters promptly telegraphed the tragic news across the country. Lt. Col. George A. Custer and the brave men of the 7th Cavalry were overwhelmed by a superior force of Sioux and Cheyenne warriors on the banks of the Little Bighorn.[61] The press accounts detailed grisly scalpings, mutilations, and stripped, bloated bodies. America received news of the tragedy just as it was preparing to celebrate its 100th birthday.

The story of George Armstrong Custer carries an interesting postscript. His widow, Elizabeth Bacon Custer – Libby, as she was known to family and friends – spent the next several decades holding lectures and writing books about her beloved husband.[62] Custer may have been denied the US presidency, but he would not be denied status as one of the more important heroes of the nineteenth century. A former general whose luster had faded since the end of the Civil War, now in death had become larger than life. Libby's books failed to include, however, the summary execution of deserters. Her accounts neglected the needless slaughter of old men, women, and children on the banks of the Washita River. And they omitted the fact that her husband's narcissistic ambitions led to the deaths of the men in his command and the handful of natives they managed to kill. Prominent narcissists rely on loyal supporters who reinforce the façade, sometimes long after the formers' moment in the sun.

Custer's defeat merely accelerated the demise of the plains tribes. Massive amounts of US troops, too many in number and too well-armed even for Sitting Bull, Crazy Horse, and their several thousand followers, hounded the Sioux and other tribes until they were forced to surrender. After the Little Bighorn, any further resistance would have meant certain annihilation, a policy advocated by many at the time.[63] The free existence of the North American tribes had come to an end.

So how does the life of a nineteenth-century US cavalry officer inform a contemporary analysis of narcissism and crime? Manifest Destiny, the manufactured but widely accepted obligation of a new nation, conveyed the notion that whites were entitled to take over the entire North American continent between Canada and Mexico. This questionable policy rested on the foundation laid by the early colonists, a policy that gave them dominion over native peoples and their lands. It granted them license to rob the eastern tribes of their homelands and forcibly relocate them to Oklahoma

Territory. The railroads provided the means to move large numbers of settlers and the material goods they would need for their new lives out west. Once Manifest Destiny gained momentum, nothing would put on the brakes. But its successful execution required a special breed of men, white men who saw themselves as superior and who felt little compunction at dispossessing, or even disposing of, nonwhites who stood in the way of personal, organizational, or national ambitions. George Armstrong Custer was just such a man.

By most historical accounts, Custer was what in contemporary terminology would be a grandiose narcissist.[64] He craved attention and visibility. He took unnecessary risks, risks that put him and those who followed him in harm's way. Despite his poor academic record at West Point, he and many others considered himself a great military tactician, one who not only could bravely distinguish himself on the battlefield but also conceivably could ascend to the highest office in the land. Even though he fought for the Union, Custer, like many other Northerners, was a racist; he considered blacks inferior to whites, and when he served in the South at the end of the war, he expressed his disdain for the freed blacks.[65] After his court-martial, his inflated sense of self gave rise to expressions of grandeur, which he penned and sent to the newspapers. Hardened by a conflict in which hundreds of thousands of Americans had suffered and died, Custer saw in western expansion the opportunity to use his military experience to subjugate the plains tribes and in doing so, regain a sense of relevance. Of glory. The symbiotic relationship between Manifest Destiny and personalities like Custer illustrates that, just like Donald Trump and MAGA, the narcissism of a movement and that of its leaders are inextricably intertwined. An entitled policy of western expansion would not have been possible without like-minded individuals who not only had demonstrated the ability to lead others but also who craved position and power, all the while lacking any meaningful measure of human empathy.

An armchair diagnosis of George Armstrong Custer as narcissistic does not require a face-to-face clinical interview by a trained professional any more than does a twenty-first-century assessment of Donald Trump. The individual's actions and words demonstrate their sense of superiority and entitlement and their lack of empathy, as well as their willingness to exploit and their compulsion to retaliate. Decades before psychology coalesced into a discipline, Custer showed the relatively young US that the self-centeredness suggested by an ancient Greek myth, whether that of an individual or of a social movement, came at a tremendous cost, often to countless innocent people who were just trying to live their lives.

Without question, the narcissistic Custer engaged in criminal behavior. After the war he once went AWOL to be with his beloved Libby, a serious offense in the military[66] and, hypocritically, one for which he had ordered men in his command to be shot. He faced a court-martial for these offenses. Such is the double standard supported by the narcissistic sense of entitlement. Custer was responsible for the needless killing of numerous noncombatants at the Battle of the Washita and elsewhere. His liaisons with Native American women and girls could not have been entirely voluntary on their part, though they were surely not considered a crime in the nineteenth-century American West. But they demonstrated that he felt entitled to satiate his libido even if that meant stepping outside his marriage with native women for whom he otherwise had contempt. And in the end, he led more than 200 soldiers and civilians to their deaths to satisfy the demands of an enormous ego. Custer's criminal behavior was met at the time less with condemnation and more with admiration, even adoration. The young "General" was hailed as a hero, his avoidable and humiliating defeat at the hands of a superior foe described as a brutal massacre. Prominent narcissists whose reckless behavior backs them into a corner are often recast as victims; hapless, helpless souls deserving of sympathy. A century and a half later, Custer remains emblematic of the havoc that superiority, arrogance, entitlement, and a lack of empathy can wreak on innocent people and their cultures.

George Armstrong Custer does not stand alone as a narcissistic leader in nineteenth-century America who committed or facilitated crimes. Other candidates include Andrew Jackson, who, despite having adopted a Native American boy whose parents his soldiers had just killed, held the tribes in contempt and helped orchestrate their expulsion through the Indian Removal Act of 1830. William Henry Harrison, who would go on to become the 9th president of the United States, as a military commander once oversaw the destruction of the massive, multi-tribe village at Prophetstown in present-day Indiana.[67] John C. Fremont, the fabled western "Pathfinder," schemed and fought to wrest California territory from Mexican control, hoping to curry favor with then President James K. Polk.[68] American contenders for narcissist-of-the-nineteenth-century must include Robert E. Lee, commander of the Confederate forces during the Civil War. As a white man who approved of and participated in slavery, he clearly saw himself as superior to people of color, blacks in particular. What some sympathetic commentators have described as his deep, abiding love of Virginia and the South,[69] may just as easily be dismissed as arrogance in thinking that he and others had the right to secede from the US, a country that less than a hundred years earlier had fought for its independence from Great Britain's oppressive rule.

The story of western expansion in the US and the treatment of native tribes is one of narcissism, a narcissism born of white ethnocentrism and the tendency to forget the tyranny the early colonists had endured at the hands of a European monarch. Analyses of contemporary narcissism and the ways in which it violates social norms must abide by the past of the country in which these traits now predominate. The institutionalized racism of the twentieth and twenty-first centuries and its many promoters finds its origins in the smoke-filled parlors of Washington, D.C., New York, Chicago, and the other cities in which white men, driven by ambition and the desire for power, influence, and money, subordinated the rights of certain others. It is not difficult, then, to ascribe narcissistic traits and motives to contemporary governmental and corporate entities when behind them lies this undeniable heritage of superiority, entitlement, exploitativeness, and retaliation.

A narcissistic sense of superiority such as that exhibited by early white Americans need not be directed toward persons of color such as blacks or Native Americans. Color simply makes discrimination easier and more obvious. Superior white men have proven themselves fully capable of targeting other whites whose cultures or religions or lifestyles conflicted with their own. Mormons in the nineteenth century, who were as white as their detractors and guilty of their own atrocities, experienced treatment more in keeping with that of lepers. They found just about every location inhospitable.[70] When they could no longer stand the abuse, the Mormons under Brigham Young chose to make the dangerous trek out west to unsettled land, inhospitable for entirely different reasons, where they might finally live unmolested.[71] Mormons, along with the Native Americans and the Chinese, were deemed unfit for land ownership and American citizenship.[72]

Analysts of the nineteenth century have not had the benefit of contemporaneous surveys employing sophisticated psychometric instruments that measure such constructs as social dominance orientation and collective narcissism. But other compelling forms of evidence suggest that in the 1800s there existed widespread prejudice. Slogans like "The only good Indian is a dead Indian"[73] represented the sentiments of many white Americans. Fourteen years after its near annihilation on the banks of the Little Bighorn, the 7th Cavalry retaliated against the Sioux at Wounded Knee,[74] this time making sure they had the military edge with sufficient troops and state-of-the-art Hotchkiss guns. In committing this final atrocity against the Sioux, the 7th vented the narcissistic rage that had been building since Custer's defeat and thereby assuaged their battered egos.

The narcissism of early America created more crime victims than can be counted. In addition to the enslaved blacks, the Native Americans, and the Chinese, many whites were casualties of the country's narcissistic posture. The more than 600,000 Americans[75] who lost their lives in the Civil War are losses due to pro-slavery narcissism. Likewise, the military casualties of the Mexican War can be linked to the arrogance of Manifest Destiny. The list of victims of American narcissistic crime goes on and on.

6.2   America since 1877

The last quarter of the nineteenth century in the US took on a decidedly different character from the earlier part.[76] The end of Reconstruction saw the withdrawal of federal troops from the South, leaving the protection of blacks in the hands of state and local authorities, the equivalent of no protection. Except for a fortunate few, most post-Civil War blacks continued to live in the boondocks and back alleys, suffering some of the worst forms of discrimination and violence of which humans are capable. Likewise, the American mistreatment of indigenous tribes would not end with their surrender and forced acceptance of reservation life. Native Americans now faced new threats to their health and well-being. Their proximity to whites exposed them to diseases for which they had no acquired immunity.[77] Unscrupulous government agents, charged with managing the funds allocated by Congress to the Bureau of Indian Affairs, routinely embezzled or otherwise mishandled resources, the result being less food, food of poorer quality, and fewer other necessities for the men, women, and children in their charge.[78] Traders without conscience sold blankets infected with smallpox.[79] In the case of both natives and blacks, assimilation works only if one survives.

6.2.1   The Forced Assimilation of Native Americans

Indigenous children, in the eyes of the US government, stood a better chance of adopting white culture. This would be accomplished through a methodical process designed to extinguish traditional native values and customs and replace them with those of the whites.[80] The children faced a strict, disciplined lifestyle that could not have been more different from that of their free life on the plains. They lived in the structures of whites.

Their long hair was cropped short like whites. They wore the clothes of white boys and girls. They were forced to speak English, the language of the whites. Indeed, any attempt to revert to their native ways would be met with disapproval and corporal punishment. They ate the food that whites served them. The worship of the Christian God would take the place of pagan rituals about the earth, animals, and the elements. Every aspect of their new existence was intended to obliterate all vestiges of Native American culture.[81]

American history has shown that any captive population of children – whether Catholic altar boys, the institutionalized disabled, Boy Scouts, or immigrants without parents – are at risk of sexual exploitation by some of the adults they should be able to trust. Reservation Indian children would be no exception. Available evidence reveals that officials and staff took advantage of the children in their care, both girls and boys.[82]

The treatment of Native Americans throughout American history bears all the signs of a maladaptive narcissistic posture. White expansionists considered themselves superior, which entitled them to exploit the tribes by taking their lands and decimating the buffalo, the very source of their existence. When the Natives resisted this exploitation, the whites retaliated without hesitation and without empathy. This modus operandi would continue to manifest toward other disfavored segments of society, particularly the freed blacks, their descendants, and other residents of color.

Box 6.6 The Rock Springs Massacre

The Union Pacific Coal Department, which owned mines in Wyoming, hired Chinese laborers willing to work for lower wages than their white counterparts. On September 2, 1885, a group of angry Irish immigrants attacked the Chinese miners. When the fighting was over, at least twenty-eight Chinese were dead and fifteen were wounded.[1] The rioters also burned numerous Chinese homes. Authorities identified the perpetrators, but none of them faced prosecution.

The incident, which would be one of many atrocities against the Chinese in nineteenth-century America, became known as the Rock Springs Massacre. It illustrates that the white sense of superiority toward people of color, including immigrants, has roots going back several centuries, and it can manifest in a myriad of ugly ways.

[1] Rea, T. (2014). The Rock Springs Massacre. www.wyohistory.org/encyclopedia/rock-springs-massacre Accessed 12-6-2024.

6.2.2 The Ku Klux Klan, Jim Crow, and the Growth of White Supremacy

The Ku Klux Klan (KKK) embodied the deep-seated American contempt for blacks. Unaccepting of the South's defeat in the Civil War, the KKK, frequently led by former Confederate officers,[83] made it their mission to terrorize into submission those they formerly had owned, exploited, and abused. Lynchings became a common occurrence, frequently attended by the community's men, women, and children.[84] Often the local officials including law enforcement who, if not actively involved in these extrajudicial hangings, looked the other way.

As black Americans gained rights and protections from the US government, local ordinances and regulations gradually took the place of widespread domestic terrorism. Jim Crow laws passed by state and local authorities restricted their behavior in virtually all realms of community life.[85] Blacks had to use separate public restrooms. They had to eat at separate lunch counters. They were forced to sit at the back of public transportation. They were unable to attend white schools and colleges. These regulations underscored the message that although blacks had technically won their freedom in the eyes of the federal government, state and local officials retained a great deal of discretion in how they dealt with the former, and they fully intended to use it to make their lives miserable.

Blacks learned that certain forms of social behavior would elicit a much stronger negative response from the local white community. It could be dangerous and frequently deadly, for example, for a black man or boy to be caught with a white female. If this did occur, and if the black man was suspected of any sort of impropriety, the community response would be immediate and severe. Such was the fate in the 1950s of Emmett Till, a black teenager visiting Mississippi from Chicago.[86] The assumption, of course, was that black men and boys were, by nature, predators waiting for the opportunity to accost vulnerable white women and girls, perhaps a form of projection by white males who themselves were quite capable of – and perhaps even guilty of – sexual assault.

6.2.3 The Robber Barons and Their Gilded Age

With the country safe from native attacks and foreign incursions and travel made easier by rail service, a tsunami of people moved westward. The discovery of valuable natural resources including gold, silver, copper, and the seemingly endless supply of timber attracted hundreds of thousands of people who, lured by the promise of land, riches, or adventure, ensured the continued exploitation of the west, albeit in different ways. It would be up to a new breed of narcissistic leader to take the baton from military generals and sprint toward economic superiority. Instead of the cold steel of cavalry sabers and exploding rounds from field artillery, the robber barons employed bribes, political influence, and, when necessary, private police to discourage any resistance to their plans to exploit the country's people and resources.

Indeed, the opening of the West created countless opportunities for capitalists to make their fortunes. Among the first of these, of course, were the railroads. Without them, people could not travel quickly and safely to their destinations. The industry this form of transportation spawned made a handful of enterprising Americans extremely wealthy. But the process of building a transcontinental railroad came at a tremendous cost, not only to the thousands of men who constructed it but also to the huge swath of real estate to which the railroad barons had been given title.[87] Real estate the native tribes had once called home.

The likes of Andrew Carnegie and Andrew Mellon stepped up to play their own respective roles in honoring the promise of Manifest Destiny. Each burgeoning industry begat ambitious entrepreneurs. The oil industry had John D. Rockefeller, who got his start with kerosene production.[88] With the invention of the internal combustion engine, his Standard Oil saw stratospheric profits in gasoline and the petroleum-based lubricants the new engines and their vehicles would require. Likewise, timber, silver, and copper barons fought one another for top spots in American business and industry.

The term robber baron suggests criminal behavior. One could not engage in large-scale entrepreneurial enterprises involving pristine, previously occupied land without cutting some ethical, moral, and even legal corners. The robber barons behaved just as narcissistically as the politicians and generals of the early nineteenth century. But instead of military might they employed backroom deals involving bribes to federal, state, and local politicians and government officials. When workers complained or challenged their authority, private security agents would enforce their claims of superiority and entitlement, sometimes with brutal efficiency.[89]

Lest anyone think the acquisition of uncommon wealth automatically translates into empathy and beneficence, the robber barons' behavior in the late nineteenth and early twentieth centuries should disabuse such thoughts. At the foundation of their success stood workforces of miners, lumberjacks, and roughnecks who did the dirty, backbreaking, and often dangerous work required to build such fortunes. Before the days of trade unions and health benefits, those who died or suffered grievous injuries on the job – and there were hundreds of them – became part of the cost of doing one's business.[90] Empathy in business and industry represented so much sentimental hogwash.

The narcissism of these powerful white robber barons was also reflected in their personal and social lives. They built opulent homes, importing marble from Italy and crystal chandeliers from France. When one of them built a mansion, another would feel compelled to build a taller, more lavish one with more rooms and fireplaces, finer chandeliers, expansive gardens, and soirees to show them off. It was not enough to exploit others in their race to the top; they broadcasted their success to the world.[91] This exhibitionism put their wealthy peers on notice that, despite their relative success, they still occupied lower rungs of the high-society ladder.

Some of the robber barons did engage in philanthropic endeavors. Andrew Carnegie gave the country hundreds of beautiful public librar-ies.[92] John D. Rockefeller endowed the University of Chicago, which would become one of the nation's preeminent institutions of higher learning.[93] Solomon Guggenheim built a museum designed by Frank Lloyd Wright and filled it with priceless works of art.[94] And indeed, the American public – arguably the entire world – benefitted from these gestures. Charitable work, of course, can be its own form of narcissis-tic exhibitionism.[95] Regardless, beneath these public demonstrations of magnanimity lay a sordid history of greed, exploitation of people and resources, and the resulting reinforcement of white superiority over oth-ers by some of the most powerful men in America.

6.2.4   The Wilmington Race Riot and the Tulsa Massacre

Despite the widespread discrimination they faced in the South and else-where, some American blacks managed to adapt white models of success within their own communities. One such place was Wilmington, North Carolina. In the latter 1800s, Wilmington had attracted many black resi-dents, some of whom had become quite prosperous. Women and men alike dressed in fine clothes. There were restaurants and salons and social clubs. Wilmington even had a black-owned newspaper, which enjoyed a wide circulation.[96] Residents there enjoyed a comfortable, middle-class life.

These manifestations of upward black mobility caused growing resent-ment among white Wilmington citizens. Blacks were not supposed to aspire to a middle-class or above standard of living. In 1898, a group of local whites decided to burn down the building in which the newspaper was published.[97] The fire could not be contained and thus spread to nearby structures, most of which were constructed of wood.

Some black residents, fearing the worst, took up arms to defend themselves, their families, and their property. Was it not only natural to believe that their livelihood and indeed their lives were at stake? Seeing armed blacks in the streets served as an excuse for local whites to "protect" themselves and their property by shooting black residents.

The surviving black residents of Wilmington had little choice but to flee. After all, the city's white residents had declared open season on any visible black resident. Once vacated by black owners fleeing for their lives, the deserted properties became fair game for eminent domain and eventual resale. And the episode largely disappeared from American history.

Several decades later, the black section of Tulsa, Oklahoma, much like that of Wilmington, teemed with business, cultural, and social activity. Blacks had moved there in the early 1900s to escape the Jim Crow policies of the South. Once relocated, they built houses and apartment buildings and created a thriving Greenwood District sprinkled with restaurants, taverns, music halls, haberdasheries, and a grand hotel.[98] Life was good for blacks in that part of Tulsa.

Box 6.7 Killers of the Flower Moon

After whites successfully subjugated the Native Americans and forced many of them to relocate to Oklahoma, an unexpected discovery was made: rich deposits of oil on Indian lands. As legal owners of the reservations, these natives, from whom everything they cared about had been taken, now faced the real prospect of becoming extremely wealthy.[1]

Certain powerful whites, not about to let Indians benefit from these rich oil reserves, plotted to methodically murder members of an Osage family who stood to benefit the most. For a ten-year period, bodies periodically turned up, but local authorities paid little attention to these killings,[2] another red flag ignored at the time. Eventually, the FBI's predecessor, the Bureau of Investigation, identified some of those responsible and charged them.

The episode became the subject of an award-winning film entitled *Flowers of the Killer Moon*. Few of the movie's viewers knew of this dark chapter in Native American history. It shows that robber barons were occasionally murder barons. Further, the incident proves that the narcissistic exploitation of, and retaliation toward, Native Americans that had begun several hundred years earlier never really stopped.

[1] Bahr, S. (2023). What to know about "Killers of the Flower Moon": A guide to the Osage murders. *The New York Times*, October 20. www.nytimes.com/2023/10/20/movies/killers-of-the-flower-moon-osage-murders-explained.html Accessed 12-7-2024.
[2] Ibid.

In May 1921, a single event would change all of this. A young black man, Dick Rowland, found himself alone with a white woman, Sarah Page, in a downtown elevator. Nothing untoward happened between them, but word got out that the two had been together. Such a situation was unacceptable at the time. Rowland was arrested and taken to jail.[99]

The male townspeople armed themselves and, acting as self-appointed deputies, decided to take law enforcement into their own hands. A shot rang out and, as so many times throughout history, incited a barrage of gunfire, resulting in the deaths of both whites and blacks. Eventually the governor mobilized the military. Airplanes dropped explosive ordnance on the black homes and businesses, starting fires that quickly swept throughout the entire Greenwood District, which was comprised largely of wooden structures. Residents who did not perish in the inferno or die by gunfire went into hiding. Any blacks who dared to show their face risked summary execution. By the end of the melee, dozens of black residents of Tulsa were dead.[100] The Greenwood District lay in smoldering ruins.

After the massacre, the deserted, formerly black district fell victim to a predictable perversion of eminent domain.[101] As in Wilmington, North Carolina, the black residents had deserted their community. Now it was up for grabs, and the whites did not hesitate to grab it.

The Tulsa Massacre, as the event came to be known, largely disappeared from US history as taught to elementary and secondary school students. From time to time, young people would learn that blacks in the South were lynched in the late nineteenth and early twentieth centuries. But most of what would be taught in schoolrooms represented a highly selective, sanitized version of American history, devoid of the many incivilities and atrocities perpetrated against blacks. It would not be until much later, when the killing of unarmed blacks by law enforcement officers gave rise to Black Lives Matter, and when there were calls from some quarters for the teaching of Critical Race Theory, that most Americans would learn the story of what happened in Tulsa so long ago.

The Tulsa Massacre carries an especially telling postscript. In 2020, two survivors, Viola Fletcher and Lessie Benningfield Randle, filed suit seeking reparations for the financial losses associated with the events of 1921.[102] After all, not only had their property been destroyed by bombs and fire, but authorities had also confiscated it when the owners had been forced to abandon it. Their legal case made it through the courts all the way to the Oklahoma Supreme Court. The Court ruled against the plaintiffs, arguing that their claim did not fall under the state's public nuisance statute.[103] This final indignity sent yet another unambiguous message about the place and importance of blacks in American society.

The events of Wilmington and Tulsa represent just two of many incidents in which black communities were attacked, their residents terrorized, and their property seized. In 1920, dozens of black residents in Ocoee, Florida, met the same fate.[104] There were many more instances of mob violence against blacks mostly, but not exclusively, in the American South. The former slaves and their descendants had been liberated only to realize that this newfound freedom carried with it exorbitant costs. Most of these atrocities would remain unknown to generations of Americans.

6.2.5   The Eugenics Movement

As noted in the case of Mormons, a narcissistic sense of superiority and its associated behaviors need not be directed solely at non-whites. Centuries of discrimination against Jews, for example, punctuates the point that whites have found inventive ways to stratify even within their own ranks: ancestry, religion, wealth, education, intelligence, physical appearance, and health, to name a few. And each comes with its own rationale.

And so another relevant sidebar to the narcissistic history of the US is the eugenics movement.[105] As far back as the nineteenth century, certain voices put forth the argument that some people in society, particularly those exhibiting mental or physical impairments, did not deserve the same place in society as those without such disabilities. As the natural and social sciences took on sophistication, it became easier to identify these undesirables by various physical measurements. Cesare Lombroso, the Italian physician, is considered by many the father of modern criminology. He took exacting physiological measurements of so-called criminals and concluded that certain physical characteristics set them apart.[106] It is but a short step, then, to justify differential treatment of such individuals, including confinement, sterilization, or worse.

Once those in power decide that the biologically or constitutionally inferior persons warrant less of society's attention and resources, it then becomes a short step toward treating these people differently. One tack, of course, is to confine them in institutions such as infirmaries or poor farms or asylums where so-called normal citizens need not be inconvenienced by their objectionable appearance and behavior. Out of sight is out of mind.

The most extreme measure consists of eliminating the undesirables from the population altogether. If they are euthanized, they will no longer pose a burden on family or public resources. Their objectionable, off-putting behavior will end. And they will not be able to propagate. Is it not in their interests to spare them a life of frustration and misery? Would they not be better off dead?

Several assumptions undergirded the eugenics movement. To consider policies like forced sterilization, those in power must assign the potential targets to a lower status. That lower status implies that while their lives may have some value, that value is less than normal citizens, particularly white citizens with social standing. Physical and mental infirmities make them inferior. This inferior status, reinforced by repulsive physical features and off-putting behaviors, entitles the superiors to take steps to cull such biological mistakes from the population. Human empathy has no place in the extermination of defectives. It is an arrogant posture, one that appears more than once throughout American history.

The eugenics movement proved that people of color, while arguably the most vulnerable to being singled out for discriminatory treatment, were not the only targets of superior-minded whites. Those considered feeble-minded or otherwise constitutionally defective made the lists of undesirables. Likewise, gays were deemed inferior and therefore fair game for ethnic cleansing.

Box 6.8 The Boy in the Attic

The Lemp family of St. Louis emigrated from Germany and made their fortune in the beer brewing industry. Like other successful entrepreneurs of their day, they built an impressive mansion in a downtown neighborhood where it still stands today.

One of the Lemp men had a son, Zeke – reportedly the offspring of a prostitute or servant – who had what now is known as Down syndrome, but at the time, he was referred to as "the monkey-faced boy."[1] As was common in the day, such family members were embarrassments to prominent families. Consequently, they were kept from public view, often confined to remote portions of the home. In Zeke's case, he stayed on the attic-like third floor of the mansion where he would look out of the small windows at passersby.

Zeke is said to have died at age sixteen. Local lore says his spirit haunts the mansion and that he still occasionally peeks out of the windows of the third floor where he spent his short life. The narcissistic sense of superiority over others, including embarrassing close relatives, coupled with a shortage of empathy, once supported the widespread ostracization of the disabled in America.

[1] www.legendsofamerica.com/mo-lempmansion/ Accessed 12-7-2024.

America thus engaged in a building spree, erecting massive institutions designed to house the undesirables. Institutions like Pennhurst State School and Hospital, which would later be featured in a widely viewed TV expose,[107] became an infamous symbol of the neglect and abusive treatment of society's mental and physical rejects. Eventually, under pressure, state governments closed these facilities, but the overgrown, decaying ruins that still dot the landscape in the twenty-first century serve as a grim reminder of how superiority, in contrast to empathy and compassion, leads to neglect, abuse, and worse.

The eugenics movement in Europe took a decidedly darker turn. In the 1930s, Adolf Hitler and the Nazi party gained popularity and power in Germany. In *Mein Kampf,* Hitler argued that the Arian race – whites of mostly northern European ancestry – were superior to Jews and people of color. Hitler read and internalized the writings of eugenicists. He already hated a growing list of what he considered inferior species. These writings provided the theoretical rationale he needed to make good on his proposed policies.

As Hitler and the Nazis amassed power in Germany, the media, as well as some of those directly affected, communicated these developments to American audiences.[108] American Jews received letters from their relatives living in Germany, Poland, and other countries about their treatment at the hands of the Nazis. Journalists wrote newspaper and magazine articles in which they chronicled the Nazis' seizure of personal and real property. On an official level, the US State Department had early confirmation of Nazi atrocities against Jewish residents. The attack on Pearl Harbor by the Japanese finally forced President Franklin Roosevelt to declare war. But by December 1941, European Jews had already suffered several years of horror, and the survivors of the Final Solution had watched millions of their relatives and friends be exterminated in the name of white supremacy.

Once the Nazi threat had been eliminated and the Second World War ended, American soldiers were able to attend college only because of the G. I. Bill; college for their children was taken more for granted. The benefits of the G. I. Bill did not, however, extend to veterans of color. They were good enough to shoulder arms against a foreign enemy, but apparently not worthy enough to receive a free education. This meant that the opportunity for upward mobility afforded by this important postwar program would only increase the existing economic disparity between whites and blacks in America.

After World War II, the ensuing prosperity permitted American families to buy the niceties of life through mail-order retailers like Sears,

---

Box 6.9 Yellow Fever

In December 1941, after the attack on Pearl Harbor by the Japanese, the US entered World War II. Stateside, the US government made the decision to round up thousands of residents of Japanese extraction and confine them in internment camps, a euphemism for a special prison surrounded by barbed wire and guarded by armed American soldiers.[1] The rationale seemed to be that these Japanese, who looked different and spoke a different language, could not be trusted. Confined and incommunicado from those outside the camps, they should not pose a threat. Once again, the US formally expressed its suspicion of, and contempt for, people of color, in this case Asians.

[1] See, for example, Sundquist, E. J. (1988). The Japanese-American internment: A reappraisal. *The American Scholar*, 57, 529–547.

Montgomery Ward, and J. C. Penney. Not only could families purchase bicycles, musical instruments, toys, and other desirable goods, but they could also do so by paying on time. This meant not having to wait for merchandise until one had saved the requisite funds.

Baby boomers enjoyed more education, better jobs, and therefore more material things than their parents. They did not experience the economic deprivation of the Great Depression, nor did they live through a world war whose outcome, at certain junctures, was uncertain. Even though many of them engaged in political activism in the 1960s, many gravitated toward rewarding jobs and comfortable, suburban lives. Along with their ability to purchase and furnish nice houses, drive nice cars, and take fun vacations, they tended to end up in metropolitan suburbs, insulated from the inner city and the problems that went with it. As children many of these more fortunate baby boomers attended school with kids who lived in shabby houses and wore wrinkled hand-me-downs. But once they had grown up and relocated to the burbs, these more fortunate Boomers lost touch with their roots, overcome by the promise of financial success and all that represented.

The Civil Rights Act of 1964 brought about a reduction in some of the overt racist killings in the US. Robert Kennedy, President John F. Kennedy's brother, served as Attorney General, and he directed the Federal Bureau of Investigation (FBI) to aggressively investigate possible civil rights violations, particularly in the South. The senseless murders of three civil rights workers in Mississippi – Michael Schwerner, James Chaney, and Andrew Goodman – brought the full weight of the US Department of Justice down on violent racism in the South.[109]

Box 6.10 A Historical Basis for Bias

The treatment of people of color, including the killing of unarmed blacks by police, according to Katrina Phillips, must be viewed not only as it has unfolded in the twenty-first century but also in its historical context. Phillips, a professor at Macalester College in Minnesota, notes that the treatment of African Americans has indisputable ties to the nineteenth-century treatment of black slaves and indigenous people in that state. Dred Scott, the slave for whom the eponymous court decision was named, was an enslaved person at Fort Snelling, located near the present-day twin cities of Minneapolis and St. Paul.[1]

[1] Phillips, K. (2025). Where two waters come together: The confluence of Black and Indigenous history at Bdote. *Saint Paul Historical.* https://saintpaulhistorical.com/items/show/416 Accessed November 24, 2025.

The recent history of the treatment of blacks in the twentieth and twenty-first centuries in America is incomplete without a mention of mass incarceration. The US ranks high among countries that have large proportions of their citizens in prison. As with arrests, outside observers might conclude that the disproportionate number of black men and women in prison results from their involvement in crime. According to author Michelle Alexander, the policies of Jim Crow simply took a different form than before.[110] The seriousness of institutionalized racism in America, mass incarceration being only one form, would take on even greater urgency with the ascendency of Trump's MAGA Movement.

6.2.6 Donald Trump and the MAGA Movement

On January 20, 2017, Donald John Trump was sworn in as the forty-fifth president of the US. As with every other presidential inauguration in modern history, the press took photos and video footage of the ceremony, including the throngs of attendees and onlookers on the Mall next to the Washington Monument. President Trump's communications director Sean Spicer addressed reporters later that evening from the White House Pressroom. In response to comments about the less-than-completely packed mall, Spicer asserted that it was the largest crowd ever to attend a presidential inauguration. It would be the first of countless untruths officially offered by President Trump or those in his administration, and it signaled not only a collective thin skin but also reinforced a fear of many observers that the new occupant of the Oval Office was a maladaptive narcissist for the ages.

Donald Trump did not have any government service in his background. He had not served as governor of New York or Florida. He had not been a member of Congress. He had not even served as mayor of a large city. And so, when he was sworn in as president of the US, he lacked in-depth knowledge about how government worked and why it worked the way it did. How was one to function not knowing anything about the federal government?

The conservative media, FOX News in particular, played a critical role in nurturing and protecting this narcissistic entity while amplifying his message. Under the leadership of CEO Roger Ailes, FOX had demonstrated its willingness to suppress or bend the truth, preferring instead to promote conspiracy theories for which there was little or no factual basis but for which the network's conservative viewers had an insatiable appetite. Ailes's own narcissistic tendencies had set the tone for the culture at FOX. His predatory sexual behavior was legendary. Those who disagreed with his exploitative and deceptive culture could either get on board or leave, and indeed, some of the Fox staff did resign.

FOX News was more than willing to exploit Donald Trump's candidacy and presidency for the sake of profit. Early on they knew the former reality TV star would be a proverbial cash cow. Trump had already made numerous appearances on the network during which he peddled his "birtherism" theory and otherwise maligned President Obama. Millions of MAGA supporters watched Fox religiously and accepted their exaggerations and lies. The degree to which the network and its anchors truly supported Trump and his ideas may never be known. What is known is that Sean Hannity and Donald Trump became quite close, the former serving as an informal adviser to the latter even after he became president.

Not all Republicans could make this pact with the devil. Joe Scarborough, former Republican US representative from Florida's panhandle and host of the MSNBC's *Morning Joe*, remained one of President Trump's most vocal critics. Former chair of the Republican National Committee, Michael Steele, a regular guest on *Morning Joe*, made it clear to the TV audience that President Trump did not represent true conservative ideals. Likewise, Nicolle Wallace, former communications director for President George W. Bush and host of MSNBC's *Deadline*, regularly called out Trump for his lying and his obliteration of political and presidential norms.

When Donald Trump became president, he approached his new role in much the same way he did in the Trump Organization. He surrounded himself with a small group of people in whom he could trust. Indeed, just as he had with his company, Trump chose to include family members including his daughter Ivanka and two sons. Donald Jr. and Eric.

Trump did not even attempt an approximation of previous presidencies. To the contrary, from the very beginning his term promised to be a one-off characterized by an absence of rectitude that posed an existential threat to the American democracy. President Donald J. Trump and his political supporters trampled upon traditional norms of appropriate behavior in the federal government. Prior to the Trump administration, the public trusted that presidents and other elected officials would honor the traditions of the past. Presidents would graciously accept the advice of their predecessors, customarily placed in the Resolute Desk by the outgoing president. They would award the Presidential Medal of Freedom only to a few deserving honorees, not because the recipients had been donors or had spoken positively of the president bestowing the award, but because of their contributions to the nation. These and other presidential norms were taken for granted. Not so for Trump.

One unique way in which Trump's narcissism expressed itself was through what appeared to be the violation of the Emoluments Clause of the US Constitution. Those who ascend to high federal service in the US do so under a longstanding assumption that they will not use their position to enrich themselves. One way to avoid this problem is to divest oneself of business interests, particularly those that potentially could pose a conflict of interest. Secret Service and other necessary support staff stayed at Trump-owned hotels and resorts, generating additional income for the family. Trump permitted his close family members to conduct business with foreign governments and their representatives, making substantial sums of money in the process.

6.2.7   *Trump Administration's Response to the COVID-19 Pandemic*

Despite having been impeached by the House of Representatives, Donald Trump had every intention of running for a second term. The US Senate, led by Senator Mitch McConnell, refused to convict him of wrongdoing. America's economy was prospering, at least for major corporations and affluent Americans. Aside from that, Trump's enormous ego demanded a second term, if not a third.

The year 2020 brought a unique and unforeseen challenge. A novel coronavirus appeared in Wuhan, China, and quickly spread to the rest of the world through air travel. As president of the US, Donald Trump received early briefings about the new disease's contagiousness and lethality. From a public health perspective, such knowledge should have prompted an immediate, proactive effort to minimize the devastating effects of the disease, including alerting and educating the public. The best public health approach would have been for everyone to quarantine for a brief period, thereby preventing the spread of the deadly disease.

After three years in office, the US economy was one of the few successes to which Trump could point. Shutting businesses down to halt the spread of the disease would negatively influence the economy, at least in the short run. So, despite the highly contagious nature of COVID-19, Trump refused to shut down businesses and schools, basically putting the health of the economy over the health of American lives.

Donald Trump could see that a widespread epidemic could have a deleterious effect on the American economy. Such a conclusion would logically lead one to institute any and all measures to control the disease as quickly as possible to minimize any economic disruption. Trump, to the contrary, concluded that minimizing the contagiousness and lethality of the disease would keep the public from panicking, thereby controlling any disruption.

And Donald Trump did know of COVID-19's lethality. In 2020, Trump agreed to an interview with Bob Woodward, the *Washington Post* journalist famous for his role in exposing the Watergate scandal during Richard Nixon's presidency. Woodward was in the process of writing another book, this one focusing on the Trump administration. In an interview for the book, Trump admitted to Woodward that he knew how deadly COVID-19 was, but he chose to "play it down."[III]

Box 6.11 Disrespect Does Not End with Death

Beginning in the 1800s, the Columbia Harmony Cemetery became the final resting place for thousands of African-Americans. The relatives of the deceased sometimes used what little savings they had to buy headstones for their loved ones. At some point, a decision was made to use the land occupied by the cemetery for another purpose. The headstones, representing a financial and emotional investment of the deceased's families, were unceremoniously sold to a contractor who used them to reinforce the shore of the Potomac.[1] A passerby noticed engraving on some of the stones and discovered that they were grave markers. He enlisted support to reclaim the tombstones. Unfortunately, the cemetery from which they had been taken had long been repurposed. This unfortunate episode in American history, one of countless indignities committed against people of color, reinforces the message that they occupy a subordinate place in society and thus do not matter.

[1] Tucker, E. & Ly, L. (2021). Headstones in historic black cemetery were desecrated. The recovery offers "symbolic justice." *CNN*, August 24. www.cnn.com/2021/08/24/us/harmony-cemetery-gravestones-repatriated.html Accessed 12-11-2024.

Trump would have to run for reelection in November 2020. Undue concern over a contagious disease could only damage his chances to hold onto the presidency. It made sense, at least to Trump, to play down the threat posed by this "China virus."

The medical and public health communities had a quite different take on the novel coronavirus. They knew that people had visited the Wuhan, China, area and had returned to the US. If these travelers had been infected, and then they had contact with others upon their return, the disease would quickly spread.

The collective relief over the end of the COVID-19 pandemic experienced by millions of Americans may have prompted them to forget the many lives needlessly lost due to President Trump's response. Hundreds of thousands of Americans died from COVID-19. Many of these people were loyal Trump followers who relied on their president for advice. A closer examination shows that he and his administration stand criminally culpable for the tragic consequences. The Trump administration had sufficient advance notice of the coming health crisis. This gave them plenty of time to devise a comprehensive strategy to minimize its devastating effects. Such a comprehensive strategy did not take place until after tens of thousands of Americans had died from the disease. Trump played it down. Nonfeasance – the criminal failure to perform one's official duties – and misfeasance – the criminally incompetent performance of one's official duties – may apply to the Trump administration's initial COVID-19 response. Trump did eventually authorize Operation Warp Speed, a project designed to accelerate the development and delivery of an effective vaccine, but it was already too late for thousands of Americans.[112]

Trump's defenders might argue that he had the discretion as president to make certain policy decisions, irrespective of their consequences. Critics, of course, could counter that his constitutional oath to protect and preserve the United States obligated him to do everything in his power to prevent unnecessary deaths. Such is the nature of narcissistic crime: much of it is not illegal per se, yet it results in substantial, sometimes incalculable harm.

Much has been written about the narcissism of President Donald J. Trump, so much so that consumers of mass media undoubtedly went numb. Indeed, during and after his term as 45th president, a virtual nonfiction cottage industry arose, generating dozens of books by journalists, pundits, academics, and even family members. But the 45th president represented perhaps the most visible and vivid example of maladaptive narcissism in the early twenty-first century. In defense of President Trump, during his candidacy, he provided a full preview of what he was and what was to come. Frequent rallies attended by adoring supporters gave proof of his outrageousness. In response to the mainstream media – including critical cable outlets like CNN and MSNBC – he worked to discredit them and their sources, successfully attaching the label "fake news." Explicit in his many criticisms of reporters was that any material critical of him was not only wrong, it must be manufactured and thus fake.

At the level of the individual, the behavior of Donald Trump reflects this retaliatory trait. No challenge or criticism ever went unanswered, even before he was elected president of the United States. Once president, with the power of that office and Twitter as the tool for his bully pulpit, Trump viciously attacked anyone who dared cross him. When members of his own administration, such as Attorney General Jeff Sessions, failed to do his bidding, he unceremoniously fired them, usually by way of a tweet on Twitter. Members of the US Congress who disagreed with him found themselves primaried or otherwise lacking sufficient political support to remain in office. No wonder members of the House of Representative and the Senate willingly kowtowed to his demands. To do otherwise meant the almost certain death of one's career. It was only at the end of his first term in office, when having incited an insurrection and having been stripped of his ability to tweet, did the country see a pause in his retaliatory instincts.

A government grounded in such a philosophy and its associated policies would exemplify a narcissistic nation-state. Those in control – mostly white, ultra-conservative Christian men who believe in their own superiority and entitlement – would exploit people and institutions for gains of power and money. Anyone who was critical of them and their policies, including the formerly free press, liberal intellectuals, and participants of the so-called deep state, would feel the narcissistic rage behind various forms of retaliation designed to get even with those who would oppose them. None of this should have been surprising. Putin did it in Russia. Erdogan did it in Turkey. And even further back in history, Hitler followed the same playbook in Germany and across Europe.

Trump and his MAGA devotees may be speaking and acting narcissistically, but they are not alone. Just before the election, a comedian at a Trump rally referred to Puerto Rico as a floating island of garbage.[113] In response, Joe Biden defended the island territory and its inhabitants and ended his remarks by saying, "The only garbage I see floating out there is [Trump's] supporters."[114], a retort reminiscent of Hillary Clinton's "basket of deplorables" remark, referring to Trump's supporters in 2016.[115]

Box 6.12 The Heritage Foundation

The Heritage Foundation was chartered as a Washington, DC, conservative think tank.[1] Its activities have included drawing up lists of conservative judicial nominees, including those for the US Supreme Court. In Donald Trump's first term as president, it played a significant role in pushing for the appointments of Neil Gorsuch, Brett Kavanaugh, and Amy Coney Barrett, Trump's three appointees to the high court.

The Trump brand of MAGA philosophy – characterized by denial of the Democrats' 2020 win, the dissemination of other demonstrable untruths, and vows to retaliate against anyone who disagreed with them – found a sympathetic ear at the Heritage Foundation. They developed and made public Project 2025, a 900-page, comprehensive plan to remake the federal government.[2]

What they recommended might not be criminal in the strictly legal sense, but it could result in a great deal of personal, organizational, and societal harm. To label Project 2025 as a blueprint for autocracy is, to many commentators, no exaggeration. Organizations such as The Heritage Foundation reinforce a narcissistic posture, one characterized by an entitled attitude toward the exercise of power and unencumbered by human empathy.

[1] www.heritage.org Accessed 1-19-2026.
[2] www.heritage.org/conservatism/commentary/project-2026 Accessed 1-19-2026.

A sense of superiority and its associated condescending behavior, it seems, can infect Americans of all political stripes.

As one of his first orders of business, Donald Trump has promised to round up and deport missllions of undocumented immigrants. If entire families fit this definition, they allegedly will face deportation together. Each era in American history, it seems, has its dangerous inferiors; immigrants, particularly those of color, have become the Native Americans of the twenty-first century.

Donald Trump learned important lessons during his first term in office. He learned that rather than surrounding himself with "the best people," he should instead rely on loyalists, those who would do his bidding even if it violates their oaths of office or even the law. He learned that the conservative Supreme Court he created with three appointees during his first term would likely rule in his favor when it came to abrogating the rights of American citizens and protecting the powerful. These decisions helped infuse the federal government with the MAGA philosophy. And he learned that the civil and criminal proceedings that once threatened his money and his mantle as narcissist-in-chief would likely disappear.

Well before being elected to his second term, Donald Trump had promised to get even with all those he perceived had stood in the way of his personal and presidential goals. Members of Congress who had served on his impeachment committee made his hit list as did those outside of government who had criticized him and his policies. Trump's second term vendetta benefitted from the organizational structure he had created in his own image. During most of his first term as president he had surrounded himself with a cadre of highly qualified individuals, most of whom took their oaths to the Constitution seriously and prevented his worst impulses from damaging the country. As the forty-seventh president of the United States, Trump had learned those lessons of the past and appointed individuals who arguably possessed weaker credentials, but they would support him without question and carry out his wishes.

One of his first orders of business was to remove from cabinet-level offices all inspectors general, individuals whose role was to ferret out and process fraud and corruption. Trump's efforts to bend or break rules during his first term had been thwarted by such individuals. It had irked him that he could not do what he wanted to do, when he wanted to do it, the way he wanted to do it. The removal of such impediments would increase the odds that his plans as 47th president would be carried out, regardless of how they might violate ethical or legal standards.

The influx of undocumented immigrants had long been one of Trump's obsessions, and during his second term he planned and carried out a plan to rid the US of as many illegals as he could, starting with those ostensibly considered to be criminal.

The political and social movement led by Donald Trump proved to be responsible for various forms of harmful behavior, much of which was clearly criminal. Most obvious is the January 6, 2021, attack on the US Capitol, which resulted in numerous deaths and injuries and ultimately multiple criminal convictions. Less infamous were the many assaults on Asians considered at least indirectly responsible for importing what Trump termed "Kung Flu." Far more serious, however, were the hundreds of thousands of unnecessary COVID-19 deaths.

Political scientists and pundits were not alone in trying to explain the authoritarian turn in twenty-first-century America. Social-personality psychologists had already accumulated an impressive array of psychometric instruments, including the Narcissistic Personality Inventory and other measures of narcissism. One such development was the identification of social dominance orientation (SDO), a construct related to narcissism in that they share superiority toward others. SDO, as discussed in Chapter 5, rests on the assumption that the social group to which the actor belongs is superior to others. Those scoring higher on SDO are more likely to hold racially prejudicial attitudes. Research shows that SDO is positively related to narcissism.

Social and behavioral scientists do not have survey or experimental data from the earlier centuries of America's history. Those tools were not developed until the twentieth century. But there are other ways to infer such constructs as SDO, authoritarianism, and collective narcissism. The archived words and actions of such luminaries as Andrew Jackson and George Armstrong Custer show that even in the early days of the American republic, prominent, powerful white men declared their superiority over Native Americans and blacks, and they backed up their words with exploitative and retaliatory behavior.

Another critical stratum that enables this consists of sycophants who not only exhibit the narcissistic traits of those they purportedly represent, but they also seek power and influence. Many of the sycophants are not as maladaptively narcissistic as the leadership; they simply make the moral, ethical, and sometimes legal compromises necessary to get what they want.

The popularity of Trump and Trumpism has relied heavily on support from intelligent, well-educated politicians, strategists, and donors who rather than blindly follow him, enabled his narcissism knowing full well that doing so would pay dividends of power and influence.

People who are high on SDO, racism, and narcissism have long been part of America's population. They have selfishly pursued their self-interests, sometimes openly, sometimes quietly, seething about those in society who are to blame for their many dissatisfactions. They do not earn enough money. They do not own enough property. They do not enjoy enough social status. Then along comes a narcissistic leader whose charisma captivates them and whose power impresses them. These leaders give them official permission to now openly express their own heretofore secret dissatisfactions. Further, and perhaps more importantly, the leaders point out segments of the population who deserve blame for these dissatisfactions. In the nineteenth century, it included indigenous people who stood in the way of American progress. They were primitive, violent, and unwilling to surrender their lands and way of life for the superior whites. Andrew Jackson, just one of many such leaders, did little to hide his hatred of the natives whom he not only fought and defeated but also forced to relocate to what later became the State of Oklahoma. Likewise, George Armstrong Custer, the exhibitionistic hero of the American Civil War whose exploits were described in laudatory detail by newspapers of the day, was considered not a champion of genocide but a hero whose bravery was opening the west for necessary expansion, an expansion justified by Manifest Destiny. But as much as contemporary narcissism has become associated with Donald Trump and his retinue, they are but symptoms of the disease. Age eventually takes its toll on someone like Trump, and once he can no longer serve as standard-bearer, the self-centered, arrogant culture he epitomized and to which he gave license will have spawned an overabundance of disciples. Others will surely step up to take his place. American narcissism is, and always has been, much bigger than any one individual.

The United States in the twenty-first century stands at an inflection point. Does it accept an increasingly narcissistic stance in which superiority, entitlement, exploitativeness, and retaliation prevail? Or does it appeal to its "better angels" and opt for fairness, decency, and civility? Even if the country passes the test, it must abide a history characterized by bouts of these maladaptive traits and the harmful, sometimes criminal, behavior that follows. The war against narcissistic crime is never won; it is only better controlled in some places and in some eras than in others.

And so it may be up to other forces within society to take on socially harmful narcissism. The likes of Warren Buffett and Bill Gates may be able to marshal support for a comprehensive strategy for moving humanity away from the more harmful traits and behaviors and toward cooperation, reconciliation, and altruism. If they can successfully use their platforms and their wealth to confront global plagues like HIV/AIDS and hunger, perhaps they are better suited to tackle problems like societal narcissism.

6.3 Conclusions

The history of America has been one of narcissistic superiority, entitlement, exploitation, and retaliation. Those who fled their home countries to escape repression at the hands of foreign monarchs soon became repressors of Natives and slaves and anyone else who fit their definitions of inferior. Long before psychiatrists affixed the term "narcissism" to a constellation of maladaptive traits and behaviors, white Americans expressed their superiority and deservedness and predictably took what did not belong to them and defied those who tried to protect themselves, their families, and their way of life.

There is an understandable temptation to regard narcissism solely as a personality style associated with individuals. Indeed, most of the popular literature on narcissism focuses on individual traits and how they can complicate social relationships. But as discussed in Chapter 5, narcissism manifests itself in complex organizations, which, particularly when led by narcissistic individuals, take on these traits, some of which are maladaptive and thus harmful to society. Regardless of the specific weaknesses in the arguments of this analyst or that, all seem to be picking up on characteristics found not solely in individuals or in organizations, but within larger society. If indeed the total is greater than the sum of the constituent parts, analysts are left with something that deserves discussion and, if possible, explanation.

The social sciences distinguish themselves with perspectives on human behavior different from other disciplines. Sociology, for example, examines social issues with a telescope, whereas psychology prefers a microscope. History argues that what occurred in the past informs the events of the present. Anthropology's forays into foreign cultures create an appreciation of both the primitive and the modern. The analysis of narcissism and crime, specifically as these intersect in the US, can benefit from moving outside psychology and psychiatry. This is particularly true when the analysis turns from individual narcissism to the ways it expresses itself more broadly.

When the camera pulls back even farther, it becomes evident that society – American society in this case – also exhibits personality traits seen at the lower levels. And as with individuals as well as organizations, societies can facilitate and commit harmful behavior. The history of the United States is fraught with multiple examples of gross insensitivity to the plight of certain peoples. Black slaves were kidnapped, bought and sold, beaten, raped, and sometimes murdered. Native Americans, who posed a threat to safety and expansion, had no real economic value and thus were disposable. To a lesser degree, groups like Chinese immigrants, another non-white population, were allowed to perform back-breaking work as long as they did not misbehave; otherwise, they, too, might face extermination.

The full-throated opening of the west created opportunities for a special breed of white men to exploit the newly discovered resources. Those who built the railroads were among the first of these opportunists. Such projects called for leaders who could take advantage of others including employees, customers, and even fellow entrepreneurs, to attain a goal. They had the leadership skills about which later experts on narcissism would write.

The fulfillment of Manifest Destiny made it possible for ambitious men to exploit the resulting opportunities. The conquest of Native Americans and the construction of railways intended to link the eastern US with the recently opened west. The railroads could move people back and forth much more efficiently, but also materials and machinery the new industries like forestry and mining would need. These abuses required a sense of superiority, not associated with just a few prominent and powerful men, but one that spread throughout much of the population. Once large numbers of people accept that they are superior to others, particularly those possessing something of value, the former feel entitled to belittle, derogate, and exploit the latter. Any ordinary empathy toward human beings is overshadowed by the threat the inferiors allegedly pose to civilized society.

Societal narcissism casts a wide net, and it employs the lower levels to carry out its nefarious plans. Manifest Destiny would have been little more than an idea, a historical footnote, without a collection of institutions, organizations, and individuals to make good on its promise. The US military, forced to take on greater sophistication due to several wars and benefitting from an industrial revolution, became the perfect vehicle to conquer any adversary that stood in the way. But this philosophy, which swept over the young country like an epidemic, required like-minded leaders whose personal ambitions and lack of human empathy were well-suited to executing the plan. Andrew Jackson and George Armstrong Custer were only two of many narcissistic leaders whose backgrounds and personalities permitted them to ascend to key roles during critical points in history. And as a result, each put his own stamp on the country, a stamp that resulted in grievous social harm.

Narcissistic superiority, entitlement, exploitation, and retaliation do not exist without consequence. Once these traits and associated behaviors have become solidified within society, they express themselves as condescension, prejudice, and discrimination. The eugenics movement serves as a case in point. Those deemed inferior because of IQ, mental disease, or physical disability would no longer be treated as legitimate members of society. Such inferiors now belonged in institutions where they did not have to be seen by the superiors. There, at least in theory, they would receive the services and care they needed. In practice, this meant neglect in the best case and abuse in the worst. So it should not have been surprising when Adolf Hitler, already predisposed to narcissistic superiority and the entitlements that accompany it, latched onto eugenics as a rationale for his plans, including his infamous final solution.

American society has long served as the exemplar of a democratic republic. Not since the war between the states in the 1860s has there been outright civil war. Americans enjoy a broad range of freedoms guaranteed by the US Constitution, a document created more than two centuries ago. The country's history boasts numerous instances of people born of modest backgrounds who rose to become success stories in business, education, public service, and other arenas. No wonder so many foreigners have risked virtually everything to make the US their new home.

But America has a darker side, one obscured by its image of a bright star on the horizon. This other side includes a long, sordid history in which certain Americans, predominantly white men, engaged in the ruthless exploitation of others, most often people of color, to achieve power, social status, and money. Exploitation demands that someone suffers a loss, and those who suffered throughout American history have included women, African slaves and their descendants, Native American tribes, immigrant Chinese laborers, and so many others.

American society continues its narcissistic behavior, much of which is directed toward marginalized groups including blacks, immigrants, non-Christians, and even women. The crimes resulting from this posture of superiority and entitlement include the killing of innocent minority suspects, the separation of immigrant families, the sexual harassment and assault of women, and the offenses of a right-wing, Christian movement headed toward authoritarian rule.

Throughout America's history, its institutions have undergone severe stress, causing some of them to bend under the strain. Yet, they have always managed to hold. The recent permutation of narcissism, however, exerts an even greater strain that threatens to break the bulwarks against autocracy, mayhem, and chaos. It remains to be seen if American society can survive the current brand of social narcissism.

The coverage of American history in a discussion of narcissism and crime has importance for another reason. Conservatives worked to remove from library shelves titles they deemed offensive because their subject matter related to race, slavery, sexual identification other than hetero, and other topics considered to infect readers, particularly young people, with liberal ideology. And so the history of slavery, lynchings, the burning of black neighborhoods, and other forms of overt and covert discrimination were to be scrubbed from school curricula and local libraries.

This movement to sanitize American history does not change the reality that played out over the last 400 years. It merely ensures that current and future generations lack knowledge about the myriad ways narcissistic actors have exploited and retaliated against those in society they regarded as inferior. Without such awareness, future Americans will feel less empathy toward segments of society who hold less power, possess fewer resources, or fit into various categories of "different." At minimum the new narcissists will overlook the plights of these people; at their worst, they will build on the history of narcissistic discrimination and abuse.

CHAPTER 7

Reflecting on the Nefarious Side of Narcissism

This analysis began as an attempt to demonstrate that narcissism – a personality style characterized by a sense of superiority and entitlement and a tendency to engage in exploitative and retaliatory behavior – bears responsibility for at least some criminal and otherwise harmful behavior. That mission was accomplished. The available evidence, informed by the work of clinicians and researchers and illustrated by actual cases reported in the media, shows that a narcissistic posture underlies a variety of socially maladaptive behaviors, many of which are defined by law as crimes.

Narcissism and the criminal behavior associated with it, however, extend well beyond entitled individuals who exploit and retaliate. Common conceptions of narcissism fail to capture the myriad ways in which it infects not only individuals, but also groups and organizations, large and small, including private corporations, government agencies, and nonprofits. The scholarly and popular literatures paint a portrait of narcissistic leaders who take their organizations down a dark path toward planning, committing, facilitating, or covering up unethical and illegal acts. As toxic as narcissistic individuals have proven themselves to be, organizations exhibiting these same traits have the potential to wreak far more havoc. They give cover to predatory offenders. They pollute and otherwise damage the environment. And they knowingly manufacture products that injure or kill. The analysis further reveals a disease that can metastasize throughout society, causing untold physical, psychological, emotional, and environmental harm and resulting in tremendous financial losses. For these reasons, narcissism more appropriately should be thought of as a highly contagious virus transmitted from person to person, generation to generation, and era to era.

Modern history offers no better exemplar of maladaptive narcissism than the forty-fifth and forty-seventh president of the United States, Donald J. Trump. For several decades the term narcissism had been part of the common lexicon used to describe arrogant, self-absorbed show-offs.

It served as water-cooler conversation and inspired popular books and blogs. But as fascinated as people may have been with narcissism as discussed in these forums, it appeared to have limited effect on their everyday lives. Donald Trump's ascent to the US presidency changed all of that. Narcissism no longer consisted solely of annoying coworkers in nearby cubicles or unfaithful partners seemingly in love with themselves. Now the narcissist of interest occupied the White House and was the *ex officio* leader of the free world, with ready access to the nation's nuclear codes. As a celebrity, Donald Trump had long basked in the public limelight and pushed the boundaries of propriety, but as president, his outrageousness now took dangerous new forms and faced new levels of scrutiny. Trump's sense of entitlement, enabled by a profound ignorance of history and the workings of government,[1] told him that his appointees and the agencies under his control existed to serve *his* needs, not those of the American people. Virtually everything he did during his terms in office reinforced armchair notions of bad narcissistic behavior, from his total disregard for time-honored norms to his well-documented attempt to overturn a legitimate election to his public promise to retaliate against his enemies,[2] most of whom had done nothing wrong.

Donald Trump's presidencies lent legitimacy to narcissism, the traits of which were shared or admired by many in his inner circle. Rudy Giuliani, a man once revered as "America's Mayor" for guiding New York City in the wake of 9/11,[3] thought nothing of stepping up to a microphone for Trump, spreading falsehoods about the 2020 election and, in doing so, ruining the lives of innocent election workers.[4] Congressman Kevin McCarthy, who briefly served as Speaker of the House and who initially blamed Trump for the events of January 6, changed course, flew to Florida, and prostrated himself before the President in hopes that his demonstrations of fealty would solidify his power within the Republican Party.[5] When in 2024 Donald Trump was forced to appear in a Manhattan criminal court, a group of prominent supporters, including Speaker of the House Mike Johnson and Senator J. D. Vance, slavishly donned blue suits and red ties in solidarity with the former president and publicly bashed the criminal justice system on his behalf.[6] These sycophants both mirrored and reinforced the behavior of the narcissist-in-chief.[7]

Those in the US who had long harbored contempt for people of color, non-Christians, immigrants, and the LGBTQ+ community now had official permission to hate from the highest authority in the land. Aggrieved whites emerged from the shadows and openly declared their allegiance to Trump and his campaign against the undesirables who were threatening the culture of *their* America. Trump's millions of MAGA devotees demonstrated that as unhealthy as he may have been, his public portrayal of narcissism was but a metaphor for a pernicious disease that has plagued America for its entire existence and continues unabated to the present day.

And thus the initial foray into the connection between narcissism and crime evolved into a study of harmful narcissistic traits and behaviors not just in the modern era, but throughout American history. Any attempt to understand contemporary narcissism, including those forms considered criminal, would be incomplete if it overlooked the country's past. Much like the film character who, upon discovering a fuse for an explosive, follows it to its source, the search for the origins of criminal narcissism traced back to the very beginnings of America.

Several centuries ago, adventurous white immigrants from far-off countries landed on the shores of the North American continent in hopes of a better life with some important, unspoken qualifiers: It would be a better life mainly for men of European heritage who held Christian beliefs. The native people who populated the New World would become enemies to vanquish, even though they had roamed freely for hundreds of years. The imported African slaves and their descendants would be tolerable so long as they accepted their status as chattel. Later arrivals, including the Chinese – never mind their willingness to leave their homeland and families thousands of miles away and take on dangerous, backbreaking work – would also feel the wrath of whites who made and enforced the written and unwritten rules. Westward expansion, inspired by Manifest Destiny and facilitated by the likes of Andrew Jackson and George Armstrong Custer, wrought irreparable harm on individuals, families, tribes, races, and the environment. These white men asserted their dominion over women, people of color, immigrants, non-Christians, and other segments of society they regarded as inferior.

The casual observer might still wonder what bearing early American history, even with its numerous examples of narcissistic behavior, has on contemporary social life. The answer is everything. A sense of superiority and entitlement, as well as a willingness to exploit and retaliate, did not just suddenly appear on the modern landscape. Like a novel virus, this posture first infected a few individuals. "We'll import some African slaves to work the tobacco, sugarcane, and cotton fields. If we don't destroy that Indian village, one day we'll be fighting their offspring. True Christians don't need Mormons with their suspect doctrine and multiple wives around here." These sentiments, frequently framed in the language of survival[8] and backed by holy scripture, spread to others, including children, who learn early in life that some people occupy a subordinate position within society and therefore have few or no rights.

Upon assigning others to an inferior status, it becomes easier to rationalize their mistreatment.

> These subhuman slaves are property we can buy, sell, beat, rape – even kill – if we so choose. The tribes occupy land we want and, besides, some of those Indians have kidnapped, raped, tortured, and killed whites.[9] They'll bend to our will or we'll obliterate them.[10] The Chinese immigrants can build railroads or work the mines, but once they challenge white authority, we'll shoot them like the vermin they are.

Inferiors must accept their place in society or suffer the consequences.

This social disease of narcissism has thus been an inextricable element of American culture from its very beginnings, despite brief periods of dormancy. Wars often bring out the best of those defending their freedoms, but once the threat subsides, the narcissism virus finds new opportunities to express itself. After the American colonists won their independence from the British Empire, they felt free to expand westward and subjugate the tribes that stood in their way. The glaring hypocrisy eluded most early Americans. Hostilities with Mexico in the 1830s and 1840s permitted greedy politicians and other opportunists to gobble up even greater expanses of the North American continent. Following the Civil War and Reconstruction, white supremacists would devise new ways to torment the recently freed blacks. After the wars of the twentieth century, African Americans and Native Americans who had fought bravely alongside their white brethren in foreign theaters faced hatred and discrimination once they returned to the US. Narcissism has taken different forms throughout history, but it has remained an ever-present element of American life.

The price paid for learning these lessons of history has been dear. Millions have died in the service of American narcissism. Countless families across several centuries have been torn apart by exploitative or retaliatory government policies.[11] Entire neighborhoods, villages, and towns have been wiped off maps by heartless whites asserting their superiority over "uppity" minorities. The Civil War, fought to free enslaved Southern blacks from narcissistic exploitation and retaliation, cost the country hundreds of thousands of lives. Even in the twenty-first century, politicians jeopardize the health and safety of the very citizens they are elected to represent – including their most ardent supporters – through executive and legislative actions designed to hold onto power and pander to their base.[12] A country rich in natural resources now battles destructive storms, wildfires, floods, and rising sea levels due in large part to selfish, exploitative stewardship of the environment.[13] The cost of narcissistic crime is incalculable.

Many of history's examples of narcissism appeared well ahead of any academic understanding of them. In time, psychoanalysts and social psychologists would piece together a clinically informed, empirically grounded set of profiles that not only refined Freud's construct but also prompted scholars and journalists to share their findings with a broader audience. Too much exposure to any social issue, however pressing, results in a sort of informational fatigue, if not exhaustion, inuring a public that otherwise might have sat up and taken better notice.[14] But despite the understandable cynicism surrounding all the attention given to narcissism, it remains a dangerous contaminant, one whose seeds formed centuries ago and have lain just beneath the surface, growing, mutating, with the implicit threat that from time to time, in this location or that, it would reemerge to infect not only individuals and their relationships but also society's institutions and the larger social order.

7.1   The Importance of Fairness and Empathy

The social order at risk consists of a fragile vessel held together with various types of normative glue that form a crucial but tenuous bond among actors and institutions.[15] One of the most important ingredients of this glue is norms governing fairness. These guide behavior not only in modern nations like the United States and the United Kingdom, but also in cultures without stable political regimes, advanced economies, or mass communication.[16] People see fairness norms operate in their everyday lives as they interact with family, friends, neighbors, coworkers, and strangers. Like air, these norms are omnipresent and invisible, so much so that people take them for granted and pay them scant attention. But their vital importance in understanding narcissistic crime cannot be overstated: fairness norms influence human interaction in virtually every sphere of endeavor, and narcissism violates them as a matter of course.

Of the ways social actors behave unfairly toward one another, exploitation and retaliation rank among the most harmful. Exploitative behavior leaves one party bereft of something of value. Something the exploiter has no right to take. In many cases, something that cannot be restored.[17] Exploitation, as well as affronts to fragile egos, elicits a desire to retaliate. These maladaptive behavioral responses – exploitation and retaliation – inhere in unhealthy narcissistic entities. This tendency to take and to seek revenge makes narcissism a serious if not existential threat to personal and social harmony. Much like acid, narcissism eats away at the normative glue that binds society together. It creates actors who put themselves above others and the rules by which others agree to abide. In this elevated position it becomes easier to assign lesser status and importance to inferior others who exist to be used if they have something of value; ignored or denigrated if they do not. If the inferiors criticize or make unreasonable demands, the narcissistic entity will strike back, frequently out of proportion to any transgression their target may have committed. Too much unfair behavior by entitled actors threatens the structural integrity of the vessel. One need only witness the effects of Trump and Trumpism on American democracy. Rarely does narcissistic exploitation or retaliation end well.

In the realm of personalities, narcissism does not stand alone. Psychology long ago discovered that society consists of a variety of personality styles, not all of which are equally capable of unfair, harmful behavior. Those who lean toward the obsessive-compulsive, for example, may come across as harsh in their judgment of others.[18] They may be fastidious about personal hygiene and organization to the point of absurdity. But most will not happily take advantage of others. If they act somewhat superior, it likely stems from perceived achievement or contribution, not entitlement. If someone offends them, they may overlook it, and if that is not possible, they will seek redress through socially appropriate channels. And although they may come across as aloof and unconcerned, their sense of empathy may well manifest when they see that others are hurting or in need.

Organizations, too, can have personalities other than narcissistic.[19] The nonprofit agency that exists to help the homeless is arguably altruistic. Rather than focusing on the preservation of its identity and the acquisition of material wealth, such an organization strives toward beneficent service as measured by clients served, clients referred to social service agencies, and clients moved from the street to safer, more permanent housing. This illustrates that large entities need not behave selfishly. To the contrary, they can do social good without expecting anything in return.

Not so with narcissistic actors. Inferior others are to be exploited if doing so meets egoistic needs. Seldom do those below deserve empathy or respect. If any members of these groups should demand the rights accorded the privileged, they need a quick, unequivocal reminder of their subordinate place in the pecking order. Donald Trump courted the African-American vote, a transparent attempt to exploit a segment of the population he otherwise held in contempt.[20] At public rallies he made sure his backdrop of adoring fans included a sprinkling of token minorities. He even cozied up to prominent black Republicans like Senator Tim Scott and Representative Byron Donalds. But in 2020, when Black Lives Matter protesters marched through the streets of American cities exercising their First Amendment right to free expression, Trump called them thugs and wondered why authorities could not employ painful, physical force to subdue them.[21] Narcissism can disguise itself only so long.

The psychological bridge linking a sense of superiority and unfair behavior against those regarded as inferior is a sense of entitlement. Once a narcissistic entity assumes a superior stance toward others, it feels free to violate rules and norms, including those related to fairness. To be sure, narcissistic actors have few qualms about exploiting or retaliating in general, but those in subordinate positions are easier to mistreat than those possessing intellect, competence, or other defensive strengths.

The intentional, unfair treatment of others also requires a shortage of empathy, the ability to put oneself in another's place. Narcissistic actors are unmoved by real-life displays of suffering or hardship. When Puerto Ricans, many of whom were left destitute by the fury of Hurricane Maria in 2017, went to see President Trump in the capital city of San Juan, he playfully tossed them packages of paper towels as though it were a game.[22] He would soon depart for the mainland on Air Force One, leaving the people of Puerto Rico – fellow Americans – to return to their devastated communities with little hope of relief. Such emotional callousness, unencumbered by guilt, permits the narcissistic entity to inflict injury or ignore tragedy until reined in by formal or informal social control.

To be sure, there have been attempts throughout history to control narcissistic actors who have shown themselves capable of causing personal and social harm, and some of these efforts have been successful. George Armstrong Custer and his invincible 7th Cavalry suffered the ultimate in humbling experiences at the hands of the Sioux and their allies. Unfortunately, a lot of innocents suffered in the process. President Richard Nixon, whose narcissistic excesses led to the Watergate scandal of the 1970s, was forced by prominent Republicans to resign from office and only escaped criminal prosecution through a pardon from his former Vice President and successor, President Gerald R. Ford.[23] Donald J. Trump finally faced multiple civil and criminal cases, though he never had to fully account for most of his alleged crimes. These examples suggest that those on the receiving end of narcissism's ravages take only so much before they invoke formal or informal means to end the harmful exploitation and retaliation.

7.2 Focusing on Narcissism Instead of Narcissists

Beginning with Freud and extending to his successors, the psychoanalysts made detailed observations of patients whose internal and external struggles with narcissistic disorders had brought them to therapy. The resulting clinical portraits by Heinz Kohut, Karen Horney, Otto Kernberg, and others added important refinements to Freud's early interpretations, and the development of the *DSM* permitted mental health professionals to embrace narcissism as a bona fide disorder deserving of diagnosis and treatment. Little did these early pioneers realize how critical this construct would become for understanding human relations.

Social-personality psychology, not yet an academic specialty when Freud first formulated his thoughts on narcissism, employed psychometrics and laboratory experiments to build a rich body of empirical knowledge about this personality style. The Narcissistic Personality Inventory (NPI) permitted researchers to delve more deeply into grandiose narcissism and correlate it with a wide array of traits and behaviors, some of which are personally and socially harmful. Later, psychologists identified other forms including vulnerable and collective narcissism. Not all types looked the same, but at the core lay a basic construct whose contours and influence could not be denied.

This analysis has argued that despite the important contributions clinicians and researchers have made in understanding narcissistic disorders, this collection of traits and the associated ways of behaving warrant a focus much broader than that of the individual, and their consequences extend far beyond the influence of any one person and their social network. Indeed, these maladaptive characteristics express themselves at higher levels of explanation. Sociology concerns itself with these structures within society that transcend the individual,[24] and it is from this view that organizational and societal narcissism may be best understood. Organizations consist of numerous individuals, and the strengths and foibles of the latter leave an undeniable imprint on the former. But once the entity justifies a mission statement and table of organization, and once it formulates policies and procedures, it takes on a personality of its own, derived in part from the leaders who have helped shape it, but one that no longer can be traced solely to the individuals who populate that space. These traits reveal themselves in business decisions, annual reports, marketing materials, legal filings, and public statements. The arrogance and entitlement expressed in such evidence may well survive the turnover of specific individuals, including those responsible for the narcissistic transformation. Psychology alone cannot explain this phenomenon.

To move toward a meaningful theory of narcissistic crime, then, it becomes necessary to view narcissism in a different light. Rather than just a specific psychological label for individuals, narcissism should be considered a worldview as well as a way of behaving. This worldview of a narcissistic entity – whether an individual, an organization, a social movement, or a nation-state – projects the idea of superiority toward others. Superiority implies that certain others are subordinate and therefore deserving of condescension and contempt. Once an entity assumes such a posture, it then exhibits the associated behaviors. The sense of entitlement and tendency to exploit surface as standard operating procedures. Bear Stearns serves as a case in point. Their subprime mortgages in the early 2000s lay in an ethical gray area. Yet lenders extended them to tens of thousands of borrowers, knowing full well that the latter could face financial ruin. The decision exploited customers' aspirations and weaknesses, and in doing so, promised irresistible returns.[25] All of this took place with little apparent compunction about the possible consequences. The result was disastrous for borrowers and for the larger economy. The narcissistic culture that had been permitted to flourish in the lending industry bore responsibility for this disastrous chain of events. And the behavior was criminal.

A parallel process operates at the societal level. Society is made up of individuals and organizations, but it, too, evidences characteristics distinct from those of the levels below. The current widespread use of social media such as Facebook, X, and Instagram has an individual element to be sure. Users access their accounts and post personal messages, photos, and videos. Organizations create, facilitate, and use social media for various purposes. But once widespread communication trends emerge, such as disinformation to support a specific political ideology, the phenomenon differs both quantitatively and qualitatively from individual posts. Prior to the January 6, 2021, insurrection, right-wing groups such as the Proud Boys and the Oath Keepers communicated with their members through social media.[26] But their messages reflected the sentiments of millions of sympathetic followers who relied on questionable information sources, some of whom were willing to engage in criminal acts to achieve their collective political and social ends. Their sense of superiority and entitlement enjoyed widespread acceptance.

And so the analysis has shown that narcissism – far beyond individual narcissists – represents the more important construct. Unhealthy narcissistic individuals can and do wreak a substantial amount of havoc in society. Some of them, like Donald Trump, have loomed large in the public eye, while most exist more anonymously as family members, friends, coworkers, neighbors, and strangers. But the maladaptive traits that constitute a narcissistic posture – including a sense of entitlement and superiority and a tendency to exploit and retaliate – move a civil, democratic society toward one characterized by arrogance, condescension, prejudice, and aggression.

Narcissism more broadly conceived serves as an integrative concept for several disciplines, including not only the obvious candidates such as clinical psychology, psychiatry, and social-personality psychology, but also history, sociology, and criminology. The clinical and experimental investigations of individual narcissism created a prototype upon which other behavioral and social sciences could base their respective models of self-centered, socially harmful behavior. To view narcissism this way does not diminish its importance as an identifiable set of individual traits and behaviors. To the contrary, by broadening its sphere of influence, narcissism becomes far more important for understanding human relations now and throughout history.

7.3   Focusing on Harms Instead of Crimes

Just as narcissism should be viewed differently, so should the concept of crime. Definitions of what society deems criminal are fluid, changing from place to place, era to era. Cannabis, as just one example, moved from a reviled substance said to induce "reefer madness"[27] to a recreational commodity legally sold in boutique dispensaries. Rather than what is defined as criminal with codified laws, society might be better served by examining the harm wrought by various kinds of behavior.

The harm associated with narcissism most often results from exploitative and retaliatory behavior. Forms of exploitation such as sexual assault and fraud, and forms of retaliation such as physical assault and murder, find condemnation in the criminal law. But outside these officially proscribed acts lie numerous forms of exploitation and retaliation not necessarily treated as criminal but which are responsible for a great deal of personal and social harm. Research misconduct, an exploitative offense discussed in Chapters 1 and 4, can result in significant financial losses, but seldom do such cases get charged as crimes.[28] Fabricating data or plagiarizing written work under a government grant wastes the grant money because it fails to yield valid and reliable information. It also wastes the time and resources of scientists who must rely on the honesty of others. It creates victims who may experience a profound sense of loss by having had their intellectual work misappropriated.[29] Such behavior also betrays the trust of the public whose tax dollars often subsidize the research. Whether handled administratively by a university or federal agency or through prosecution in state or federal courts, research misconduct committed by a narcissistic actor results in the same degree of harm to society, a degree that warrants its classification as criminal behavior.

A similar argument can be made about offenses committed by perpetrators who have been shielded from criminal liability. The hundreds of Boy Scout troop leaders who, for more than a century, sexually abused tens of thousands of boys in their care were guilty of serious crimes. Some of these cases resulted in civil actions against the perpetrators. Relatively few offenders faced criminal charges. Until the 2019 lawsuit, most cases were ignored or swept under the proverbial rug. The physical, psychological, and emotional harm to the victims, however, remains regardless of disposition. The definition of what is harmful and criminal, therefore, should not be limited solely to offenses embodied in formal criminal statutes or those coming to the attention of criminal justice authorities. Scholars interested in studying criminal behavior, including those employing victimization surveys, might be better served by focusing their attention on serious wrongful behavior – whether legally defined as crime or not – as well as the various harms that result from it, rather than solely on traditional, legal definitions of crime.[30] The victims of such behaviors arguably will be.

Finally, a theory of narcissistic crime does not imply that all crime results from this personality style. The individual who steals in order to eat engages in exploitation by taking something to which they have no legal right, but they need not behave narcissistically. They may do so to survive or to ensure the survival of those they love. Likewise, the person under the influence of alcohol, unable to think clearly or rationally, who retaliates against the bartender who cuts off his drinking, need not be a narcissist. Not every social actor who engages in exploitative or retaliatory behavior deserves this label. But many criminal forms of exploitation and retaliation, particularly those undergirded by an air of superiority and sense of entitlement, do account for a great deal of criminal, unethical, and otherwise harmful behavior in society.

7.4   Preventing Narcissism

No fleam exists for bleeding the narcissism virus from an afflicted entity. So as with other viruses, prevention makes more sense than treatment. If those concerned about narcissistic crime accept the disease metaphor, then it warrants a public health approach including primary, secondary, and tertiary prevention.[31] Primary prevention efforts aim to keep a potential patient from contracting the disease in the first place. Secondary prevention identifies members of the population who have already been exposed and attempts to keep them from getting worse. In recognition that some people inevitably become fully infected, tertiary prevention consists of treatment efforts to save them from the disease's more devastating effects. Taken together, these three forms of prevention represent a comprehensive strategy to reduce the suffering associated with a disease, in this case, narcissism.

Prevention spares victims the physical, psychological, and emotional trauma, as well as any financial loss. Prevention also conserves the limited resources of the systems needed to process behavior not prevented. The foregoing discussion of narcissism at all levels implies potential strategies for preventing it in the future.

Box 7.1 Preventing Ethics Violations

Clarence Thomas was confirmed by the US Senate as Associate Justice on the United States Supreme Court in 1991. It was a contentious process, in part because Anita Hill, a former law clerk, alleged that Thomas had engaged in inappropriate sexual conduct toward her.[1] Despite this and other concerns, Thomas made it through the confirmation process.

Fast forward to 2022 when *Politico* investigated allegations that Justice Thomas had accepted lavish gifts from conservative billionaire Harlan Crow.[2] These included travel on private jets and a loan for a recreational vehicle which was never repaid. Inasmuch as Mr. Crow's extensive business interests could conceivably be litigated before the Court, the potential for conflicts of interest should have been clear. Thomas's behavior was entitled and it was wrong.

As a result of public pressure, the US Supreme Court finally adopted a code of ethics, one which permits the justices to police themselves.[3] Given the implicit arrogance and sense of entitlement, why should the American public believe a code of ethics with no enforcement mechanism will prevent future misconduct?

[1] See CBS News (2010). Anita Hill vs. Clarence Thomas: The backstory. *CBS News*, October 20. www.cbsnews.com/news/anita-hill-vs-clarence-thomas-the-backstory/ Accessed 8-8-2025.
[2] Kaplan, J., Elliot, J & Mierjeski, J. (2023). Clarence Thomas and the billionaire. *ProPublica*, April 6. www.propublica.org/article/clarence-thomas-scotus-undisclosed-luxury-travel-gifts-crow.html Accessed 1-23-2024.
[3] VanSickle, A. & Liptak, A. (2023). Supreme Court adopts ethics code after reports of undisclosed gifts and travel. *The New York Times*, November 13. www.nytimes.com/2023/11/13/us/politics/supreme-court-ethics-code.html Accessed 1-23-2024. See also Liptak, A. (2023). Supreme Court's new ethics code is toothless, experts say. *The New York Times*, November 14. www.nytimes.com/2023/11/14/politics/supreme-court-ethics-code-clarence-thomas-sotomayor.html Accessed 5-14-2024.

7.4.1　Preventing Individual Narcissism

7.4.1.1　Parenting Education and Training

People frequently observe that parenting is the only job for which there is no training manual.[32] To the contrary, experts have penned hundreds of how-to books on parenting, some of which have gone on to become bestsellers.[33] It could be argued that some parents who would stand to benefit most from such books never read them. Regardless, first-time parents find themselves thrust into a role as caregivers for a human life, often ill-prepared for the huge responsibility they now face.

The literature on individual narcissism offers convincing evidence that parenting style exerts a significant influence on whether children later exhibit narcissistic traits and behaviors. Permissive parenting, wherein parents give in to the child's preferences and demands, helps create in them a sense of specialness, born not of accomplishment but of entitlement, which later manifests itself in maladaptive attitudes and behaviors. Snowplow parents – those who, often with the best of intentions, remove barriers for their children – do a disservice to their children and to society. Ethan Couch, the "affluenza" teen whose drunken, reckless driving took the lives of four people and injured nine others, was the product of overindulgent parents. Likewise, it could be argued that Fred Trump, Sr., left to parent alone by a depressed, disengaged wife, not only failed to inculcate in his son Donald the importance of honesty, integrity, and empathy, but instead steeped him in an ethic of avarice and revenge. Not setting appropriate limits and enforcing standards of appropriate behavior sends a signal to young, developing minds that no matter what they do or say, it is okay with Mom and Dad and therefore permissible. This puts such youths on an inevitable collision course with teachers, parents of friends, and other adults who individually and collectively try to enforce society's rules. Children raised in such a manner will inevitably learn that the world does not necessarily share in their belief of specialness. Without such training, they can do a great deal of damage.

Knowing the importance of this connection, nonprofits such as Planned Parenthood could offer instruction on how to parent authoritatively by setting and enforcing reasonable rules, disciplining firmly but fairly, all the while making sure the children never doubt how much they are loved. Given the availability of programming designed to help parents and caregivers raise children in a nurturing, consistent way, people who are planning to give birth to or adopt should undergo in-depth parenting training. Operating under the assumption that most first-time parents know little or nothing about how to inculcate and reinforce positive behavior, sponsors could hold parenting classes. Parents should have easy access to such classes just as they do for Lamaze and childbirth.[34] Preparedness increases the odds of better outcomes.

7.4.1.2   *Universal, School-Based Programs*

Some delinquency prevention programs take a universal approach wherein a large swath of children participate in the intervention.[35] Preventionists advocate this under the assumption that most or all the children face at least some risk of exposure and therefore stand to benefit from the treatment. Using a similar rationale, a narcissism prevention program could impart messages such as "Children are not entitled to break the rules," "Why taking advantage of others is wrong," and "Alternative responses to getting even."

Students in preschool through high school already undergo a variety of educational experiences, some of which do not relate to traditional academic subjects. Health classes, for example, acquaint students with the benefits of good hygiene and a balanced diet and the risks associated with alcohol, tobacco, and other drugs and unprotected sex. Physical education classes emphasize the importance of regular exercise. Students take classes that can help them in adult life, such as personal financial management. Likewise, courses in home economics and industrial arts equip students with knowledge and skills to take on day-to-day necessities such as meal preparation, sewing, and how to use various tools one might need for home maintenance and repair. Such information theoretically facilitates the students' transition from adolescence and dependence to adulthood and independence.

The twenty-first century has witnessed a strong backlash against the teaching of certain academic subject matter, such as social emotional learning and what has incorrectly but widely been labeled critical race theory (CRT).[36] The CRT situates the contemporary problems of structural racism and discrimination in the history of the United States, some of which has been covered in this analysis. Beyond the importance of how social narcissism has targeted numerous groups including people of color, Jews, Native Americans, and immigrants, an appreciation of history admonishes potential consumers – echoing the advice of philosopher George Santayana – to learn the mistakes of the past so as not to repeat them.[37] Until the pendulum swings back to a place where such subjects can once again be taught in schools, it may be up to parents and other caregivers to share with children a more complete, non-sanitized version of American and world history.

Other courses for children could focus on the more maladaptive behavioral responses of exploitation and retaliation. Research suggests that children can learn not to get even.[38] Indeed, it is possible to choose other, more positive, socially adaptive behavioral responses to a perceived grievance. Likewise, children can learn that taking without asking and taking without reciprocating will not serve their interests in the long run.

Given the close empirical connection between narcissism and social dominance orientation, a persuasive argument can be made for higher education as an antidote against the internalization of narcissism's more maladaptive thinking patterns and associated traits and behaviors. For one, college students learn critical thinking skills, which teach them to evaluate the many sources of information to which they will be exposed, ideally permitting them to reject overtly biased sources in favor of those committed to verification and a balanced view.

A strategy for the secondary prevention of narcissism faces some substantial challenges. A college education in the US has become so expensive that it is out of reach for many aspirants. For those willing to take the plunge, they very well may be saddled with tens of thousands of dollars in student loans, which will take years if not decades to repay. This reality argues for an alternative forum to learn how to critically think and to better evaluate various sources of information.

Tertiary prevention, that is, the treatment of narcissistic individuals, presents greater challenges. By virtue of their personality style, narcissists

---

Box 7.2 Safe Streets Baltimore

Preventionists working in inner cities know well the role revenge plays in gang violence. In Baltimore, Maryland, Catholic Charities has spearheaded an initiative designed to prevent gang-related shootings. Founded on the evidence-based Cure Violence program,[1] Safe Streets employs specially trained individuals who pay visits to shooting victims in the hospital or in their homes soon after the incident. In discussions with the victims, their families, and friends, these "violence interrupters" strive to make the case that retaliation is not the best or only option to address victimization.[2] These efforts are not always successful, but research reveals that they have reduced the amount of retaliatory violence.[3]

[1] For information on the Cure Violence program see https://cvg.org/about Accessed 2-10-2022.
[2] For information on how violence interrupters contribute, see https://monse.baltimorecity.gov/safe-streets-0 Accessed 2-10-2022.
[3] For information on how this works, see https://popcenter.asu.edu/content/violent-retaliatory-disputes

tend not to be introspective about the personal problems that brought them to treatment. If one has a deeply ingrained sense of superiority, it may well extend to treatment professionals. Narcissists in therapy may well consider themselves vastly superior to the professionals trying to help them. This fact should not dissuade qualified therapists from trying, but the treatment community must be realistic about the prospects for successful intervention. Promising modalities at the individual level include cognitive behavior therapy and group therapy. Cognitive behavior therapy rests on the assumption that an individual's thoughts, some of which might be based on erroneous information, lead to behavior that can be maladaptive and harmful to oneself and to others. If the individual can replace the erroneous information with facts, it should lead to more appropriate behavior. If the narcissist, subclinical or officially disordered, believes they are superior, it then becomes easier to derogate and mistreat others who are deemed inferior. A cognitive-behavioral approach would endeavor to change the individual's feelings of superiority. Ideally, this would bring about a change in behavior such as treating others fairly, respectfully, and, ideally, with empathy.

Parenting training may help correct narcissism in children. The widespread push for evidence-based interventions suggests a need to identify additional successful treatment modalities for individual narcissism. Prevention, as noted, is always preferable to treatment, but any serious strategy needs to address the large number of people who prefer a narcissistic posture and who pose a risk to others.

Evidence suggests that narcissists harbor a fear of humiliation.[39] Could such knowledge be employed for prevention? Australian criminologist John Braithwaite maintains that traditional forms of criminal punishment involve humiliation, but a form that stigmatizes rather than rehabilitates. As an alternative, Braithwaite put forth the concept of "reintegrative shaming."[40] In contrast to public humiliation, officials instead provide the offender the opportunity to acknowledge what they have done and how it has hurt individuals and the community. Rather than stigmatizing the accused, which can lead to yet additional wrongdoing, the public would accept the apology and facilitate the offender's future adjustment. Given narcissistic actors' fear of humiliation, might it be possible to devise a program designed to shame them in a reintegrative way?

Psychologist Christina M. Jones argues to the contrary. In an interesting synthesis of the literature on shaming and personality, she makes a convincing case that narcissists' bad behavior cannot be successfully checked by shaming – including reintegrative shaming – because they become angrier and react with more aggression when experiencing shame.[41] If she is correct, then what might society do to keep individuals who behave narcissistically in check?

In their book, *Scholarly Crimes and Misdemeanors: Violations of Fairness and Trust in the Academic World*, sociologist Bonnie Berry and this author suggest that one possible strategy for controlling research misconduct might be to employ prosocial gossip.[42] In contrast to malicious gossip, which serves no purpose other than hurting others, prosocial gossip alerts potential victims about the threat posed by the social actor who is the subject of the gossip. The academic world is small in the sense that negative information tends to travel quickly. For lab-coat offenders like those discussed in Chapters 1 and 4, perhaps one of the few ways to prevent future offending is to let the scientific community know what they have done and the damage they have wrought.

Likewise, individuals who seem to delight in breaking rules, violating norms, and victimizing those in their paths may be stoppable only by sharing their maladaptive behavior and the harm it has done with potential victims. Indeed, such prosocial gossiping already occurs. But if done strategically, it may well prevent a great deal of narcissistic harm.

7.4.2   Preventing Organizational Narcissism

From the growing body of evidence, organizations also behave narcissistically. They evidence a sense of entitlement that frees them to engage in exploitative practices that result in harm to their clients, their employees, collateral victims, and society in general. The narcissism evident in organizations parallels that in individuals in that they often take advantage of the weak and vulnerable and retaliate against anyone or anything that challenges their right to do so.

Private corporations, by their very nature, compete against one another in the marketplace. A quest for superiority and winning inheres in what they do. Their products and services must surpass those of their competitors. Their profits must satisfy their owners or stockholders. Corporations unwilling or unable to set and meet high bars often do not survive. This inherent narcissistic nature of the business world attracts and nurtures like-minded individuals. This may in part explain why some criminologists are so critical of capitalist society: Someone gets exploited through this economic system, and it is not those who control the means of production.

The work of Jennifer Chatman of UC Berkeley and her colleagues confirms what some in the business world have been asserting for some time.

When narcissistic leaders take over the reins of corporations, nonprofits, or government agencies, they exert an influence capable of corrupting the entire organization, so much so that it evidences similar maladaptive traits and behaviors. Removal of the narcissistic leader may become necessary, but it may not be sufficient to heal an infected organization.

Business schools, however, now realize that as inevitable as these traits may be among the students they train, they need to identify ways to address the more maladaptive side.[43] Whether such attempts at amelioration catch on and whether they yield the desired result remains to be demonstrated. But such efforts reveal a growing unease about narcissism within their ranks and its more negative consequences for individuals, for the corporation, and for society.

Knowing the negative outcomes associated with narcissistic leadership, private corporations and other organizations should take steps to weed out from candidate pools individuals whose words and behavior bespeak a maladaptive narcissistic posture. Such candidates may possess exemplary leadership qualities, but this strength may not be worth what the candidate will ultimately cost the organization and society.

Box 7.3 A Different Brand of Justice?

On November 18, 2021, twenty-year-old Christopher Belter appeared in court in Niagara County, New York, for sentencing. When he was seventeen, he raped and sexually molested four girls then 15–16 years of age. He faced up to eight years in prison for his crimes.[1]

Belter hailed from an affluent upstate family. He had attended a prep school. He was white. Judge Matthew Murphy announced in court that day that Belter did not belong in prison. In lieu of prison, the judge sentenced the defendant to eight years of probation.

Steven Cohen, an attorney for one of the female victims, said: "If this individual was not a rich white kid from a privileged background and an influential family, he would be in prison right now."[2] This case seems to illustrate the findings from social-personality psychology that pampered children can grow up to be narcissistic adults who do harm. The implications for prevention seem obvious.

[1] Fitz-Gibbons, J. (2021). Former prep-school student gets off with probation for raping teen girls. *New York Post*, November 18. https://nypost.com/2021/11/18/christopher-belter-gets-probation-for-rape-of-teens Accessed 11-18-2021.
[2] Lenghi, M. (2021). A judge sentenced a rapist to probation. One of his victims warns "he will offend again" *CBS News*, November 18. https://cbsnews.com/news/christopher-belter-mm-rape-victim-probation/ Accessed 11-18-2021.

This commitment to addressing narcissism must extend beyond the recruitment, training, and socialization of executives and managers. The idea that organizations possess personalities has moved beyond an intriguing metaphor to the realization that the corporate whole consists of much more than a sum of the individuals comprising it, and that like individuals, these unique organizational personalities are capable of a range of behaviors, some of which may not serve either the organizations or society very well.

Narcissists' tendency to retaliate points to other possible preventive strategies. For example, whereas most workers object to unfairness, the anger of narcissistic individuals is more likely to manifest itself in retaliatory behavior[44] such as malingering, pilfering, or in extreme cases, retaliatory violence. Such a finding reinforces the importance of promoting distributive, procedural, and interactional justice within organizations.

That narcissism became the personality style of choice was no accident. Despite efforts to apply other personality types to organizational analysis,[45] the traits of grandiosity, arrogance, and exhibitionism fit too many corporate profiles too well, as do the exploitation and ethical violations. While research on the personality of organizations remains in its infancy, the theoretical and empirical work to date depicts corporations whose image and behavior offer uncanny parallels to that of narcissistic individuals.

When the narcissistic behavior of corporate leaders moves into maladaptive territory, corporate boards and owners must be willing to make the necessary midcourse corrections, even if doing so temporarily hurts the proverbial bottom line. In fact, failing to act may well invite legal and public relations consequences that prove far more costly than replacing a narcissistic CEO.[46]

Whistleblowers have played and will continue to play a crucial role in exposing unethical and illegal narcissistic behavior. Understandably, many individuals prefer not to blow the whistle. Some employees may fear loss of their jobs or be involved in the wrongdoing and have legal exposure. They may face legal exposure even if they are innocent of any wrongdoing. A small percentage, however, knows of the wrongdoing and is willing to put their jobs, even their entire careers, on the line to do the right thing. Countless instances of organizational misconduct likely would not have surfaced were it not for insiders blowing the whistle.

Human resource specialists will never succeed in weeding out all unhealthy narcissistic individuals. To think otherwise is unrealistic. The ranks of employees within an organization will include those with narcissistic traits, from the top of the table of organization down to the bottom. Are there ways to harness narcissism and take advantage of its more adaptive aspects?

One tactic for dealing with individual narcissistic tendencies centers on trying to identify opportunities for those with such leanings to perform well while satisfying their unique ego needs. As acknowledged in the Introduction, narcissistic individuals are not all bad. Indeed, some are talented individuals capable of making important contributions. Leadership, for example, suggests an adaptive trait capable of inspiring respect and confidence and motivating productivity. Might it be possible to channel traits such as exhibitionism in positive directions? If an individual prefers to bask in the limelight, can the organization in which they work find suitable roles that permit them to perform before appreciative audiences? Organizations have a long history of administering aptitude tests to identify workers' strengths and preferences. HR specialists should be able to identify specific jobs that are best suited to individuals with narcissistic traits. And if these ego needs find expression, will the happy employee be less likely to engage in maladaptive behavior?

Possible vehicles for addressing organizational narcissism are unions and trade organizations, which work to serve the interests of their constituent members. They do so through such activities as education, training, and legislative lobbying. If organizational narcissism poses potential safety or legal risks for organizations' employees, customers, or constituents, could not trade associations serve their members' interests by undertaking initiatives designed to mitigate such risks? In the case of colleges and universities hit by sex abuse scandals, could not trade organizations such as the Association of American Colleges & Universities,[47] or perhaps its subdivision, The Presidents' Trust,[48] make it a priority to address sexual assault, abuse, and harassment in its members' athletic departments, Greek organizations, and elsewhere on campuses? Such a role assumes the trade organization itself is not infected with narcissistic leadership and characteristics that would prevent it from fulfilling this role.

The handling of the COVID-19 mask mandate in Florida serves as a case in point. Governor Ron DeSantis issued an executive order that prohibited any Florida school district from issuing a mask mandate.[49] In early 2021, Florida was one of several states experiencing a surge of COVID cases, ostensibly due to low vaccination rates. Despite this spike in cases and a corresponding increase in hospitalizations, DeSantis insisted that he would not permit mask mandates to infringe on individual freedoms. The American Federation of Teachers, the national organization representing teachers across the US, showed a willingness to take on government officials whose policies threatened teachers, staff, and students.[50]

Business schools, as training grounds for future corporate leaders, bear at least some responsibility for preventing CEOs from corrupting the organizations they lead. Their curricula incorporate all that is known about the connections between narcissism and bad corporate behavior. The business literature suggests that there not only is recognition of this challenge, but also that business schools have taken steps to address it.

7.4.3   Preventing Societal Narcissism

Societal narcissism represents, at least partially, unchecked individual and organizational narcissism. Put another way, if those other forms did not exist, it is less likely that signs of societal narcissism would emerge. The prevention strategies aimed at individual and organizational levels may well go a long way toward reducing societal narcissism. However, in recognition that societal narcissism represents more than simply the sum of the other two levels, it requires its own strategy.

The United States cannot turn back the pages of the calendar and recreate its history. Mistakes and abominations of the past serve only as object lessons, reverse role models for future generations. If Americans detest what they see in the mirror, they must commit to a total makeover. They must make a firm, unwavering commitment to fairness. Short of such a commitment, nations should fully expect to relive the past with all its arrogance, condescension, exploitation, and associated human suffering.

Tackling such an immense challenge understandably overwhelms even the most competent and caring in society. The task parallels other seemingly insurmountable problems such as ending world hunger. Where exactly does one start? Should authorities begin with a bottom-up, grassroots initiative? Or does a governmentally driven, federally funded, top-down approach promise better results?

Exactly which topics belong in the primary and secondary educational experience is subject to some debate. One camp argues to limit curricula to the more traditional three Rs. Others, however, assert that living and thriving in a complex society requires a broad array of knowledge and skills that go beyond the basics.

Social-personality psychology has produced convincing evidence that narcissistic traits express themselves in young people. Further, the link between narcissism – even the subclinical, collective narcissism of the masses – and prejudice suggests that this personality style, with its sense

---

Box 7.4 The Narcissism of Minor Differences

Dr. Seuss, the alter ego of author-illustrator of books for children, Theodore Geisel, spoke to the sense of superiority in his 1961 book, *The Sneetches and Other Stories*[1] about two groups of imaginary creatures. In the first story, some of the sneetches had plain bellies, whereas the bellies of others were adorned with big stars. Those with stars, of course, exhibited a sense of superiority toward their plain-bellied counterparts. The book relates efforts to add and then remove stars to differentiate one group from the other.[2]

One interpretation of this story is that one group is not superior to another. Could such simple but entertaining devices be used to discourage superiority in society and instead teach acceptance?

[1] Seuss, D. (1961). *The Sneetches and Other Stories*. New York: Random House Books for Young Readers.
[2] Jennings, C. R. (1965). Dr. Seuss: "What am I doing here?" *Saturday Evening Post, 238* (21), 105–109. October 23, 1965.

---

of superiority, may be responsible for more social harm than good. If children could gain exposure to adaptations to social exchange that promote social harmony versus condescension and prejudice, society might experience less division based on superiority.

What might such a curriculum look like? School officials and parents might demand that it be integrated within existing courses rather than constitute a new course. At most schools the day is already filled with required courses. The addition of more coursework likely is not an option.

History remains important for understanding the current contours and prevalence of narcissistic prejudice. These courses should not only encompass the ways marginalized peoples have been subjected to exploitation, retaliation, and spite, but also class discussions about how these practices set the stage for later conflict.

Mass media and social media play a significant, if not determinative, role in spreading the messages of influential, narcissistic social actors. Even before he was elected president, Donald Trump harnessed the power of social media, X (Twitter) in particular, to spread misinformation and stoke the fears and aspirations of his followers. Objective analyses of Trump's messages, including those echoed by Fox News, confirm that lie upon lie made their way to his supporters, many of whom accepted the messages as gospel.

In the era of Donald Trump, Fox News and certain other conservative media outlets went to great lengths to echo and reinforce the president's messages. Fox's audience numbers in the tens of millions, many of whom believe those messages and behave accordingly. When such large swaths of the population act on the advice of voices like those of popular Fox anchors, and when narcissistic impulses underlie the original message, the manifestation is no longer just individual or organizational; it infects a significant portion of American society.

This widespread form of narcissism is a much tougher nut to crack. The strategies that hold promise for addressing individual and organizational narcissism are barely relevant to social pathology on such a scale. Even if society holds figures like President Donald Trump responsible for the exacerbation of national narcissism, replacing him does little to address what is already firmly in place. His deposition will not immediately cause regular users of Facebook, X, or Instagram to stop sharing their likenesses and their trivial day-to-day activities with what they believe are adoring fans.

Despite the immensity of the challenge, there are a few strategies that might help fight against maladaptive social narcissism. There is a long-standing tradition of protest in democracies. In the twenty-first century, protesters have made their voices heard. Another obvious tactic to confront narcissism on a grand scale is voting. If narcissism gets support from institutions such as the White House and Congress, then those fighting narcissistic impulses must go to the polls and make their preferences known. In a democracy like the United States, voting is one obvious vehicle for counteracting narcissism at the highest levels of government. If one has access to the polls, and if one's vote still counts, elections serve as one important means by which citizens can replace officials whose narcissistic behavior threatens freedom with autocracy. A narcissistic government moving toward authoritarianism only gains power when the opposition stays home at election time.

In Chapter 3, much of the discussion focused on exploitativeness and retaliation as maladaptive behavioral responses, responses closely associated with grandiose narcissism. But in the array of behavioral responses available to social actors lie alternatives considered far more adaptive. Among these are reconciliation, the behavioral manifestation of forgiveness, and altruism.

7.5   Future Research on Narcissistic Harm

As impressive as the extant body of research on narcissism is, the current analysis points to other opportunities to make unique contributions to understanding individual, organizational, and societal narcissism.

7.5.1 Researching Individual Narcissistic Harm

In the early years of empirical research on narcissism, the NPI was the primary measure for exploring the contours and correlates of narcissism. However, over time, researchers developed new, arguably better measures capable of assessing narcissistic traits.

One problem that has characterized narcissism research on individuals is the lack of uniformity in measures. One study of narcissism and bullying may employ the NPI, whereas another uses the Pathological Narcissism Inventory, and still others use scales that assess distinct narcissistic traits such as entitlement or exploitativeness. It is good that through the study of narcissism so many valid and reliable psychometric measures have emerged. But it becomes problematic when one tries to synthesize the state of knowledge. The analysis becomes an apples-to-oranges comparison. New knowledge results from such research, but the exact nature of the contribution remains fuzzy at best.

One step toward standardizing measures would be to phase out use of the NPI. When the NPI was developed in the 1980s, few alternative measures of narcissism or its constituent traits were available. Once validated, the NPI permitted personality researchers to correlate this personality style with a wide variety of traits, attitudes, and behaviors, building a large, impressive literature. But noteworthy limitations inhere in the NPI, several of which were discussed in Chapter 2. The initial developers based the constituent traits on the description of the narcissistic personality disorder (NPD) as it appeared in the Diagnostic and Statistical Manual of Mental Disorders (DSM). As a personality disorder, the NPD does not represent subclinical narcissism, the form most likely found in the general population. Its subscales, then, also grounded in the DSM-III, carry the same limitations. Regardless, countless researchers employed the NPI to assess what some later described as grandiose narcissism. The immense contribution of this body of literature notwithstanding, the time has come to set it aside in favor of more precise measures of the various forms of narcissism and their specific sub-traits that do not have the same limitations.

Another strategy would be to study not just how individuals score on psychometric measures of narcissism, but the ways in which their everyday words and deeds convey this style. Diary studies, wherein subjects – not just university psychology students, but others in the population – would record their daily exchanges with others. Such an approach might reveal a maladaptive narcissistic posture irrespective of any scores on psychometric tests.

The National Longitudinal Survey of Adolescent Health[51] represents an extremely rich data on the health-related behaviors of adolescents. Researchers from a variety of disciplines have used Add Health to explore myriad issues including academic performance, adolescent sexual behavior, and the role of genetics in violent behavior. As of mid 2024, scholars had published more than 6,000 articles and chapters using the Add Health data.[52] The author and social-personality psychologist Amy B. Brunell developed and validated a measure, the Add Health Narcissism Scale, using variables originally included for other purposes.[53] This measure could be used to examine narcissism and how it relates to higher levels of explanation.

In the US, the Society for Personality and Social Psychology (SPSP) is the primary scholarly association for those interested in personality types such as narcissism. The SPSP members number more than 7,500 and several thousand attend its annual meetings.[54] Perhaps the SPSP could convene a committee of narcissism specialists for the purpose of identifying and reaching consensus on a suitable set of measures for future research on grandiose narcissism. The same could be done for vulnerable, communal, and other forms of narcissism.

There is more work to be done to understand and respond to narcissistic crime. Prospective longitudinal research would offer one of the strongest approaches to understanding the developmental causes and short- and long-term consequences of individual narcissism, including the role of specific parenting styles, peer relationships, and neighborhood influences. This includes a more thorough examination of genetic factors and how they might interact with environmental factors to produce maladaptive narcissistic traits.

7.5.2 Researching Organizational Narcissistic Harm

Researchers should also pay greater attention to the narcissism of organizations, including entities whose exploitative actions result in injury and death, damage to the environment, and untold financial losses.

The measurement challenge extends to organizational narcissism. Much like individual narcissism, organizational researchers have arrived at more than one way to measure narcissistic traits and behaviors in organizations. Again, uniformity of measures, particularly those that have well-established validity and reliability, will move this field of inquiry further than every researcher employing his or her unique set of data collection instruments.

The body of research on organizational narcissism remains in a nascent stage. Nevertheless, a small group of theorists and researchers have found inventive ways to assess narcissistic traits of organizations and those of their CEOs. Archival documents, including annual reports, press releases, and website content, all have been used to substantiate narcissistic traits and behaviors in complex organizations. The strength of unobtrusive measures includes the fact that they are unbiased by the researchers' measurement. As it turns out, these strengths are also a weakness in that the researcher must make do with what these sources provide.

One set of methods, Hierarchical Linear Modeling (HLM), is particularly well-suited to analyzing phenomena at more than one level of analysis. It permits the analyst to link variables of interest.[55] Criminologists, for example, have looked at individual-level data on youth in large cities.[56] But they were also interested in the neighborhoods in which these young people have grown up and where they interact with peers and engage in delinquent activities. HLM permitted these researchers to simultaneously analyze the variables from both levels. A further advantage is that it can also be used to examine phenomena longitudinally over time. This makes it a powerful statistical technique.

Applying this set of methods to the study of organizational narcissism, researchers could devise a study wherein the constructs of interest were measured at various levels throughout the organization including line workers, supervisors, mid-level managers, and executives. Aside from assessing personalities, the strategy would collect detailed data on the organizational climate. Armed with such data, the analyst could explore a wide range of issues. Are narcissistic organizations more likely to attract and retain narcissistic employees at all levels? Do organizations that exploit their customers or the environment also exploit their employees? If so, do narcissistic organizations experience more counterproductive work behavior than non-narcissistic organizations?

In the wake of the 1986 Challenger disaster, sociologist Diane Vaughn undertook an in-depth organizational analysis of NASA to understand what exactly went wrong. The book reporting the results of her research laid the blame squarely at the feet of the organizational culture that made possible a series of missteps and oversights which led to this tragedy.[57] Future studies of organizational narcissism could similarly employ detailed analyses of how organizations become infected, how narcissism spreads, and how it results in various types of harm.

7.5.3   Researching Societal Narcissistic Harm

What began as an analysis of the connections between narcissism and various forms of criminal behavior in individuals and organizations evolved into a more comprehensive historical case study in which the United States and its past played and continue to play an irrefutable role. This focus in no way implies that the US is uniquely narcissistic or that it maintains a monopoly on narcissistic traits and behaviors, including those associated with criminal behavior.

The measurement of narcissistic tendencies within the larger society poses a unique but not insurmountable challenge. Researchers have not been investigating societal narcissism for very long, even though it has been decades since Christopher Lasch made a convincing case for doing so. His analysis was quite admirable because he had available much less data than what are available to contemporary analysts.

There are existing datasets that lend themselves to the analysis of narcissism and its various traits. The General Social Survey (GSS),[58] administered

---

Box 7.5 Putting Foreign Movements Under the Microscope

Boko Haram, more formally known as the Islamic State in West Africa, has gained notoriety for kidnapping and raping hundreds of women and girls.[1] The known association between narcissism and sexual assault takes on new significance when sanctioned by a fanatical movement as a means to establish dominance and superiority and is practiced on a grand scale.

In its perversion of Islam, Boko Haram believes impregnation through rape will ensure an enduring legacy of their extremist views.[2] This is accomplished by exploiting women and girls who have done nothing other than find themselves in the middle of a conflict zone, unable to fight, with nowhere to flee.

Examples such as Boko Haram illustrate that the West does not have a monopoly on narcissistic crime. Those interested in researching the narcissism of groups and nation-states might benefit from studying extremist religious movements such as Boko Haram and the societies in which they are permitted to flourish.[3]

---

[1] Oriola, T. B. (2017). "Unwilling cocoons": Boko Haram's war against women. *Studies in Conflict & Terrorism, 40,* 99–121. https://doi.org/10.1080/1057610X.2016.1177998

[2] Nossiter, A. (2015). Boko Haram Militants Raped Hundreds of Female Captives in Nigeria. *The New York Times,* May 18. www.nytimes.com/2015/05/19/world/africa/boko-haram-militants-raped-hundreds-of-female-captives-in-nigeria.html Accessed 6-1-2024.

[3] For a comprehensive analysis of these events, see Habila, H. (2014). *The Chibok Girls: The Boko Haram Kidnappings and Islamist Militancy in Nigeria.* New York: Columbia Global Reports.

by the National Opinion Research Center at the University of Chicago for several decades, is one such possibility. The GSS contains variables that could be employed to assess narcissistic attitudes over time.

7.5.4 Researching Narcissistic Harm Outside the US

The present book has used the United States as a case study to illustrate individual, organizational, and societal narcissism, but future analyses could perform similar analyses on other nation-states. Germany, with its history of Nazism and the perpetration of the Holocaust, is one obvious candidate. Germany's resurgence of far-right-wing political activity has been accompanied by physical violence against Jews, people of color, and members of the LGBTQ+ community.

7.5.5 Nation-State Narcissism Abroad: The Russian Federation

The Russian Federation represents another nation-state worthy of analysis. President Vladimir Putin's grandiose narcissism has shown itself in his bare-chested ride atop a horse and his pretending to play professional-level ice hockey.[59] The exploitativeness of Putin and his supporters has transformed a postcommunistic, planned democracy into little more than an oligarchy and kleptocracy: He and his favored supporters enrich themselves at the expense of the Russian people. Putin buys lavish homes that a lifelong public servant should not be able to afford.[60] Those who challenge his ruling style find themselves the objects of his retaliation, imprisoned or executed.[61]

Putin's Russia offers an example of narcissistic behavior by a corrupt nation-state. Those in the twenty-first-century US might study the Russian Federation to understand what happens when a democracy moves toward autocracy. The resulting totalitarian government shows itself capable of serious forms of exploitative and retaliatory acts, the effects of which are often felt in other parts of the world.

7.5.6 2016 Election Interference

Donald J. Trump faced Hillary Rodham Clinton in the 2016 US presidential election. Early on, Trump had labeled her "Crooked Hillary" to paint her as a criminal and to dissuade voters from supporting her.[62] While serving as Secretary of State in the Obama administration, Hillary

---

Box 7.6 Putin's Revenge?

Alexei Navalny had long been a vocal critic of Russian President Vladimir Putin.[1] Navalny called out Putin for his obvious corruption and lavish lifestyle.

In 2020, Navalny became seriously ill and was hospitalized. Doctors discovered that he had been poisoned with Novichok, a lethal nerve agent and favorite weapon of Russian operatives.[2] Navalny recovered and eventually returned to Russia to resume his public critique of Putin and his corrupt allies.

Upon returning to his native Russia in 2021, Navalny was immediately arrested and charged with extremism.[3] He had a trial, and no one was surprised he was found guilty on all counts and was sentenced to prison.[4]

Alexei Navalny had been transferred to a Yamalo-Nenets prison in Western Siberia. In February of 2024, he became suddenly ill and died.[5] Russian experts, including former US Ambassador to Russia Michael McFaul, put the blame for Navalny's death squarely on President Putin,[6] who had finally gotten his retaliation. Federal investigators, however, later revealed that their intelligence told them that Putin was not responsible.[7] But could he have created a culture in which such actions were encouraged and rewarded?

[1] For a good overview of Navalny's opposition to Putin, see Gupta, G. (2024). Who was Alexei Navalny? *The New York Times*, February 16. www.nytimes.com/2024/02/16/world/europe/aleksei-navalny-career-russia.html Accessed 4-3-2024.

[2] Schwirtz, M. & Eddy, M. (2020). Alexei Navalny was poisoned with Novichok, Germany says. *The New York Times*, September 2. www.nytimes.com/2020/09/02/world/europe/navalny-poison-novichok.html Accessed 5-27-2024.

[3] Troianovski, A. & Nechepurenko, I. (2021). Navalny arrested on return to Moscow in battle of wills with Putin. *The New York Times*, January 17. www.nytimes.com/2021/01/17/world/europe/navalny-russia-return.html Accessed 4-3-2024.

[4] Treisman, R. (2022). Russian court finds jailed Kremlin critic Alexei Navalny guilty of fraud. *NPR*, March 22. www.npr.org/2022/03/22/1088009817/putin-critic-alexei-navalny-guilty Accessed 4-3-2024.

[5] Hopkins, V. & Kramer, A. E. (2024). Aleksei Navalny, Russian opposition leader, dies in prison at 47. *The New York Times*, February 16. www.nytimes.com/2024/02/26/world/europe/aleksei-navalny-dead.html Accessed 4-1-2024.

[6] Irwin, L. (2024). Former ambassador to Russia: "Putin killed Navalny, let's be crystal clear." *The Hill*, February 16. https://thehill.com/policy/international/4472127-former-ambassador-to-russia-putin-killed-navalny/ Accessed 4-1-2024.

[7] De Luce, D. (2024). Putin likely did not directly order Navalny's killing, U.S. intelligence agencies conclude. *NBC News*, April 27. www.nbcnews.com/news/world/putin-likely-not-directly-order-navalnys-killing-rcna149663 Accessed 5-27-2024.

Clinton had used a private email service, the contents of which were stored on a private server at her New York residence. Most federal government employees use their respective agencies' official email accounts; indeed, they are expected to do so for work. When she turned the server over to federal investigators, a portion of the emails was nowhere to be found. At one point, then-candidate Trump publicly announced, "Russia, if you're listening, I hope you're able to find the 30,000 emails that are missing."[63] Presidential candidates often make outrageous statements, but this was perhaps the first time one openly invited a hostile foreign power to commit a crime against the United States.

It was no secret that Vladimir Putin preferred Donald Trump to the other presidential candidates. On more than one occasion, Trump had paid Putin compliments, stating well before becoming president, "It is always a great honor to be so nicely complimented by a man so highly respected within his own country and beyond."[64] As a former KGB operative, Putin was not a fool. His early years in counterintelligence work had made him an extremely cunning and capable adversary, one who undoubtedly knew multiple paths to achieving an objective. In Donald Trump he clearly saw someone who craved and responded to flattery. In short, Putin quite likely had Trump's number. He would have been more than receptive to Trump's invitation to ferret out Clinton's potentially damaging emails, thereby improving Trump's chances of winning the Presidency.

During this same time, the GRU, the intelligence arm of the Russian government, infiltrated the information systems of the Democratic National Committee, the Democratic Congressional Campaign Committee, as well as various officials of Hillary Clinton's campaign. The GRU made much of the hacked data available to the public in order to put Hillary Clinton in a bad light.[65]

These and related efforts by Russia to interfere with the 2016 US presidential election prompted the US Department of Justice to initiate an investigation, which was spearheaded by Special Counsel Robert Mueller, a well-respected former head of the FBI.[66] Mueller and his legal team conducted an exhaustive investigation, and, as a result, Russian operatives were charged with specific crimes.[67] The likelihood that they would face justice in the US was slim, but the indictments sent a message to the Russians that the US would not overlook election tampering by a nation-state, not even one as large and powerful as Russia.

The Russian Federation under Vladimir Putin represents an example of arrogance and entitlement out of control. Putin and his supporting cast of wealthy oligarchs have enriched themselves far beyond what should be possible under a constitutional republic. In fact, Putin's personal wealth has been estimated at more than $200 billion, which, if accurate, would make him one of the wealthiest men in the world.[68]

7.5.7 The Olympics Doping Scandal

The Olympic Games held every four years represent the pinnacle of international athletic competition. Hundreds of athletes representing countries large and small do their best to win medals for themselves and the nations they represent. In between the Olympic years are other games in which athletes have opportunities to compete internationally and hone their skills, but the Olympic Games stand apart by their heritage and prestige.

Such keen competition creates incentives to deviate from accepted practice. In the past athletes have been known to take performance-enhancing drugs to give them an edge over competitors.[69] These and related shortcuts have forced Olympic officials to implement rigorous drug-testing protocols.

Prior to the 2018 Olympic Games, Russia was rumored to have circumvented the testing process by secretly substituting blood samples. Russian insiders finally came forth and described in detail the methods by which the Russians had subverted the system for testing athletes.[70] Instead of owning up to its misdeeds, the Russian government denied the allegations and made it known that those whistleblowers who had revealed the inner workings of the doping scheme would face Putin's wrath.[71]

Something as seemingly healthy and wholesome as the quadrennial Olympic Games served as yet another opportunity for the Russians under Vladimir Putin to pursue criminal activity. Although it has long been known that Olympic athletes have tried to gain various unfair edges, the problem has largely been considered one of individuals. Recent investigations have made it clear that rather than the isolated incidents involving a handful of individuals, the doping scandal was a well-orchestrated, government-sponsored conspiracy to circumvent rules to win Olympic gold.

7.5.8 Russia's Invasion of Ukraine

In the fall of 2021, Russian President Vladimir Putin began moving military troops and equipment to the eastern border of Ukraine. The world's unease with this development proved to be well-founded: In 2014, Putin had ordered a Russian military invasion of the Crimean Peninsula. Although his aggression brought about sanctions from the US, Russia retained Crimea as its own.

By early 2022, the estimates of Russian troops surrounding three sides of Ukraine numbered more than 150,000.[72] The Russian government tried to explain the military maneuvers as war games, an explanation contradicted by other indicators, including the influx of blood supplies.[73]

President Biden and US Secretary of State Antony Blinken reached out to NATO and the European Union to establish unity in the face of the Russian aggression. One outcome of these efforts was a graduated list of economic sanctions the West would impose on Russia if it chose to invade. In February of 2022, President Putin declared two eastern regions of Ukraine, Donetsk and Luhansk, to be independent. Having done so, he concluded that Russia would send troops into both regions as "peacekeepers."[74] This was, of course, a pretext for war.

The US and its NATO partners regarded Putin's declaration and associated military deployment as a de facto invasion. In response, the United States, NATO, and the European Union imposed economic sanctions on Russia to make them change course. Although the increasing sanctions caused substantial disruption to the Russian economy, Putin's military attacks continued unchecked.

Russia's military has undoubtedly committed war crimes in Ukraine. They have targeted civilians in their attacks, destroying residential neighborhoods, churches, schools, and even hospitals. Numerous mass graves have been discovered, some containing hundreds of murdered Ukrainians. Many of the survivors and the deceased have suffered atrocities, including rape and torture. As a result of Russia's actions, the International Criminal Court in The Hague, the Netherlands, opened an investigation into possible war crimes.

The behavior of the Russian government and of the actors operating with their implied consent leads to several conclusions. Russia acted arrogantly and with a sense of entitlement in trying to influence the US election, as they did in trying to cheat in the Olympics. Both incidents represent efforts to achieve outcomes Russia did not deserve.

President Vladimir Putin has turned Russia into a kleptocracy. Putin has real estate holdings and other wealth that cannot be explained by his presidential salary or his earlier career in the KGB. Many of his most prominent supporters are wealthy Russian businessmen Putin has permitted to operate quasi-legal corporate empires.

The crimes of the Russian Federation are many and varied. It is well-known that the Kremlin has ordered the assassinations of numerous individuals, some of whom were critics of Vladimir Putin. One such critic was shot dead within yards of the Kremlin. They have even shown a willingness to go beyond their borders to eliminate those they perceive as critical or disloyal. The crimes coming out of Putin's Russia suggest several conclusions about nation-states that engage in such behavior. It amounts to nothing short of arrogance to attempt to influence another country's election, particularly a country as powerful as the United States. Likewise, the same arrogance and sense of entitlement told the Russian government that Olympic gold – and the international recognition associated with it – was well worth taking ethical and legal shortcuts. The Russian Federation conspired to subvert the rules of the Olympic Games by giving their athletes a performance-enhancing edge to win gold. What emerges is a country willing to substitute cunning and deceit for competence and achievement. The personality infects not only the Olympics, but other games and sports, proving that these traits have moved well beyond individuals to infect an entire government.

The Russian Federation has engaged in many forms of exploitative behavior. It has the misappropriated data belonging to countless individuals and organizations and used those data for illicit purposes. It used deception in multiple attempts to garner gold medals during the Olympic Games. Russian oligarchs have enriched themselves at the expense of ordinary Russian citizens. Russia invaded and occupied Crimea, and it tried to do the same in Ukraine. Nation-states, therefore, can and do engage in exploitative behavior that results in a range of significant harms. Given the increasingly authoritarian direction the US has taken under the leadership of President Trump, an in-depth analysis of Russia may prove instructive.

Among countries conspiring to commit crimes, none has more suspected involvement than China. Their ruthless pursuit of foreign intellectual property could perhaps best be described as shameless. It has been well-known for several decades that China puts substantial resources into identifying inventions and products which to exploit. Once they successfully seize the secret code or formula, they quickly convert it into mass production, flooding the international marketplace with goods whose intellectual provenance belongs to another.

The United States has called out China multiple times in the last several decades, eliciting official responses ranging from denials to promises that they will take every possible step to keep it from happening again. And then the next incident occurs, starting the cycle anew.

Of the candidates for future research, North Korea is an obvious possibility. Its leader, Kim Jong Un, demands constant praise and adoration. When he perceives the slightest criticism or failure to show deference, he retaliates swiftly and severely. He and his regime exploit the North Korean people in myriad ways, not the least of which is a so-called communist leader who enjoys a lavish lifestyle. It is a country worthy of further study.

7.5.9   *Researching Narcissism and Artificial Intelligence*

The analysis in this book has focused on more traditional levels of explanation that can and do take on a narcissistic posture: individuals; groups and organizations, and; social movements and nation-states. Technological advances, however, have created yet another one with which society must reckon: artificial intelligence (AI). There was a time when the notion of computers becoming so intelligent that they threatened humankind was the stuff of science fiction, such as HAL 9000 in *2001: A Space Odyssey*. Fast forward to the present and society is there. AI has reached a scary degree of sophistication within a short period of time. In the twenty-first century the world has had to confront an array of risks AI poses.

AI receives its training through input from subject matter experts. On behalf of AI, these individuals may react to questions and scenarios, which in turn teach the AI how to consider such complex problems and issues. The more comprehensive and detailed the input, the more AI's ability approximates that of a human.

The current analysis has advanced the notion that from its very beginnings, the US has been a highly narcissistic country, and its narcissism has taken a variety of forms throughout history. Chapter 2 discussed research that suggests American college students have become more narcissistic over time. Those who develop AI recruit their experts from among the educated American population. It stands to reason that, unless personality screening procedures eliminate those with narcissistic leanings, AI theoretically receives much of its training from those with a narcissistic posture.

If the AI training proposes a scenario in which the trainer must supply answers to a moral or ethical dilemma, or one in which superiority toward a racial or ethnic minority could be brought to bear, what are the implications for AI and the decisions it makes for humankind in the future? Could AI become so maladaptively narcissistic that it gives advice and makes decisions that result in personal or social harm? Those interested in the AI-personality nexus could devise studies to explore some of these issues. It is only going to play a greater role in the lives of Americans.

7.6   Conclusions

Narcissism in all its forms and at all its levels has been, and continues to be, responsible for a great degree of harm in American society. Rather than simply an individual personality style, narcissism expresses itself at organizational and societal levels, and it is at these levels where it arguably does the most damage. The narcissistic sense of superiority and entitlement has permitted generation after generation of white Americans to not only look down on blacks, Indigenous peoples, women, non-Christians, and immigrants, but also free whites – men in particular – to take what they want including land, sex, individual freedom, and natural resources.

Society now knows enough about narcissism to undertake efforts aimed at prevention and control. The civil and criminal justice systems serve as vehicles for making narcissistic actors accountable for the harm they do. Far better, however, would be efforts to prevent narcissistic attitudes and behavior, beginning as early as possible.

Further research on narcissism is important, and it should include not only individual and organizational studies in the US but also other countries like the Russian Federation, which, under Putin, has transformed from a democracy to an autocracy. The US under Trump has moved in a similar direction, and it might be instructive to understand how such deleterious changes take place in order to prevent their occurrence in America.

Notes

Introduction

1. Riso, D. R. (1987). *Personality Types: Using the Enneagram for Self-Discovery.* Boston: Houghton Mifflin.
2. In a later book, Riso gave the type three a more positive label: The motivator. See Riso, D. R. (1990). *Understanding the Enneagram: The Practical Guide to Personality Types.* Boston: Houghton Mifflin.
3. Riso, *Personality Types*, p. 79.
4. Ibid.
5. www.enneagraminstitute.com/ Accessed 2-18-2021.
6. In 1972 the US Supreme Court in *Furman* v. *Georgia* declared the death penalty unconstitutional in the way it was being administered, leading to a moratorium. The *Furman* case was overturned in *Gregg* v. *Georgia* in 1976, permitting executions to resume.
7. Riso's 1987 book is a well-written, impressive piece of scholarship. However, even though the descriptions seem to have face validity, they lack grounding in empirical research. Despite this, the Enneagram enjoys a great deal of acceptance, including among therapists. Efforts to establish the validity and reliability of this system include: Wagner, J. P. & Walker, R. E. (1983). Reliability and validity study of a Sufi personality typology: The Enneagram. *Journal of Clinical Psychology, 39,* 712–717; https://doi.org/1097-4679(198309)39:5<712::AID-JCLP2270390511>3.0.CO;2-3 and Newgent, R. A., Parr, P. E., Newman, I. & Higgins, K. K. (2004). The Riso-Hudson Enneagram Type Indicator: Estimates of reliability and validity. *Measurement and Evaluation in Counseling and Development, 36,* 226–237. https://doi.org/10.1080/07481756.2004.11909744
8. For a description of obsessive-compulsive symptoms, see https://my.clevelandclinic.org/health/diseases/9490-ocd-obsessive-compulsive-disorder Accessed 12-9-25.
9. For an overview of equity theory, see Walster, E. & Walster, G. W. (1978). *Equity: Theory and Research.* Boston: Allyn & Bacon.
10. For an overview of this perspective, see Wellford, C. (1975). Labeling theory and criminology: An assessment. *Social Problems 22,* 332–345. https://doi.org/10.2307/799814

11. Twenge, J. M. & Campbell, W. K. (2010). *The Narcissism Epidemic: Living in the Age of Entitlement*. New York: Atria Books.
12. Burgo, J. (2015). *The Narcissist You Know: Defending Yourself against Extreme Narcissists in an All-about-Me Age*. New York: Touchstone.
13. Kluger, J. (2014). *The Narcissist Next Door: Understanding the Monster in Your Family, in Your Office, in Your Bed – in Your World*. New York: Riverhead Books.
14. See, for example, Wright, J. P. & Beaver, K. (2014). Teaching a criminological taboo. *ACJS Today*, *39*, 1–13 (10 pp.).
15. See Rosenfeld, R. (2011). The big picture: 2010 Presidential Address to the American Society of Criminology. *Criminology*, *49*, 1–26. https://doi.org/10.1111/j.1745-9125.2010.00216.x
16. For an excellent essay on the importance of neighborhood for understanding crime, see Sampson, R. J. (2013). 2012 Presidential Address to the American Society of Criminology: The place of context: A theory and strategy for criminology's hard problems. *Criminology*, *51*, 1–31. https://doi.org/10.1111/1745-9125.12002
17. Duchon, D. & Burns, M. (2008). Organizational narcissism. *Organizational Dynamics*, *37*, 354–364. https://doi.org/10.1016/j.orgdyn.2008.07.004
18. For a dictionary definition of personality, see www.merriam-webster.com/dictionary/personality. Accessed 5-9-2016.
19. Brunell, A. B., Gentry, W. A., Campbell, W. K., Hoffman, B. J., Kuhnert, K. W. & Demaree, K. G. (2008). Leader emergence: The case of the narcissistic leader. *Personality and Social Psychology Bulletin*, *34*, 1663–1676. https://doi.org/10.1177/0146167208324101
20. Lasch, C. (1979). *The Culture of Narcissism: American Life in an Age of Diminishing Expectations*. New York: W. W. Norton.
21. Young, S. M. & Pinsky, D. (2006). Narcissism and celebrity. *Journal of Research in Personality*, *40*, 463–471. https://doi.org/10.1016/j.jrp.2006.05.005
22. Thanks Prof. Amy B. Brunell of The Ohio State University at Mansfield for bringing this interpretation to my attention in a face-to-face discussion.
23. Fehr, E. & Gintis, H. (2007). Human motivation and social cooperation: Experimental and analytical foundations. *Annual Review of Sociology*, *33*, 43–64. https://doi.org/10.1146/annurev.soc.33.040406.131812
24. Davis, M. S. (2024). *Fairness and Crime: A Theory*. Abingdon, Oxon, and New York: Routledge.

1 The Character of Contemporary Crime

1. Perez-Pena, R. (2017). Sentenced to death: A look at Dylann Roof's rampage and its aftermath. *The New York Times*, January 10. www.nytimes.com/2017/01/10/us/dylann-roof-trial-sentencing-verdict.html Accessed 8-10-2023.
2. Horowitz, J., Corasaniti, N. & Southall, A. (2015). Nine killed in shooting at black church in Charleston. *The New York Times*, June 17. www.nytimes.com/2015/06/18/us/church-attacked-in-charleston-south-carolina.html Accessed 11-30-2021.

3. Apuzzo, M. (2015). Dylann Roof, Charleston shooting suspect is indicted on federal hate crime charges. *The New York Times*, July 22. www.nytimes .com/2015/07/23/us/dylann-roof-charleston-shooting-suspect-is-expected-to-face-federal-hate-crime-charges.html Accessed 2-10-2022.

4. Robles, F. (2015). Dylann Roof photos and a manifesto are posted on website. *The New York Times*, June 20. www.nytimes.com/2015/06/21/ us/dylann-storm-roof-photos-website-charleston-church-shooting.html Accessed 12-18-2021.

5. Sack, K. & Harris, G. (2015). President Obama eulogizes Charleston pastor as one who understood grace. *The New York Times*, June 26. www.nytimes .com/2015/06/27/us/thousands-gather-for-funeral-of-clementa-pinckney-in-charleston.html Accessed 8-23-2024.

6. Ibid.

7. Sack, K. (2017). Trial documents show Dylann Roof had mental disorders. *The New York Times*, February 2. www.nytimes.com/2017/02/02/us/dylann-roof-charleston-killing-mental.html Accessed 2-10-2022.

8. Ibid.

9. Ted Bundy, who attended but did not graduate from law school, insisted on representing himself in his last trial in Florida. He was convicted, sentenced to death, and executed. For a biography of Bundy, see Rule, A. (2008). *The Stranger beside Me: The Shocking Inside Story of Serial Killer Ted Bundy*. New York: Pocket Books.

10. This expression has been attributed to various sources including Abraham Lincoln. For a scholarly analysis, see Duffy, C. D. & Gray, M. (2021/2022). He who represents himself has a fool for a client: The right to counsel and the right to self-representation in New York. *Albany Law Review, 85*, 891–923.

11. Shapiro, E., Emerson, A. & McFann, K. (2017). Dylann Roof sentenced to death, 1st to get death penalty for federal hate crimes. *ABC News*, January 10. www.abcnews.go.com/US/charleston-church-shooter-dylann-roof-sentenced-death/story?id=44674575 Accessed 11-30-2021.

12. Dylann Roof sentenced to death for Charleston church shooting. *CBS NEWS*, January 10. www.cbsnews.com/news/dylann-roof-death-sentence-charleston-church-shooting/ Accessed 10-21-2024.

13. For an overview of what criminology encompasses, see the dated but still relevant: Wolfgang, M. E. (1963). Criminology and the criminologist. *Journal of Criminal Law, Criminology & Police Science, 54*, 155–162. https:// scholarlycommons.law.northwestern.edu/jclc/vol54/iss2/3

14. That there are academic units offering instruction and advanced degrees in criminology, as well as specialized scholarly journals in which criminologists publish their work, argues that it has arrived as a distinct discipline.

15. To see the extent of criminology and criminal justice programs, see www .adpccj.com/documents/2020survey.pdf Accessed 12-18-2021.

16. For a brief discussion of sociology's influence within criminology, see Chapter 2 of Davis, M. S. (2024). *Fairness and Crime: A Theory*. Abingdon, Oxon, & New York: Routledge.

17. Examples of prominent twentieth century criminologists whose work illustrated an interest in the behavior of individuals include Simon Dinitz of The Ohio State University, who conducted award-winning research on schizophrenics, in addition to his more mainstream work in criminology. Other criminologists whose scholarship suggested they appreciated a psychological perspective include John Monahan and Hans Toch.

18. In Oregon's Crime Seriousness Scale, for example, aggravated murder is at the very top, followed by murder and other forms of homicide. See https://oregon.public.law/rules/oar_213-017-0001 Accessed 3-5-2021.

19. Smart, R. & Schell, T. L. (2021). Mass shootings in the US. RAND Corporation, April 15. www.rand.org/research/gun-policy/analysis/essays/mass-shootings.html Accessed 11-29-2021. See also: www.gunviolencearchive.org/explainer/mass-shooting-methodology-and-reasoning Accessed 1-18-2024 and; Berk, R. (no date). What is a mass shooting? What can be done? https://crim/sas/upenn.edu/fact-check/what-mass-shooting-what-can-be-done Accessed 2-2-2021.

20. Cases of mass shootings in which the shooter was taken alive include the Charleston church shooting, the Texas Walmart shooting, and the Parkland, Florida high school shooting.

21. See, for example, Peters, J. W. & Luo, M. (2013). Mental health again an issue in gun debate. *The New York Times*, September 18. www.nytimes.com/2013/09/19/us/politics/mental-health-again-an-issue-in-gun-debate.html Accessed 12-18-2021.

22. Steinmetz, K. (2017) Why "thoughts and prayers" is a double-edged sword. *TIME*, November 9. https://time.com/5016382/thoughts-and-prayers-mass-shootings-language/ Accessed 4-20-2025.

23. Bradbury, S. (2018). Timeline of terror: A moment-by-moment account of Squirrel Hill mass shooting. *Pittsburgh Post-Gazette*, October 28. www.post-gazette.com/news/crime-courts/2018/10/28/TIMELINE-20-minutes-of-terror-gripped-Squirrel-Hill-during-Saturday-synagogue-attack/stories/201810281028097 Accessed 11-30-2021.

24. Roose, K. (2018). On Gab, an extremist-friendly site, Pittsburgh shooting suspect aired his hatred in full. *The New York Times*, October 28. www.nytimes.com/2018/10/28/us/gab-robert-bowers-pittsburgh-synagogue-shootings.html?searchResultPosition=127 Accessed 2-3-2021.

25. www.adl.org/resources/blog/deadly-shooting-pittsburgh-synagogue Accessed 6-21-2024.

26. Sousa, S., Brown, N. & Levenson, E. (2023). Pittsburgh synagogue shooter sentenced to death for killing 11 worshippers in 2018 massacre. *CNN*, August 2. www.cnn.com/2023/08/02/us/pittsburgh-synagogue-shooting-trial-sentencing-deliberations/index.html Accessed 11-11-2023.

27. Romero, S., Fernandez, M. & Padilla, M. (2019). Massacre at crowded Walmart in Texas leaves 20 dead. *The New York Times*, August 3. https://nytimes.com/2019/08/03/us/el-paso-shooting.html Accessed 12-18-2021.

28. Arango, T., Bogel-Burroughs, N. & Benner, K. (2019). Minutes before El Paso killing, hate-filled manifesto appears online. *The New York Times*,

August 3. www.nytimes.com/2019/08/03/us/patrick-crusius-el-paso-shooter-manifesto.html Accessed 11-29-2021.

29. Sandoval, E. (2023). Gunman in El Paso shooting sentenced for federal hate crimes. *The New York Times*, July 7. www.nytimes.com/2023/07/07/us/el-paso-walmart-shooting-sentencing.html Accessed 1-18-2024.

30. Baker, P. & Shear, M. D. (2019). El Paso shooting suspect's manifesto echoes Trump's language. *The New York Times*, August 4. www.nytimes.com/2019/08/04/us/politics/trump-mass-shootings.html Accessed 3-7-2021.

31. Arango, T., Bogel-Burroughs, N. & Benner, K. (2019). Minutes before El Paso killing, hate-filled manifesto appears online. *The New York Times*, August 3. www.nytimes.com/2019/08/03/us/patrick-crusius-el-paso-shooter-manifesto.html Accessed 8-23-2024.

32. www.arithmeticofcompassion.org/blog/2020/08/25/confronting-the-deadly-arithmetic-of-compassion Accessed 6-2-2025.

33. Gun Violence Archive. https://gunviolencearchive.org/explainer Accessed 5-5-2025.

34. The New York Times (2022). What to know about the school shooting in Uvalde, Texas. *The New York Times*, August 25. For a comprehensive analysis of these events, as well as details about the victims, see U. S. Department of Justice (2024). *Critical Incident Review: Active Shooter at Robb Elementary School*. Washington, DC: Office of Community Oriented Policing Services.

35. Bogel-Burroughs, N. (2022). The Texas gunman had few friends in high school, classmates say. *The New York Times*, May 25. www.nytimes.com/2022/05/25/us/texas-shooting-gunman-bullied.html Accessed 1-18-2024.

36. See Skeem, J. & Mulvey, E. (2020). What role does serious mental illness play in mass shootings, and how should we address it? *Criminology & Public Policy*, *19*, 85–108.

37. Szabo, L. (2012). Newtown tragedy could put mental health in spotlight. *USA Today*, December 17. www.usatoday.com/story/news/nation/2012/12/16/newtown-mental-health/1773479/ Accessed 6-12-2025.

38. See Madison, J. H. (2020). *The Ku Klux Klan in the Heartland*. Bloomington: Indiana University Press.

39. www.justice.gov/crt/hate-crime-laws Accessed 11-30-2021.

40. The Civil Rights Act of 1968 included provisions for what later were called hate crimes. See https://uslaw.link/citation/us-law/public/90/284 Accessed 2-28-2022.

41. www.justice.gov/crt/matthew-shepard-and-james-bird-jr-hate-crimes-prevention-act-2009-0 Accessed 2-28-2022.

42. Spencer H. & Stolberg, S. G. (2017). White nationalists march on University of Virginia. *The New York Times*, August 11. www.nytimes.com/2017/08/11/us/white-nationalists-rally-charlottesville-virginia.html Accessed 1-18-2024.

43. Stolberg, S. G. & Rosenthal, B. M. (2017). Man charged after white nationalist rally in Charlottesville ends in deadly violence. *The New York Times*, August 12. www.nytimes.com/2017/08/12/us/charlottesville-white-nationalist-protest.html Accessed 9-30-2021.

44. Shear, M. D. & Haberman, M. (2017). Trump defends initial remarks on Charlottesville; again blames "both sides." *The New York Times*, August 15. https://nytimes.com/2017/08/15/us/politics/trump-press-conference-charlotteville.html Accessed 2-28-2022.

45. Fausset, R. (2022). What we know about the shooting death of Ahmaud Arbery. *The New York Times*, August 8. www.nytimes.com/article/ahmaud-arbery-shooting-georgia.html Accessed 1-18-2024.

46. Fausset, R. (2020). Two weapons, a chase, a killing and no charges. *The New York Times*, April 26. www.nytimes.com/2020/04/26/us/ahmed-arbery-shooting-georgia.html Accessed 9-30-2021.

47. Fausset, R. (2022). Three men sentenced to life in prison in Arbery killing. *The New York Times*, January 7. www.nytimes.com/2022/01/07/us/mcmichael-bryan-sentencing-ahmaud-arbery-killing.html Accessed 2-10-2022.

48. Mzezewa, T., Burch, A. D. S. & Fausset, R. (2022). Three men are found guilty of hate crimes in Arbery killing. *The New York Times*, February 22. www.nytimes.com/2022/02/22/us/gregory-mcmichael-travis-mcmichael-william-bryan.html Accessed 3-1-2022.

49. Carrega, C. & Krishnakumar, P. (2021). Hate crime reports in US surge to the highest level in 12 years, FBI says. *CNN*, October 26. www.cnn.com/2021/08/30/us/fbi-report-hate-crimes-rose.2020/index.html Accessed 11-29-2021.

50. See, for example, Gover, A. R., Harper, S. B. & Langton, L. (2020). Anti-Asian hate crime during the COVID-19 Pandemic: Exploring the reproduction of inequality. *American Journal of Criminal Justice, 45*, 647–667.

51. Wee, S.-L. & McNeil, Jr., D. G. (2020). From Jan. 2020: China identifies new virus causing pneumonialike illness. *The New York Times*, January 8. www.nytimes.com/2020/01/08/health/china-pneumonia-outbreak-virus .html Accessed 11-30-2021.

52. Blum, J. (2020). Trump doubles down on calling COVID-19 "Kung Flu" in Phoenix rally. *Huffpost*, June 24. www.huffpost.com/entry/trump-kung-flu-phoenix_n_5ef3756fc5b6c5bf7c58ca7b Accessed 9-30-2021.

53. Saletan, W. (2021). Sickening decisions: A new congressional report shows how Donald Trump sabotaged the country's early response to COVID. *SLATE*, December 20. www.slate.com/news-and-politics/2021/12/the-sad-new-details-of-how-trump-sabotaged-the-countrys-response-to-covid.html Accessed 11-4-2024.

54. For one opinion, see Blow, C. M. (2018). Trump is a racist. Period. *The New York Times*, January 14. www.nytimes.com/2018/01/14/trump-racist-shithole .html Accessed 12-18-2021.

55. See, for example, Associated Press (2021). More than 9,000 anti-Asian incidents have been reported since pandemic began. *NPR*, August 12. www .npr/2021/08/12/1027236499/anti-asian-hate-crimes-assaults-pandemic-incidents-aapi Accessed 1-18-2024.

56. For biographical information on Larry Nassar, see www.biography.com/crime-figure/larry-nassar Accessed 11-30-2021.

57. Salam, M. (2019). How Larry Nassar "flourished unafraid" for so long. *The New York Times*, May 3. www.nytimes.com/2019/05/03/sports/larry-nassar-gymnastics-hbo-doc.html Accessed 8-23-2024.

58. Nassar faced a raft of charges. See, for example, www.justice.gov/usao-wdmi/pr/2016_1219_Nassar Accessed 10-01-2021.

59. Connor, T. (2018). Simone Biles says she was molested by gymnastics doctor Larry Nassar. *NBC News*, January 15. www.nbcnews.com/news/us-news/simone-biles-says-she-was-molested-gymnastics-doctor-larry-nassar-n837806 Accessed 5-20-2024.

60. Hoffman, B. (2017). Gymnastics doctor Larry Nassar pleads guilty to molestation charges. *The New York Times*, November 22. www.nytimes.com/2017/11/22/larry-nassar-gymnastics-molestation.html Accessed 12-18-2021.

61. Cacciola, S. & Mather, V. (2018). Larry Nassar sentencing: "I just signed your death warrant." *The New York Times*, January 24. www.nytimes.com/2018/01/24/sports/larry-nassar-sentencing.html Accessed 1-29-2021.

62. See Hauser, C. (2018). Larry Nassar Is Sentenced to Another 40 to 125 Years in Prison. *The New York Times*, February 5. www.nytimes.com/2018/02/05/sports/larry-nassar-sentencing-hearing.html Accessed 6-12-2025.

63. Friess, S. and Smith, M. (2018). Larry Nassar's Former Boss at Michigan State Faces Charges. *The New York Times*, March 26. www.nytimes.com/2018/03/26/us/nassar-michigan-state-dean-strampel.html Accessed 5-6-2025.

64. Saul, S. (2018). Calls Grow for Michigan State University President to Resign over Nassar Case. *The New York Times*, January 19 www.nytimes.com/2018/01/19/us/michigan-state-nassar.html Accessed 1-28-2024.

65. Smith, M. & Davey, M. (2018). Ex-President of Michigan State Charged with Lying About Nassar Case. *The New York Times*, November 20. www.nytimes.com/2018/11/20/us/lou-anna-simon-michigan-state-nassar.html Accessed 5-6-2025.

66. Smith, M. & Hartocollis, A. (2018). Michigan State's $500 million for Nassar victims dwarfs other settlements. *The New York Times*, May 16. www.nytimes.com/2018/05/16/us/larry-nassar-michigan-state-settlement.html Accessed 9-30-2021.

67. Ibid.

68. For a historical overview of the beginnings of the Boy Scouts of America, see www.scouting.org/programs/venturing/about-venturing/history Accessed 9-30-2021.

69. No author (1911). The Boy Scouts. *The New York Times*, August 21. https://timesmachine.nytimes.com/timesmachine/1911/08/21/issue.html Accessed 6-21-2024.

70. This phrase appears on Boy Scout letterhead contained in one of the so-called perversion files of alleged abusers. See https://crewjanci.com/files/0489.pdf Accessed 8-13-2023.

71. For a list of famous eagle scouts, see https://nesa.org/for-eagle-scouts/famous-eagle-alumni/ Accessed 12-18-2021.

72. Johnson, K. (2012). Oregon justices approve release of Boy Scouts' perversion files. The *New York Times*, June 14. www.nytimes.com/2012/06/15/us/court-approves-release-of-boys-scouts-perversion-files.html Accessed 9-29-2021.

73. Fausset, R. (2019). Lawsuit says former Boy Scouts have named 350 more abusers. *The New York Times*, August 7. www.nytimes.com/2019/08/07/us/boy-scouts-abuse-lawsuit.html Accessed 9-30-2021.

74. Baker, M. (2020). Sex abuse claims against Boy Scouts now surpass 82,000. *The New York Times*, November 15. www.nytimes.com/2020/11/15/us/boy-scouts-abuse-claims=bankruptcy.html Accessed 1-18-2024.

75. Crary, D. & McCombs, B. (2020). Boy Scouts seek bankruptcy, urge victims to step forward. *AP*, February 18. https://apnews.com/article/d65e98062be130ceeb73a2581cc21d3f Accessed 5-5-2025.

76. Fortin, J. & Grullon Paz, I. (2021). Boy Scouts agree to $850 million settlement over abuse claims. *The New York Times*, July 2. www.nytimes.com/2021/07/02/us/boy-scouts-of-america-sexual-abuse-settlement.html Accessed 9-30-2021.

77. See the Trust Distribution Procedures at https://scoutingsettlementtrust.my.salesforce.com

78. Scurria, A. & Biswas, S. (2021). Boy Scouts insurer Chubb to pay $800 million in sex-abuse compensation. *Wall Street Journal*, December 13. www.wsj.com/articles/boy-scouts-insurer-chubb-to-pay-800-million-in-sex-abuse-compensation-deal-11639434626 Accessed 12-18-2021.

79. See, for example, Horowitz, J., Povoledo, E. & Pianigiani, G. (2022). Benedict faulted for handling of abuse cases when he was archbishop. *The New York Times*, January 20. www.nytimes.com/2022/01/20/world/europe/benedict-germany-sexual-abuse.html Accessed 2-10-2022.

80. Leitsinger, M. (2012). Boy Scouts release secret child abuse files – "the pain and anguish of thousands." *NBC News*, October 18. www.nbcnews.com/news/us-news/boy-scouts-release-secret-child-abuse-files-pain-anguish-thousands-flna1C6550722 Accessed 11-21-2024.

81. Sponsoring organizations for the Boy Scouts include those such as local churches that provide space for meetings and financial support. One of the largest sponsoring organizations of the past, the Church of Jesus Christ of Latter-day Saints, was named in the lawsuit and ultimately contributed $250 million to the victims' trust. See Asbury, N. (2021). Boy Scouts reach agreement with Mormon Church, insurers in sex abuse case. *The Washington Post*, September 15. www.washingtonpost.com/dc-md-va/2021/09/15/boy-scourt-mormons-settlement/ Accessed 2-5-2024.

82. Barron, J. (2010). In New York, Cuomo wins easily. *The New York Times*, November 3. www.nytimes.com/2010/11/04/nyregion/04nyelect.html Accessed 09-29-2021.

83. Ward, R. B. (2011). Governor Cuomo's three big achievements. https://rockinst.org/blog/governor-cuomo-three-big-achievements/ Accessed 1-18-2024.

84. Wang, V. (2019). Sexual harassment laws toughened in New York: "Finally, this is happening." *The New York Times*, June 20. https://nytimes.com/2019/06/20/nyregion/sexual-harassment-laws-ny.html Accessed 09-29-2021.

85. McKinley, J. (2021). Cuomo is accused of sexual harassment by a 2nd former aide. *The New York Times*, February 27. www.nytimes.com/2021/02/27/nyregion/ cuomo-charlotte-bennett-sexual-harassment.html Accessed 9-29-2021.

86. O'Donnell, N., Kaplan, M., Morse, J., Verdugo, A. & Yilek, C. (2021). "The governor's trying to sleep with me": Cuomo accuser recalls alleged harassment. *CBS News*, March 5. www.cbsnews.com/news/cuomo-accuser-charlotte-bennett-interview-sexual-harassment/ Accessed 6-21-2024.

87. Ferre-Sadurni, L. (2021). As Cuomo fights for survival, he revives his combative image. *The New York Times*, May 10. www.nytimes.com/2021/05/10/ nyregion/cuomo-sexual-harassment-strategy.html Accessed 09-29-2021.

88. Gold, M. & Rashbaum, W. K. (2021). Cuomo harassed a state trooper in his protective detail, the report said. *The New York Times*, August 3. www .nytimes.com/2021/08/03/nyregion/cuomo-state-trooper.html   Accessed 9-30-2021.

89. Ferre-Sadurni, L. (2021). Cuomo's last stand: What he and his accusers told investigators. *The New York Times*, November 10. www.nytimes.com/2021/11/10/ nyregion/cuomo-investigation-testimony.html Accessed 8-23-2024.

90. For Attorney General Letitia James's full announcement, see https://ag.ny .gov/press-release/2021/attorney-general-james-receives-referral-letter-investigate-allegations-sexual Accessed 10-2-2021.

91. Goodman, J. D. & Ferre-Sadurni, L. (2021). "I believe these 11 women": Letitia James says as she reveals the report's finding. *The New York Times*, August 3. https://nytimes.com/2021/08/03/nyregion/letitia-james-ag.html Accessed 09-30-2021.

92. Lach, E. (2021). The vindication of Andrew Cuomo's accusers. *The New Yorker*, August 13. www.newyorker.com/news/our-local-correspondents/the-vindication-of-andrew-cuomos-accusers Accessed 6-12-2025.

93. Ferre-Sadurni, L. & Goodman, J. D. (2021). Cuomo resigns amid scandals, ending decade-long run in disgrace. *The New York Times*, August 10. https:// nytimes.com/2021/08/10/nyregion/andrew-cuomo-resigns.html   Accessed 09-29-2021.

94. Ferre-Sadurni, L. (2021). Kathy Hochul wants to make one thing clear: She is not Cuomo. *The New York Times*, August 30. www.nytimes.com/2021/08/30/ nyregion/kathy-hochul-cuomo.html Accessed 3-1-2022.

95. Shanahan, E. (2021). Prosecutor won't charge Cuomo over trooper's sexual harassment claim. *The New York Times*, December 23. www.nytimes .com/2021/12/23/nyregion/prosecutor-cuomo-trooper-sexual-harassment-claim.html Accessed 2-28-2022.

96. Sepkowitz, K. (2020). Why New York has been hit so hard by coronavirus. *CNN*, April 13. www.cnn.com/2020/04/11/opinions/new-york-hit-hard-coronavirus-sepkowitz/index.html Accessed 3-6-2024.

97. Cuomo's alleged leadership during the pandemic is discussed in McKinley, J. (2021). Cuomo faces inquiry over use of state resources for pandemic book. *The New York Times*, April 19. www.nytimes.com/2021/04/19/nyregion/ andrew-cuomo-book-investigation.html Accessed 2-10-2022.

98. Gold, M. & Shanahan, E. (2021). What we know about Cuomo's nursing home scandal. *The New York Times*, August 4. www.nytimes.com/article/ andrew-cuomo-nursing-home-death.html Accessed 2-10-2022.

99. McKinley, J. (2021). See Note 85.

100. Ashford, G. & Ferre-Saduri (2021). Cuomo is ordered to forfeit earnings from $5.1 million book deal. *The New York Times*, December 14. www.nytimes.com/2021/12/14/nyregion/andrew-cuomo-book-deal.html Accessed 2-28-2021.

101. To see how Cuomo's responses have changed, see Rubinstein, D. & McFadden, A. (2025). Revisiting the sexual harassment complaints against Cuomo. *The New York Times*, June 6. www.nytimes.com/ interactive/2020/06/06/nyregion/andrew-cuomo-sexual-harassment-claims .html Accessed 6-18-2025.

102. Krieg, G., Cole, D. & Joseph, E. (2021). Cuomo says he's "truly sorry" for workplace comments he says were "misinterpreted as unwanted flirtation" following sexual harassment claims. CNN, updated March 1. www.cnn .com/2021/02/28/politics/cuomo-harassment-claims-independent-lawyer/ index.html Accessed 6-9-2025.

103. Fandos, N. & Glueck, K. (2022). Cuomo portrays himself as a victim in a six-figure TV ad blitz. *The New York Times*, February 28. www.nytimes .com/2022/02/28/nyregion/andrew-cuomo-tv-ad.html Accessed 2-28-2022.

104. Fandos, N. (2023). The secret hand behind the women who stood by Cuomo? *The New York Times*, August 7. www.nytimes.com/2023/08/07/ nyregion/cuomo-women-sister-madeline.html Accessed 1-18-2024.

105. Ibid.

106. For a dictionary definition of fraud, see /www.merriam-webster.com/ dictionary/fraud Accessed 3-3-2022.

107. Parloff, R. (2014). New blood. *Fortune, 169,* 64–72.

108. For information on Elizabeth Holmes's childhood, see www.forbes.com/sites/ petercohan/2019/02/17/4-startling-insights-into-elizabeth-holmes-from-psychiatrist-whos-known-here-since-childhood/ Accessed 9-9-2025.

109. For an example of how Holmes was promoted, see Arrillaga-Andreesen, L. (2015). Five visionary tech entrepreneurs who are changing the world. *The New York Times Style Magazine*, October 12. www.nytimes.com/ interactive/2015/10/12/t-magazine/elizabeth-holmes-tech-visionaries-brian-chesky.html Accessed 3-1-2022.

110. Carreyrou, J. (2018). *Bad Blood: Secrets and Lies in a Silicon Valley Startup.* New York: Alfred A. Knopf.

111. Kunthara, S. (2021). A closer look at Theranos' big-name investors, partners and board as Elizabeth Holmes' trial begin. *Crunchbase*, September 14. www.news.crunchbase.com/health-wellness-biotech/theranos-elizabeth-holmes-trial-investors-board/ Accessed 8-19-2024.

112. See, for example, Carreyrou, J. (2015). Hot startup Theranos has struggled with its blood-test technology. *Wall Street Journal*, October 16. www.wsj.com/articles/ theranos-has-struggled-with-blood-test-144488i901 Accessed 2-28-2022.

113. Carreyrou, J. (2018). See Note 110.

114. Ibid.

115. Griffith, E. & Woo, E. (2022). Elizabeth Holmes is found guilty of four counts of fraud. *The New York Times*, January 3. www.nytimes.com/2022/01/03/technology/elizabeth-holmes-guilty.html Accessed 2-10-2022.

116. For the U.S. Department of Justice's formal statement on the case, see www.justice.gov/usao-ndca/pr/theranos-founder-elizabeth-holmes-found-guilty-investor-fraud Accessed 6-18-2025.

117. Griffith, E. (2020). Elizabeth Holmes is sentenced to more than 11 years for fraud. *The New York Times*, November 18. www.nytimes.com/2022/11/18/technology/elizabeth-holmes-sentence-theranos.html Accessed 1-22-2024.

118. Morrow, A. (2024). Elizabeth Holmes, Silicon Valley's most famous convict, makes her long-shot appeal. *CNN*, June 11. www.cnn.com/2024/06/11/business/elizabeth-holmes-appeal/index.html Accessed 8-24-2024.

119. Moench, M. (2025). Theranos founder Elizabeth Holmes loses fraud appeal. *BBC*, February 25. www.bbc.com/news/articles/c1jpg0069wg0 Accessed 7-19-2025.

120. No author (2021). Elizabeth Holmes testifies she 'never' misled investors. *BBC*, December 8. www.bbc.com/news/world-us-canada-59587919 Accessed 7-20-2025.

121. Kaplan, S. (2018). Doctors urge elite academy to expel a member over charges of plagiarism. *The New York Times*, April 9. www.nytimes.com/2018/04/09/health/academy-medicine-plagiarism.html Accessed 11-18-2021.

122. Ibid.

123. Ibid.

124. Ibid.

125. Ibid.

126. Science News Staff (2021). Medical groups hushes ouster. *Science*, October 7. www.science.org/content/article/news-glance-telescope-s-namesake-questioned-flood-risk-maps-and-extinct-woodpecker Accessed 11-18-2021.

127. Wadman, M. (2021). Top secret: U.S. National Academy of Medicine keeps expulsions quiet. *Science*, September 29. www.science.org/content/article/top-secret-u-s-national-academy-medicine-keeps-expulsions-quiet Accessed 1-12-2022.

128. For how research misconduct is typically charged, see see Davis, M. S. & Berry, B. (2018). *Scholarly Crimes and Misdemeanors: Violations of Fairness and Trust in the Academic World*. Abingdon, Oxon, & New York: Routledge.

129. Ibid.

130. https://oig.nsf.gov/investigations/research-misconduct/by-the-numbers Accessed 1-22-2-24.

131. Strain theory, including Robert Agnew's General Strain Theory, does not adequately explain a case like Noji's. Noji had already proven his ability to withstand the strains of medical school and a research career. It seems just as plausible that he felt entitled to the rewards of a career as a physician-scientist and thus decided not to do the requisite work.

132. Schmidt, M. S. & Benner, K. (2020). Justice Dept. eases election fraud inquiry constraints as Trump promotes false narrative. *The New York Times*, October 7. www.nytimes.com/2020/10/07/us/politics/justice-department-election-fraud.html Accessed 5-15-2024.

133. Haberman, M. (2021). Trump told crowd "You will never take back our country with weakness." *The New York Times*, January 6. www.nytimes.com/2021/01/06/us/politics/trump-speech-capital.html Accessed 7-18-2025.

134. Edmondson, C. & Broadwater, L. (2021). Before Capitol riot, Republican lawmakers fanned the flames. *The New York Times*, January 11. www.nytimes.com/2021/01/11/us/politics/republicans-capitol-riot.html Accessed 6-16-2025.

135. Savage, C. (2021). Incitement to riot? What Trump told supporters before mob stormed Capitol. *The New York Times*, January 10. www.nytimes.com/2021/01/10/us/trump-speech-riot.html Accessed 5-15-2024.

136. CBS News (2021). Capitol chaos: Anti-semitic apparel worn during riot traced to website based in New York City. *CBS News*, January 11. www.cbsnews.com/newyork/news/anti-semitic-sweatshirts-camp-auschwitz-6wme-shirt-hate-speech-apparel-us-capitol-protests/ Accessed 8-10-2025.

137. Chappell, B. (2021). Architect of the Capitol outlines $30 million in damages from pro-Trump riot. *NPR*, February 24. www.npr.org/sections/insurrection-at-the-capitol/2021/02/24/970977612/architect-of-the-capitol-outlines-30-million-in-damages-from-pro-trump-riot Accessed 5-15-2024.

138. Goldman, A. & Dewan, S. (2021). Inside the deadly Capitol shooting. *The New York Times*, January 23. www.nytimes.com/2021/01/23/us/capitol-police-shooting-ashli-babbitt.html Accessed 5-15-2024.

139. Jackson, J. (2021). 4 Capitol Police officers have died by suicide since the January 6 insurrection. Newsweek, August 2. www.newsweek.com/3-capitol-police-officers-have-died-suicide-since-january-6-insurrection-1615452 Accessed 9-27-2025.

140. Barnes, D., Brown-Kaiser, L., Gregorian, D. & Jester, J. (2023). Four Oath Keepers convicted of seditious conspiracy in Jan. 6 attack. www.nbcnews.com/politics/justice-department/oath-keepers-members-convicted-seditious-conspiracy-rcna66622 Accessed 5-15-2024.

141. Feuer, A. (2022). In Capitol attack, over 900 people have been criminally charged. *The New York Times*, December 19. www.nytimes.com/2022/12/19/us/politics/jan-6-capitol-attack-charges.html Accessed 8-25-2024.

142. Richer, A. D. & Kunzelman, M. (2025). Trump grants sweeping pardon of Jan. 6 defendants, including rioters who violently attacked police. *AP*, January 21. https://apnews.com/article/capitol-jan-6-pardons-trump-justice-department-8ce8b2a8f8cb602d5eaf85ac7b969606 Accessed 7-18-2025.

143. For an overview of the post-election litigation, see https://the2020election.org/voting-related-litigation Accessed 9-27-2025.

2 Narcissism from Freud to Facebook

1. Kacel, E. L., Ennis, N. & Pereira, D. B. (2017). Narcissistic Personality Disorder in clinical psychology practice: Case studies in comorbid psychological distress and life-limiting illness. *Behavioral Medicine, 43,* 156–164. https://doi.org/10.1080/08964289.2017.1301875
2. Schellenberg, J. A. (1978). *Masters of Social Psychology.* New York: Oxford University Press.
3. Crockatt, P. (2006). Freud's "On narcissism: An introduction." *Journal of Child Psychotherapy, 32,* 4–20. https://doi.org/10.1080/00754170600563638
4. Kohut, H. (1966). Forms and transformations of narcissism. *Journal of the American Psychoanalytic Association, 14,* 243–272. https://doi.org/10.1177/000306516601400201
5. Kohut, H. (1971). *The Analysis of the Self: A Systematic Approach to the Psychoanalytic Treatment of Narcissistic Personality Disorders.* Madison, CT: International Universities Press.
6. Kohut, H. (1973). *The Restoration of the Self.* Madison, CT: International Universities Press.
7. DeRosis, L. E. (1981). Horney theory and narcissism. *The American Journal of Psychoanalysis, 41*(4), 337–346. https://doi.org/10.1007/BF01258947
8. Kernberg, O. (1975). *Borderline Conditions and Pathological Narcissism.* New York: Jason Aronson.
9. For information on Elsa Ronningstam and her work, see www.mccleanhospital.org/profile/elsa-ronningstam
10. Ronningstam, E. (2016). New insights into narcissistic personality disorder. *Psychiatric Times,* February 29.www.psychiatrictimes.com/view/new-insights-narcissistic-personality-disorder Accessed 8-31-2025.
11. For a chronology of the development of the DSM, see www.psychiatry.org/psychiatrists/practice/dsm/about-dsm/history-of-the-dsm
12. Ibid.
13. www.psychiatry.org Accessed 9-23-2021.
14. These criteria have been taken from the DSM-IV. For the approach used in the DSM-5, see www.mind-diagnostics.org/blog/narcissistic-personality/narcissistic-personality-disorder-dsm-5-criteria-and-treatment-options Accessed 11-22-2024.
15. Levy, K. N., Chauhan, P., Clarkin, J. F., Wasserman, R. H. & Reynoso, J. S. (2009). Narcissistic pathology: Empirical approaches. *Psychiatric Annals, 39,* 203–213. https://doi.org/10.3928/00485713-20090401-03
16. Aftab, A. & Ryznar, E. (2021). Conceptual and historical evolution of psychiatric nosology. *International Review of Psychiatry, 33,* 486–489. https://doi.org/10.1080/09540261.2020.1828306
17. Junewicz, A. & Billick, S. B. (2020). Conduct disorder: Biology and developmental trajectories. *Psychiatric Quarterly, 91,* 77–90. www.doi.org/10.1007/s11126-019-09678-5

18. Farber, B. A. (2012). Afterword: Our narcissistic age – or not. *Journal of Clinical Psychology*, *68*, 954–959. https://doi.org/10.1002/jclp.21899

19. Zanor, C. (2010). A fate that narcissists will hate: Being ignored. *The New York Times*, November 29. www.nytimes.com/2010/11/30/health/views/30mind.html Accessed 8-30-2024.

20. Ibid.

21. See the discussion in Morey, L. C. & Stagner, B. H. (2012). Narcissistic pathology as core personality dysfunction: Comparing the DSM-IV and the DSM-5 proposal for narcissistic personality disorder. *Journal of Clinical Psychology*, *68*, 908–921. https://doi.org/10.1002/jclp.21895

22. Ibid.

23. For an overview of Thurstone's contributions to psychometrics, see Gulliksen, H. (1968). Louis Leon Thurstone, experimental and mathematical psychologist. *The American Psychologist*, *23*, 786–802. https://doi.org/10.1037/h0026696

24. Cattell, R. B. (1945). The life and work of Charles Spearman. *Journal of Personality*, *14*, 85–92. https://doi.org/10.1111/j.1467-6494.1945.tb01040.x

25. Raskin, R. & Hall, C. S. (1981). The Narcissistic Personality Inventory: Alternate form reliability and further evidence of construct validity. *Journal of Personality Assessment*, *45*, 159–162. https://doi.org/10.1207/s15327752jpa4502_10

26. Raskin, R. & Terry, H. (1988). A principal-components analysis of the Narcissistic Personality Inventory and further evidence of its construct validity. *Journal of Personality and Social Psychology*, *54*, 890–902. https://doi.org/10.1037/0022-3514.54.5.890

27. Emmons, R. A. (1984). Factor analysis and construct validity of the Narcissistic Personality Inventory. *Journal of Personality Assessment*, *48*, 291–300. https://doi.org/10.1207/s15327752jpa4803_11

28. Campbell, W. K., Bonacci, A. M., Shelton, J., Exline, J. J. & Bushman, B. J. (2004). Psychological entitlement: Interpersonal consequences and validation of a self-report measure. *Journal of Personality Assessment*, *83*, 29–45. https://doi.org/10.1207/s15327752jpa8301_04

29. Brunell, A. B., Davis, M. S., Schley, D. R., Eng, A. L., van Dulmen, M. H. M. & Flannery, D. J. (2013). A new measure of interpersonal exploitativeness. *Frontiers in Psychology*, *4*, 299. https://doi.org/10.3389/fpsyg.2013.00299

30. Gauch, Jr., H. G. (2015). *Scientific Method in Practice*. Cambridge: Cambridge University Press.

31. Konrath, S., Meier, B. P. & Bushman, B. J. (2014). Development and validation of the Single Item Narcissism Scale (SINS). *PLoS ONE*, *9*(8) e103469. https://doi.org/10.1371/journal.pone.0103469

32. Twenge, J. M. & Campbell, W. K. (2010). *The Narcissism Epidemic: Living in the Age of Entitlement*. New York: Atria Books.

33. For the GSS sampling methodology, see https://gss.norc.org/content/dam/gss/get-documentation/pdf/codebook/GSS_Codebook_AppendixA.pdf

34. Foster, J. D., McCain, J. L., Hibberts, M. F. Brunell, A. B. & Johnson, R. B. (2015). The Grandiose Narcissism Scale: A global and facet-level measure of

grandiose narcissism. *Personality and Individual Differences, 73*, 12–16. https://doi.org/10.1016/j.paid.2014.08.042

35. Crowe, M. L., Edershile, E. A., Wright, A. G. C., Campbell, W. K., Lynam, D. R. & Miller, J. D. (2019). Development and validation of the Narcissistic Vulnerability Scale: An adjective rating scale. *Psychological Assessment, 30*, 978–983. https://doi.org/10.1037/pas0000578

36. Campbell, W. K. & Miller, J. D. (eds.) (2011). *The Handbook of Narcissism and Narcissistic Personality Disorder*. New York: Wiley.

37. Otway, L. J. & Vignoles, V. L. (2006). Narcissism and childhood recollections: A quantitative test of psychoanalytic predictions. *Personality and Social Psychology Bulletin, 32*, 104–116. https://doi.org/10.1177/0146167205279907

38. Ramsay, A., Watson, P. J., Biderman, M. D., & Reeves, A. L. (1996). Self-reported narcissism and perceived parental permissiveness and authoritarianism. *Journal of Genetic Psychology, 157*, 227–238. https://doi.org/10.1080/0022 1325.1996.9914860

39. Horton, R. S., Bleau, G. & Drwecki, B. (2006). Parenting Narcissus: What are the links between parenting and narcissism? *Journal of Personality, 74*, 345–376. https://doi.org/10.1111/j.1467-6494.2005.00378.x

40. Brunell A. B., Robison, J., Deems, N. P. & Okdie, B. M. (2018) Are narcissists more attracted to people in relationships than to people not in relationships? *PLoS ONE 13*(3), e0194106. https://doi.org/10.1371/journal .pone.0194106

41. Baumeister, R. F., Bushman, B. J. & Campbell, W. K. (2000). Self-esteem, narcissism, and aggression: Does violence result from low self-esteem or from threatened egotism? *Current Directions in Psychological Science, 9*, 26–29. https://doi.org/10.1111/1467-8721.00053

42. Fanti, K. & Henrich, C. C. (2015). Effects of self-esteem and narcissism on bullying and victimization during early adolescence. *The Journal of Early Adolescence, 35*, 5–29. https://doi.org/10.1177/0272431613519498

43. Barry, C. T., Grafeman, S. J., Adler, K. K. & Pickard, J. D. (2007). The relations among narcissism, self-esteem, and delinquency in a sample of at-risk adolescents. *Journal of Adolescence, 30*, 933–942. https://doi.org/10.1016/j .adolescence.2006.12.003

44. Mouilso, E. R. & Calhoun, K. S. (2012). Narcissism, psychopathy and the five-factor model in sexual assault perpetration. *Personality and Mental Health, 6*, 228–241. https://doi.org/10.1002/pmh.1188

45. Crouch, J. L., Hiraoka, R., Rutledge, E., Zengel, B., Skowronski, J. J. & Milner, J. S. (2015). Is narcissism associated with child physical abuse risk? *Journal of Family Violence, 30*, 373–380. https://doi.org/10.1007/s10896-015-9672-3

46. Lasch, C. (1979). *The Culture of Narcissism: American Life in an Age of Diminishing Expectations*. New York: W. W. Norton.

47. Ibid.

48. Riso, *Personality Types*, p. 78.

49. Boorstin, D. (1992). *The Image: A Guide to Pseudo-Events in America*. New York: Vintage.

50. For background on this movement, see Baumeister, R. F., Campbell, J. D., Krueger, J. I. & Vohs, K. D. (2003). Does high self-esteem cause better perfor-mance, interpersonal success, happiness, or healthier lifestyles? *Psychological Science in the Public Interest, 4,* 1–44. https://doi.org/10.1111/1529-1006.01431

51. For a critique of self-esteem training, see Baumeister, R. F., Campbell, J. D., Krueger, J. I. & Vohs, K. D. (2005). Exploding the self-esteem myth. *Scientific American, 292,* 84–91. PMID: 15724341.

52. Robert Lull and Ted Dickinson, "Obsessed with reality TV? You may be a narcissist" in *The Conversation.* https://theconversation.com/obsessed-with-reality-tv-you-may-be-a-narcissist-57702 Accessed 6-12-2016.

53. Rowe, S. D. (2016). Consumer narcissism is on the rise. *CRM Magazine, 20,* 10–10.

54. This is the motto of The Toy Barn, a luxury auto dealership based in Dublin, Ohio. www.cars.com/dealers/105981/toy-barn/. Accessed 6-12-2016. A Google search reveals that other businesses have also used this or a similar phrase.

55. Gentile, B., Twenge, J. M., Freeman, E. C., & Campbell, W. (2012). The effect of social networking websites on positive self-views: An experimen-tal investigation. *Computers in Human Behavior, 28,* 1929–1933 https://doi.org/10.1016/j.chb.2012.05.012; Walters, N. T. & Horton, R. (2015). A diary study of the influence of Facebook use on narcissism among male college students. *Computers in Human Behavior, 52,* 326–330 https://doi.org/10.1016/j.chb.2015.05.054 Winter, S. et al. (2014). Another brick in the Facebook wall – How personality traits relate to the content of status updates. *Computers in Human Behavior, 34,* 194–202. https://doi.org/01.1016/j.chb.2014.01.048

56. Halpern, D., Valenzuela, S. & Katz, J. E. (2016). "Selfie-ists" or "Narci-selfiers"?: A cross-lagged panel analysis of selfie taking and narcissism. *Personality and Individual Differences, 97,* 98–101. https://doi.org/10.1016/j.paid.2016.03.019 and Sorokowski, P., Sorokowski, A., Oleszkiewicz, A., Frackowiak, T., Huk, A. & Pisanski, K. (2015). Selfie posting behaviors are associated with narcissism among men. *Personality and Individual Differences, 85,* 123–127. https://doi.org/10.1016/j.paid.2015.05.004

57. Halpern, D. et al. (2016). p. 99

58. Carr, D. (2015). Selfies on a stick and the social-content challenge for the media. *The New York Times,* January 4. www.nytimes.com/2015/01/05/business/media/selfies-on-a-stick-and-the-social-content-challenge-for-the-media.html Accessed 10-01-2021.

59. Lasch, C. (1979). See Note 46.

60. Sisario, B. (2015). Justin Bieber's "Purpose" debuts at No. 1, with huge streaming numbers. *The New York Times.* http://artsbeat.blogs.nytimes.com/2015/11/23/justin-bieber-purpose-billboard-streaming/ Accessed 8-13-2016.

61. Caligor, E., Levy, K. N. & Yeomans, F. E. (2015). Narcissistic personality dis-order: Diagnostic and clinical challenges. *The American Journal of Psychiatry, 172,* 415–422. https://doi.org/10.1176/appi.ajp.2014.14060723

62. Twenge, J. M., Konrath, S., Foster, J. D., Campbell, W. K. & Bushman, B. J. (2008). Egos inflating over time: A cross-temporal meta-analysis of the Narcissistic Personality Inventory. *Journal of Personality, 76,* 875–901. https://doi.org/j.1467-6494.2008.00507.x

63. Trzesniewski, K. H., Donnellan, M. B. & Robins, R. W. (2008). Is "Generation Me" really more narcissistic than previous generations? *Journal of Personality, 76,* 903–917. https://doi.org/10.1111/j.1467-6494.2008.00508.x

64. Rovenpor, J., Kopelman, R. E., Brandwein, A. C., Quach, P. & Waldman, M. (2016). The best-seller as an indicator of societal narcissism. *Society, 53,* 414–421. https://doi.org/10.1007/s12115-016-0035-2

65. Blasco-Bellad, A., Rogoza, R. & Alsinet, C. (2022). Vulnerable narcissism is related to the fear of being laughed at and to the joy of laughing at. *Personality & Individual Differences, 190.* https://doi.org/10.1016/j.paid.2022.111536

66. Bernardi, R. & Monica, E. (2018). Thin-skinned or vulnerable narcissism and thick-skinned or grandiose narcissism: Similarities and differences. *International Journal of Psychoanalysis, 99,* 291–313. https://doi.org/10.1080/00207578.2018.1425599

67. Jordan, C. H., Nevicka, B. & Sedikides, C. (2021). The many faces of narcissism: Phenomenology, antecedents, and consequences. *Self & Identity, 20,* 145–151. https://doi.org/10.1080/15298868.2019.1680427

68. Duchon, D. & Burns, M. (2008). Organizational narcissism. *Organizational Dynamics, 37,* 354–364. https://doi.org/10.1016/j.orgdyn.2008.07.004

69. Golec de Zavala, A. & Lantos, D. (2020). Collective narcissism and its social consequences: The bad and the ugly. *Current Directions in Psychological Science, 29,* 273–278. https://doi.org/10.1177/0963721420917703

3 A Matter of Fairness

1. Adapted from Hod-Shemer, O., Zimerman, H., Hassunah-Arafat, S. & Wertheim, C. (2018). Preschool children's perceptions of fairness. *Early Childhood Education Journal, 46,* 179–186. https://doi.org/10.1007/s10643-017-0855-9

2. See the discussion in Lund, D. J., Scheer, L. K. & Kozlenkova, I. V. (2013). Culture's impact on the importance of fairness in interorganizational relationships. *Journal of International Marketing, 21,* 21–43. https://doi.org/10.1509/jim.13.0020

3. van der Meij, L., Klauke, F., Moore, H. L., Ludwig, Y. S., Almela, M. & van Lange, P. A. M. (2015). Football fan aggression: The importance of low basal cortisol and a fair referee. *PLoS ONE, 10,* 1–14. https://doi.org/10.1371/journal.pone.0120103

4. Evangelidis, I. (2024). Shrinkflation aversion: When and why product size decreases are seen as more unfair than equivalent price increases. *Marketing Science, 43,* 280–288. https://doi.org/10.1287/mksc.2023.0269

5. Grape, L., Skoglund, J., Haugen, G. M. D. & Thornblad, R. (2024). Adolescents' negotiations of loyalty and fairness in relation to parents' separation process. *Child & Family Social Work*. https://doi.org/10.1111/cfs.13215 See also Loeser, M., Whiteman, S. & McHale, S. (2016). Siblings' perceptions of differential treatment, fairness, and jealousy and adolescent adjustment: A moderated indirect effects model. *Journal of Child & Family Studies*, 25, 2405–2414. https://doi.org/10.1007/s10826-016-0429-2

6. Alda, E., Bennett, R., Marion, N., Morabito, M. & Baxter, S. (2020). Antecedents of perceived fairness in criminal courts: A comparative analysis. *International Journal of Comparative and Applied Criminal Justice*, 44, 201–219. https://doi.org/10.1080/01924036.2019.1615521

7. This overview is adapted from Davis, M. S. (2024). *Fairness and Crime: A Theory*. Abingdon, Oxon & New York: Routledge.

8. Ibid.

9. Witte, A. (2014). Co-operation – the missing value of business education. *Journal of Management Development*, 33, 357–373. https://doi.org/10.1108/JMD-02-2013-0027

10. Lunden, M. (2007). When does cooperation improve public policy implementation? *Public Policy Journal*, 35, 629–652. https://doi.org/10.1111/j.1541-0072.2007.00240.x

11. Kakkireni, B. K, (2024). The power of strategic partnerships: Driving business growth through collaboration. *Forbes*, November 26. www.forbes.com/councils/forbesbusinesscouncil/2024/11/26/the-power-of-strategic-partnerships-driving-business-growth-through-collaboration/ Accessed 7-10-2024.

12. For an overview of the World Food Programme's efforts in Gaza, see www.wfp.org/emergencies/palestine-emergency Accessed 8-20-2024.

13. Ehrenberg, M. F., Hunter, M. A. & Elterman, M. F. (1996). Shared parenting agreements after marital separation: the roles of empathy and narcissism. *Journal of Consulting and Clinical Psychology*, 64, 808–818. https://doi.org/10.1037/0022-006X.64.4.808

14. For an overview of this game, see Frischman, B. M., Marciano, A. & Ramelo, G. B. (2019). Retrospectives: Tragedy of the commons after 50 years. *Journal of Economic Perspectives*, 33, 211–228. https://doi.org/10.1257/jep.33.4.211

15. Campbell, W. K., Bush, C. P., Brunell, A. B. & Shelton, J. (2005). Understanding the social costs of narcissism: The case of the tragedy of the commons. *Personality and Social Psychology Bulletin*, 31, 1358–1368. https://doi.org/10.1177/0146167205274855

16. Melesza, M. (2020). Grandiose narcissism and vulnerable narcissism in prisoner's dilemma game. *Personality & Individual Differences*, 158, 109841. https://doi.org/10.1016/j.paid.2020.109841

17. Gouldner, A. W. (1960). The norm of reciprocity: A preliminary statement. *American Sociological Review*, 25, 161–178. https://doi.org/10.2307/2092623

18. See, for example, Levi-Strauss, C. (1969). *The Elementary Structures of Kinship*. Boston: Beacon Press.

19. For an interesting history of this practice, see Aubert, S. (2022). Symbolic and problematic: Gifts in diplomacy. *Harvard International Review*, April 20. https://hir.harvard.edu/symbolic-and-problematic-gifts-in-diplomacy/ Accessed 8-20-2024.

20. Meier, L. L. & Semmer, N. K. (2013). Lack of reciprocity, narcissism, anger, and instigated workplace incivility: A moderated mediation model. *European Journal of Work and Organizational Psychology*, 22, 461–475. https://doi.org/1 0.1080/1359432X.2012.654605

21. Gouldner, A. W. (1960). See Note 17.

22. For a dictionary definition of exploitation, see https://merriam-webster.com/ dictionary/exploitation Accessed 11-19-2021.

23. For an overview of Marxian exploitation, see Zwolinski, M., Ferguson, B. & Wertheimer, A. (2022). "Exploitation," *The Stanford Encyclopedia of Philosophy* (Winter 2022 Edition), Edward N. Zalta & Uri Nodelman (eds.). https://plato.stanford.edu/archives/win2022/entries/exploitation/

24. Battersby, S. (2017). Can humankind escape the tragedy of the commons? *Proceedings of the National Academy of Sciences*, 114, 7–10. https://doi .org/10.1073/pnas.1619877114

25. For an analysis of this event, see Phillips, A. S., Hung, Y-T. & Bosela, P. A. (2007). Love Canal tragedy. *Journal of Performance of Constructed Facilities*, 21, 313–319. https://doi.org/10.1061/(ASCE)0887-3828(2007)21:4(313)

26. Brunell, A. B., Davis, M. S., Schley, D. R., Eng, A. L., van Dulmen, M. H. M., Wester, K. L. & Flannery, D. J. (2013). A new measure of interpersonal exploitativeness. *Frontiers in Psychology*, 4, 299. https://doil.org/10.3389/ fpsyg.2013.00299

27. Ibid.

28. Shabecoff, P. (1989). Largest U.S. tanker spill spews 270,000 barrels of oil off Alaska. *The New York Times*, March 25. www.nytimes.com/1989/03/25/us/ largest-us-tanker-spill-spews-270000-barrels-of-oil-off-alaska.html Accessed 8-28-2024.

29. For examples in the defense industry, see Chasan, A. (2023). How the Pentagon falls victim to price gouging by military contractors. *CBS News*, May 21. www .cbsnews.com/news/pentagon-budget-price-gouging-60-minutes-2023-05-21/ Accessed 6-24-2025.

30. See Thakor, A. V. (2015). The financial crisis of 2007–2009: Why did it happen and what did we learn? *The Review of Corporate Finance Studies, 4*, 155–205. https://doi.org/10.1093/rcfs/cfv001

31. Feuer, A. (2019). Trump ordered to pay $2 million to charities for misuse of foundation. *The New York Times*, November 7. www.nytimes.com/2019/11/07/ nyregion/trump-charities-new-york.html Accessed 8-28-2024.

32. For a dictionary definition of retaliation, see https://merriam-webster.com/ dictionary/retaliation Accessed 11-19-2021.

33. Walster, E. & Walster, G. W. (1978). *Equity: Theory and Research*. Boston: Allyn & Bacon.

34. Gouldner, A. W. (1960). See Note 17.

35. King, D. (2013). *The Feud: The Hatfields and McCoys: The True Story*. New York: Little, Brown and Co.

36. Wang, V. (2017). Senator Rand Paul assaulted at his home in Kentucky, police say. *The New York Times*, November 4. www.nytimes.com/2017/11/04/rand-paul-assaulted.html Accessed 8-12-2023.

37. Brunell, A. B. & Davis, M. S. (2016). Grandiose narcissism and fairness in social exchanges. *Current Psychology*, *35*, 220–233. https://doi.org/10.1007/s12144-016-9415-5

38. Rasmussen, K. (2016). Entitled vengeance: A meta-analysis relating narcissism to provoked aggression. *Aggressive Behavior*, *42*, 362–379. https://doi.org/10.1002/ab.21632

39. For a dictionary definition of withdrawal, see www.merriam-webster.com/withdrawal Accessed 8-25-2024.

40. Merton, R. K. (1938). Social structure and anomie. *American Sociological Review*, *3*, 672–682. https://doi.org/10.2307/2084686

41. Ibid.

42. Davis, M. S., Callanan, V. J., Lester, D. & Haines, J. (2009). An inquiry into relationship suicides and reciprocity. *Suicide and Life-Threatening Behavior*, *39*, 482–498. https://doi.org/10.1521/suli.2009.39.5.482

43. For a dictionary definition of acquiescence, see www.merriam-webster.com/dictionary/acquiescence Accessed 8-25-2024.

44. For a dictionary definition of spite, see www.merriam-webster.com/dictionary/spite Accessed 8-25-2024.

45. Marcus, D. K., Zeigler-Hill, V., Mercer, S. H. & Norris, A. L. (2014). The psychology of spite and the measurement of spitefulness. *Psychological Assessment*, *26*, 563–574. https://doi.org/10.1037/a0036039

46. Ibid.

47. For a discussion of both reconciliation and forgiveness, see Exline, J. J., Worthington, Jr., E. L., Hill, P. & McCullough, M. E. (2003). Forgiveness and justice: A research agenda for social and personality psychology. *Personality and Social Psychology Review*, *7*, 337–348. https://doi.org/10.1207/S15327957PSR0704_06

48. For a recent overview, see Boehle, J. (2021). Forgiveness, restorative justice and reconciliation in sustainable peacebuilding: Contemporary debates and future possibilities. *Global Change, Peace & Security*, *33*, 103–123. https://doi.org/10.1080/14781158.2021.1910226

49. For an early overview by pioneers of this movement, see Zehr, H. & Umbreit, M. (1982). Victim offender reconciliation – An incarceration substitute? *Federal Probation*, *46*, 63–68.

50. Brown, R. P. (2004). Vengeance is mine: Narcissism, vengeance, and the tendency to forgive. *Journal of Research in Personality*, *38*, 576–584. https://doi.org/10.1016/j.jrp.2003.10.003; See also Fatfouta, R., Gerlach, T. M., Schroder-Abe, M. & Merkl, A. (2015). Narcissism and lack of interpersonal forgiveness: The mediating role of state anger, state rumination, and state empathy. *Personality and Individual Differences*, *75*, 36–40. https://doi.org/10.1016/j.paid.2014.10.051

51. Brunell, A. B. & Davis, M. S. (2016). See Note 37.

52. For a dictionary definition of altruism, see www.merriam-webster.com/dictionary/altruism Accessed 8-25-2024.

53. McClenahen, J. S. (2005). Defining social responsibility. *Industry Week*, *254(3)*, 64–65.

54. Al-Shammari, M., Rasheed, A. & Al-Shammari, H. A. (2019). CEO narcissism and corporate social responsibility: Does CEO narcissism affect CSR focus? *Journal of Business Research*, *104*, 106–117. https://doi.org/10.1016/j.busres.2019.07.005

55. White, D., Szabo, M. & Tiliopoulos, N. (2018). Exploring the relationship between narcissism and extreme altruism. *American Journal of Psychology*, *131*, 65–80. https://doi.org/10.5406/amerjpsyc.131.1.0065

56. Oakley, B. A. (2013). Concepts and implications of altruism bias and pathological altruism. *Proceedings of the National Academy of Sciences, Supplement 2*, *110*, 10408–10415. https://doi.org/10.1073/pnas.1302547110

57. O'Gorman, R. & Silke, A. (2016). Terrorism as altruism: An evolutionary model for understanding terrorist psychology. In M. Taylor, J. Roach & K. Pease (eds.), *Evolutionary Psychology and Terrorism* (pp. 149–163). Abingdon, Oxon: Routledge.

58. Davis, M. S. (2024). See Note 7.

59. Thibault, J. W. & Walker, L. (1975). *Procedural Justice: A Psychological Analysis*. Hillsdale, NJ: Lawrence Erlbaum Associates.

60. Tyler, T. R. (1990). *Why People Obey the Law*. New Haven: Yale University Press.

61. For a dated but still informative review, see Tyler, T. R. (2000). Social justice: outcome and procedure. *International Journal of Psychology*, *35*, 117–125. https://doi.org/10.1080/002075900399411

62. To see some of the ways Tom Tyler has worked with his collaborators to apply his research on legitimacy and procedural justice, go to www.justicehappenshere.yale.edu

63. Bies, R. J. & Shapiro, D. L. (1987). Interactional fairness judgments: The influence of causal accounts. *Social Justice Research*, *1*, 199–218. https://doi.org/10.1007/BF01048016

64. Burton, J. P. & Hoobler, J. M. (2011). Aggressive reactions to abusive supervision: The role of interactional justice and narcissism. *Scandinavian Journal of Psychology*, *52*, 389–398. https://doi.org/10.1111/j.1467-9450.2011.00886.x

65. Botelho, G. (2012). What happened the night Trayvon Martin died. *CNN*, May 23. www.cnn.com/2012/05/18/justice/florida-teen-shooting-details/index.html Accessed 5-21-2024.

66. Alvarez, L. (2012). A Florida law gets scrutiny after a teenager's killing. *The New York Times*, March 20. www.nytimes.com/2012/03/21/us/justice-department-opens-inquiry-in-killing-of-trayvon-martin.html Accessed 8-13-2023.

67. Shear, M. D. (2012). Obama speaks out on Trayvon Martin killing. *The New York Times*, March 23. https://archive.nytimes.com/thecaucus.blog.nytimes.com/2012/03/23/obama-makes-first-comments-on-tryvon-martin-shooting/ Accessed 8-13-2023.

68. The first usage of the phrase Black Lives Matter may not be known, but at the protests in Ferguson, Missouri in the aftermath of Michael Brown's death in 2014, posters bore this phrase. See Eligon, J. (2014). Anger, hurt and moments of hope in Ferguson. *The New York Times*, August 20. www.nytimes.com/2014/08/21/us/in-ferguson-anger-hurt-and-moments-of-hope.html Accessed 8-25-2024.

69. For an official version of Michael Brown's death, see U.S. Department of Justice (2015). *Department of Justice Report Regarding the Criminal Investigation into the Shooting Death of Michael Brown by Ferguson, Missouri Police Officer Darren Wilson.* Washington, DC: Author.

70. Hauser, C., Taylor, D. B. & Vigdor, N. (2020). "I can't breathe": 4 Minneapolis officers fired after black man dies in custody. *The New York Times*, May 26. www.nytimes.com/2020/05/26/us/minneapolis-police-man-died.html Accessed 9-15-2024.

71. Eligon, J., Furbur, M. & Robertson, C. (2020). Appeals for calm as sprawling protests threaten to spiral out of control. *The New York Times, May 30.* www.nytimes.com/us/george-floyd-protest-minneapolis.html Accessed 9-15-2024.

72. For one black mother's take on "the talk," see Sanders, S. & Young, K. (2020). A black mother reflects on giving her 3 sons "the talk"... again and again. *NPR*, June 28. www.npr.org/2020/06/28/882383372/a-black-mother-reflects-on-giving-her-3-sons-the-talk-again-and-again Accessed 5-21-2024.

73. Condon, S. (2012). Obama: "If I had a son, he'd look like Trayvon" *CBS News*, March 23. www.cbsnews.com/news/obama-if-i-had-a-son-hed-look-like-trayvon Accessed 9-19-2024.

74. Krupenkin, M., Yom-Tov, E. & Rothschild, D. (2025). Gun purchase interest as backlash to Black Lives Matter protests. *Social Forces*, soaf096. https://doi.org/10.1093/sf/soaf096

75. Gjelten, T. (2020). Peaceful protesters tear-gassed to clear way for Trump church photo-op. *NPR*, June 1. www.npr.org/2020/06/01/867532070/trumps-unnounced-church-visit-angers-church-officials Accessed 5-21-2024.

76. U.S. Department of the Interior (2023). *Alleged Excessive Use of Force, NPS, DC.* Washington, DC: Office of Inspector General. www.doioig.gov/sites/default/files/2021-migration/AllegedExcessiveUseofForceNPSDC_Public.pdf Accessed 5-21-2024.

77. Browne, M., Kelso, C. & Marcolini, B. (2020). How Rayshard Brooks was fatally shot by the Atlanta police. *The New York Times*, June 14. www.nytimes.com/us/2020/06/14/videos-rayshard-brooks-shooting-atlanta-police.html Accessed 9-17-2024.

78. For an analysis of this position, see O'Connor, B., Cox, L. & Cooper, D. (2024). The ideology of American exceptionalism: American nationalism's nom de plume. *Journal of Political Ideologies*, 29, 634–655. https://doi.org/10.1080/13569317.2022.2112126

79. Adams, T. (2017). Casting-couch tactics plagued Hollywood long before Harvey Weinstein. *Variety*, October 17. https://variety.com/2017/film/features/casting-couch-hollywood-sexual-harassment-harvey-weinstein-1202589895/ Accessed 5-15-2025.

80. Mcintosh, S. & Davis, J. P. (2022). The "casting couch" scenario: Impact of perceived employment benefit, reporting delay, complainant gender, and participant gender on juror decision-making in rape cases. *Journal of Interpersonal Violence, 37*, NP6676-NP6696. https://doi.org/10.1177/0886260520966679

81. Kantor, J. & Twohey, M. (2019). *She Said: Breaking the Sexual Harassment Story that Helped Ignite a Movement.* New York: Penguin Press.

82. No Author. TIME's 25 most influential Americans. *TIME Magazine*, April 21, 1997.

83. Hayak, S. (2017). Harvey Weinstein is my monster too. *The New York Times*, December 12. www.nytimes.com/interactive/2017/12/13/opinion/contributors/salma-hayak-harvey-weinstein.html Accessed 4-1-2022.

84. Levenson, M. (2020). Who's who in the Harvey Weinstein trial. *The New York Times*, February 19. www.nytimes.com/2020/02/19/nyregion/weinstein-trial.html Accessed 4-1-2022.

85. For an overview of these events, see Ransom, J. (2025). A timeline of the Harvey Weinstein case. *The New York Times*, June 11. www.nytimes.com/2025/06/11/nyregion/harvey-weinstein-timeline.html Accessed 7-28-2025.

86. For an overview of this movement, see Chapman, M. & Mills. A. (2006). Eighty years and more: Looking back at the Nineteenth Amendment. *Canadian Review of American Studies, 36*, 1–15. https://doi.org/10.1353/crv.2006.0022

87. See No Author (2019). Equal Rights Amendment overview: Origins and subsequent actions in Congress and the states. *Congressional Digest, 98(3)*, 5–8.

88. Grynbaum, M. M. & Koblin, J (2017). Matt Lauer firing caps a difficult time at NBC News. *The New York Times*, November 29. www.nytimes.com/2017/11/29/business/media/matt-lauer-nbc-news-firing.html Accessed 9-14-2024.

89. Koblin, J. & Grynbaum, M. M. (2017). Charlie Rose fired by CBS and PBS after harassment allegations. *The New York Times*, November 21. www.nytimes.com/2017/11/21/business/media/charlie-rose-fired-cbs.html Accessed 9-23-2024.

4 Narcissistic Crimes of Individuals

1. Fernandez, M. & Schwartz, J. (2013). Teenager's sentence in fatal drunken-driving case stirs "affluenza" debate. *The New York Times*, December 13. www.nytimes.com/2013/12/14/us/teenagers-sentence-in-fatal-drunken-driving-case-stirs-affluenza-debate.html Accessed 10-19-2024.

2. Ibid.

3. Fernandez, M., Perez-Pena, R. & Ahmed, A. (2015). Ethan Couch, "affluenza" teenager, had last party before fleeing. *The New York Times*, December 29. www.nytimes.com/2025/12/30/us/affluenza-ethan-couch-mexico.html Accessed 10-19-2024.

4. Garza, L. M. & Williams, T. (2016). Teenager who used "affluenza" defense is sentenced to jail. *The New York Times*, April 13. www.nytimes.com/2016/04/14/us/teenager-who-used-affluenza-defense-is-sentenced-to-jail.html Accessed 10-19-2024.

5. Victor, D. (2018). Ethan Couch, "affluenza teen" who killed 4 while driving drunk, is freed. *The New York Times*, April 2. www.nytimes.com/2018/04/02/us/ethan-couch-affluenza-jail.html Accessed 10-19-2024.

6. Rothman, L. (2016). The "affluenza" defense is older than you think. *TIME*, September 2. https://time.com/4206296/affluenza-leopold-loeb/ Accessed 6-14-2025.

7. Gray, M. (2013). The affluenza defense: Judge rules rich kid's rich kid-ness makes him not liable for deadly drunk driving accident. *TIME*, December 13. https://newsfeed.time.com/2013/12/12/the-affluenza-defense-judge-rules-rich-kids-rich-kid-ness-makes-him-not-liable-for-deadly-drunk-driving-accident/ Accessed 6-14-2025.

8. For some quotes on science from an eminent, award-winning scientist, see https://scarc.library.oregonstate.edu/coll/pauling/peace/quotes/linus_pauling.html Accessed 6-26-2025.

9. Merton, R. K. (1965). *On the Shoulders of Giants: A Shandean Postscript*. New York: The Free Press.

10. For an example of the expectation of external grant funding, see https://jobs.chronicle.com/job/37860509/assistant-professor/ Accessed 7-22-2025.

11. Holtfreter, K., Reisig, M. D., Pratt, T. C. & Mays, R. D. (2020). The perceived causes of research misconduct among faculty members in the natural, social, and applied sciences. *Studies in Higher Education*, 45, 2162–2174. https://doi.org/10.1080/03075079.2019.1593352

12. Yeo-Teh, N. S. L. & Tang, B. L. (2022). Perceived publication pressure and research misconduct: Should we be too bothered with a causal relationship? *Research Ethics*, 18, 329–338. https://doi.org/10.1177/17470161221125097

13. For an overview and history of this practice, see Hooper, M. (2019). Scholarly review, old and new. *Journal of Scholarly Publishing*, 51, 63–75. https://doi.org/10.3138/jsp.51.1.04

14. Broad, W. & Wade, N. (1982). *Betrayers of the Truth: Fraud and Deceit in the Halls of Science*. New York: Simon and Schuster.

15. Steneck, N. H. (2007). *ORI Introduction to the Responsible Conduct of Research*. Washington, DC: U.S. Government Printing Office. https://oir.hhs.gov/sites/default/files/rcintro.pdf Accessed 9-25-2025.

16. Broad, W. & Wade, N. (1982). See Note 14.

17. Banerjee, T., Partin, K. & Resnik, D. B. (2022). Authorship issues when articles are retracted due to research misconduct and then resubmitted. *Science and Engineering Ethics*, 28(4), 31. https://doi.org/10.1007/s11948-022-00386-1

18. https://retractionwatch.com

19. Broad, W. & Wade, N. (1982). See Note 14.

20. Debarment, a possible consequence of being found guilty of research misconduct, involves being prohibited from receiving federal grants for a specified period of time. See www.gsa.gov/policy-regulations/policy/acquisition-policy/office-of-acquistion-policy/gsa-acq-policy-integrity-workforce/suspension-debarment-and-agency-protests/suspension-debarment-faq Accessed 6-14-2025.

21. For an account of one who felt violated, see Davis, M. S. & Berry, B. (2018). *Scholarly Crimes and Misdemeanors: Violations of Fairness and Trust in the Academic World.* Abingdon, Oxon, & New York: Routledge.

22. For an example of a faculty mentoring program and its rationale, see https:// facultydevelopment.cornell.edu/faculty-development/mentorship/best-practices-in-faculty-mentoring/#why-establish Accessed 7-23-2025.

23. Researchers that undergo ethics training prior to undertaking research, access the CITI program at https://about.citiprogram.org/get-to-know-citi-program/ Accessed 7-29-2025.

24. Boffey, P. M. (1987). U.S. study finds fraud in top researcher's work on mentally retarded. *The New York Times*, May 24. www.nytimes.com/1987/05/24/us/us-study-finds-fraud-in-top-researcher-s-work-onmentally-retarded.html Accessed 1-12-2022.

25. Sprague, R. L. (1993). Whistleblowing: A very unpleasant avocation. *Ethics & Behavior*, *3*, 103–133. https://doi.org/10.1207/s15327019eb0301_4

26. Brand, D. (1987). Medicine: It was too good to be true. *TIME*, June 1. https://time.com/archive/6709321/medicine-it-was-too-good-to-be-true/ Accessed 7-31-2025.

27. Breuning denies via telephone interview: AP (1988). Scientist given a 60-day sentence for false data. *The New York Times*, November 12. www.nytimes.com/1988/11/12/us/scientist-given-a-60-day-term-for-false-data.html Accessed 1-12-2022.

28. AP (1988). U.S. indicts researcher over grant data. *The New York Times*, April 16. www.nytimes.com/1988/04/16/us/us-indicts-researcher-over-grant-data.html Accessed 1-12-2022.

29. AP (1988). Scientist given a 60-day term for false data. *The New York Times*, November 12. www.nytimes.com/1988/11/12/us/scientist-given-a-60-day-term-for-false-data.html Accessed 1-12-2022.

30. Ibid.

31. Dahlberg, J. E. & Mahler, C. C. (2006). The Poehlman case: Running away from the truth. *Science and Engineering Ethics*, *12*, 157–173. https://doi.org/10.1007/s11948-006-0016-9

32. ORI (2005). "Findings of Scientific Misconduct: Case Summary – Eric T. Poehlman." The Office of Research Integrity. Department of Health and Human Services. https://ori.hhs.gov/case-summary-eric-t-poehling Accessed 6-16-2025.

33. United States Attorney District of Vermont (March 17, 2005). "Dr. Eric T. Poehlman | ORI" (Press release). Burlington, Vermont, U.S.: U.S. Department of Justice – via The Office of Research Integrity. https://ori.hhs.gov/press-release-dr-eric-t-poehlman Accessed 6-16-2025.

34. For the U.S. Department of Justice's version of the Duke misconduct case, see www.justice.gov/usao-mdnc/pr/duke-university-agrees-pay-us-1125-million-settle-false-claims-act-allegations-related Accessed 7-27-2025.

35. Prof. James M. DuBois of Washington University in St. Louis has pioneered in the rehabilitation of those with ethical challenges. See https:// intergrityprogram.org/coachingprogram/ Accessed 7-24-2025.

36. Antes, A. L., Brown, R. P., Murphy, S. T., Waples, E. P., Mumford, M. D., Connelly, S. D. & Devenport, L. D. (2007). Personality and ethic decision-making in research: The role of peceptions of self and others. *Journal of Empirical Research on Human Research Ethics, 2*, 15–34. https://doi.org/10.1525/jer.2007.2.4.15

37. Tijdink, J. K., Bouter, L. M., Veldkamp, C. L., van den Ven, P. M. Wicherts, J. M. & Smulder, Y. M. (2016). Personality traits are associated with research misbehavior in Dutch scientists: a cross-sectional study. *PLoS One, 11*, e0163251 https://doi.org/10.1371/journal.pone.0163251

38. Davis, M. S., Wester, K. L. & King, B. (2008). Narcissism, entitlement, and questionable research practices in counseling: A pilot study. *Journal of Counseling & Development, 86*, 200–210. https://doi.org/10.1002/j.1556-6678.2008.tb00498.x

39. For a statistical argument for the benefits of a college education, see www.bls.gov/careeroutlook/2021/data-on-display/education-pays.htm   Accessed 6-29-2025.

40. Amponsah, M. N. & Haidar, E. H. (2023). Harvard College accepts 3.41% of applicants to Class of 2027. *The Harvard Crimson*, March 31. www.thecrimson.com/article/2023/03/31/admissions-decisions-2027/   Accessed 6-18-2025.

41. www.usnews.com/best-colleges/university-of-michigan-ann-arbor-9092 Accessed 7-22-2025.

42. *The New York Times* (2019). College admissions scandal: Your questions answered. *The New York Times*, March 14. www.nytimes.com/2019/03/14/us/college-admissions-scandal-questions.html Accessed 1-12-2022.

43. Ibid.

44. Trump, M. L. (2020). *Too Much and Never Enough: How My Family Created the World's Most Dangerous Man*. New York: Simon & Schuster.

45. For a history of college admission cheating, see Carlon, K. (2019). Stress test. *Corridor Business Journal*, April 1–7. https://research-ebsco-com.webproxy3.columbuslibrary.org/c/bfcip5/viewer/pdf/k7ssfmziu5 Accessed 6-29-2025.

46. *The New York Times* (2019). See Note 42.

47. Taylor, K. (2020). Lori Loughlin and Mossimo Giannulli get prison in college admissions case. *The New York Times*, August 21. www.nytimes.com/2020/08/21/us/lori-loughlin-mossimo-giannulli-sentencing.html Accessed 4-1-2021.

48. Hartocollis, A. (2021). 2 parents are convicted in the Varsity Blues admission trial. *The New York Times*, October 8. www.nytimes.com/us/varsity-blues-trial-wilson-abdelaziz.html Accessed 1-12-2022.

49. Press Release (2019). First parent in college admissions case sentenced to prison. United State Attorney's Office, District of Massachusetts, September 13. www.justice.gov/usao-ma/pr/first-parent-college-admissions-case-sentenced-prison Accessed 7-29-2025.

50. Hartocollis, A. (2019). A trial about wealth, privilege and the murkiness of college admissions. *The New York Times*, October 6. www.nytimes.com/2021/10/06/us/varsity-blues-college-admissions-trial-usc.html Accessed 1-12-2022.

51. See Trammell, R. & Chenault, S. (2009). "We have to take these guys out": Motivations for assaulting incarcerated child molesters. *Symbolic Interaction*, *32*, 334–350. https://doi.org/10.1525/si.2009.32.4.334

52. The Associated Press (2022). A timeline of the Jeffrey Epstein, Ghislaine Maxwell scandal. *The Associated Press*, June 28. https://apnews.com/article/epstein-maxwell-timeline-b9f15710fabb72e8581c71e94acf513e Accessed 12-11-2024.

53. Steel, E., Eder, S., Maheshwari, S. & Goldstein, M. (2019). How Jeffrey Epstein used the billionaire behind Victoria's Secret for wealth and women. The New York Times, July 25. www.nytimes.com/2019/07/25/business/jeffrey-epstein-wexner-victorias-secret.html Accessed 8-30-2025.

54. Enrich, D., Goldstein, M. & Silver-Greenberg, J. (2025). How JPMorgan enabled the crimes of Jeffrey Epstein. *The New York Times*, September 8. www.nytimes.com/2025/09/08/magazine/jeffrey-epstein-jp-morgan.html Accessed 9-25-2025.

55. Karni, A. & Haberman, M. (2019). Jeffrey Epstein was a 'terrific guy,' Donald Trump once said. Now he's 'not a fan.' *The New York Times*, July 9. www.nytimes.com/2019/07/09/us/politics/trump-epstein.html Accessed 6-18-2025.

56. Finnegan, M. (2025). See Epstein's full 'birthday book,' with alleged personal messages from Trump, Clinton and others. PBS News, September 10. www.pbs.org/newshour/nation/see-epsteins-full-birthday-book-with-alleged-personal-messages-from-trump-clinton-and-others Accessed 9-11-2025.

57. The U.S. Department of Justice maintained a file on Jeffrey Epstein, one which President Trump said would eventually be disclosed. Attorney General Pam Bondi did not make public the file despite widespread demand for its disclosure. Unless and until this happens, the public may never know the extent of Epstein's friends' involvement in his sex trafficking crimes.

58. Dockterman, E. (2021). Ghislane Maxwell's trial centers on allegations of 'grooming' young girls. Here's what that means. *TIME*, December 2. https://time.com/6125081/ghislane-maxwell-grooming-trial/ Accessed 8-31-2025.

59. Ibid.

60. U.S. Attorney's Office, Southern District of New York (2019). Jeffrey Epstein charged in Manhattan Federal Court with sex trafficking of minors. www.justice.gov/usao-sdny/pr/Jeffrey-epstein-charged-manhattan-federal-court-sex-trafficking-minors Accessed 9-10-2025.

61. McKinley, Jr., J. C. (2021). What is known about Jeffrey Epstein's suicide. *The New York Times*, December 1. www.nytimes.com/2021/12/01/nyregion/jeffrey-epstein-suicide.html Accessed 12-11-2024.

62. Weiser, B., Davis O'Brien, R. & Moynihan, C. (2021). Ghislaine Maxwell is found guilty of aiding Epstein's sex abuse. *The New York Times*, December 29. www.nytimes.com/2021/12/29/nyregion/ghislaine-maxwell-guilty-verdict.html Accessed 12-11-2024. United States Attorney's Office, Southern District of New York (2022). Ghislaine Maxwell sentenced to 20 years in prison for conspiring with Jeffrey Epstein to sexually abuse minors. www.justice.gov/usao-sdny/pr/ghislaine-maxwell-sentenced-20-years-prison-conspiring-jeffrey-epstein-sexually-abuse Accessed 7-19-2025.

63. Fitzpatrick, S. & Schapiro, R. (2025). Virginia Giuffre, one of Jeffrey Epstein's most prominent abuse survivors, dies by suicide. *NBC News*, April 25. www.nbcnews.com/news/us-news/virginia-giuffre-one-jeffrey-epsteins-prominent-abuse-survivors-dies-s-rcna203027 Accessed 9-29-2025.
64. Trump, M. L. (2020). *Too Much and Never Enough: How My Family Created the World's Most Dangerous Man.* New York: Simon & Schuster.
65. Ibid.
66. Ibid.
67. For an overview, see https://en.wikipedia.org/wiki/Trump_University.
68. Price, E. (2018). Trump allegedly lied about his wealth to get on the Forbes 400 List in the 1980. *Fortune*, April 20. https://fortune.com/2018/04/20/trump-lied-wealth-forbes-400-list/ Accessed 7-28-2025.
69. Svetkey, B. (2011). Could this man be president? *Newsweek*, May 6. 18-18.
70. Buettner, R. & Bagli, C. V. (2016). How Donald Trum bankrupted his Atlantic City casinos, but still earned millions. The New York Times, June 11. www.nytimes.com/2016/06/11/nyregion/donald-trump-atlantic-city.html Accessed 8-30-225.
71. Ibid.
72. Lee, M. (2016). Fact check: Has Trump declared bankruptcy four or six times? *Washington Post*, September 26. www.washingtonpost.com/politics/2016/live-updates/general-election/real-time-face-checking-and-analysis-of-the-first-presidential-debate/fact-check-has-trump-declared-bankruptcy-four-or-six-times/ Accessed 7-22-2025.
73. Bustillo, X. (2024). Adult film star Stormy Daniels testifies against Trump in New York trial. NPR, May 7. www.npr.org/2024/05/07/1249318101/stormy-daniels-trump-trial-new-york Accessed 8-30-2025.
74. Dorn, S. (2023). Trump denies affair with Stormy Daniels – as he could reportedly face criminal charges in hush-money scheme. *Forbes*, March 10. www.forbes.com/sites/saradorn/2023/03/10/trump-denies-affair-with-stormy-daniels-as-he-could-reportedly-face-criminal-charges-in-hush-money-scheme/ Accessed 9-25-2025.
75. Carroll, E. J. (2019). *What Do We Need Men For? A Modest Proposal.* New York: St. Martin's Press.
76. Associated Press (2019). "She's not my type," Trump says of E. Jean Carroll, who accused him of sexual assault. *NBC News*, June 25. www.nbcnews.com/politics/donald-trump/she-s-not-my-type-trump-says-e-jean-carroll-n1021331 Accessed 8-30-2025.
77. Ibid.
78. Weiser, B., Fadulu, L. & Christobek, K. (2023). Donald Trump sexually abused and defamed E. Jean Carroll, jury finds. *The New York Times*, May 9. www.nytimes.com/2023/05/09/nyregion/trump-carroll-trial-sexual-abuse-defamation.html Accessed 12-11-2024.
79. Weiser, B., Bromwich, J. E., Cramer, M. & Cristobek, K. (2024). Jury orders Trump to pay Carroll $83.3 million after years of insults. *The New York Times*, January 26. www.nytimes.com/2024/01/26/nyregion/trump-defamation-trial-carroll-verdict.html Accessed 12-11-2024.

80. Scannell, K. (2025). Appeals court upholds $83 million verdict against Trump for defaming E. Jean Carroll. *CNN*, September 8. www.cnn.com/2025/09/08/politics/e-jean-carroll-jury-award-trump Accessed 9-11-2025.

81. McAdams, D. P. (2016). The mind of Donald Trump. *The Atlantic*. www.theatlantic.com/magazine/archive/2016/06/the-mind-of-donald-trump/480771/ Accessed 8-13-16.

82. Bustillo, X. & Fung, H. (2024). Trump is found guilty on 34 felony counts. Read the counts here. NPR, May 30. www.npr.org/2024/05/30/g-s1-1848/trump-hush-money-trial-34-counts Accessed 9-25-2025.

83. Criminologist and author Gregg Barak has analyzed Donald Trump's criminal behavior in detail. See Barak, G. (2022). *Criminology on Trump*. New York: Routledge.

5 Narcissistic Crimes of Organizations

1. Paybarah, A. (2021). Fraternity hazing led to death of Bowling Green student. *The New York Times*, March 7. www.nytimes.com/2021/03/07/us/stone-foltz-hazing-dead.html Accessed 11-4-2024.

2. Columbus Dispatch (2021). Stone Foltz: What we know about the BGSU student who died after an alleged fraternity hazing incident. *Columbus Dispatch*, March 8.

3. Bentley, Q. & Bruner, B. (2021). Delaware County grad on life support after Bowling Green hazing incident. *Columbus Dispatch*, March 6.

4. Bentley, Q., Bruner, B. & Cooley, P. (2021). Delaware student Stone Foltz dies after alleged BGSU hazing incident left him on life support. *The Columbus Dispatch*, March 6. www.dispatch.com/story/news/local/2021/03/06/delaware-county-grad-life-support-after-bowling-green-hazing-incident/4613344001/ Accessed 7-27-2025.

5. King, M. (2023). Bowling Green reaches $2.9 million settlement in hazing death. *The New York Times*, January 23. www.nytimes.com/2023/01/23/us/bowling-green-state-university-hazing-settlement.html Accessed 11-4-2024.

6. Diaz, J. (2021). 8 indicted in fraternity hazing death of Bowling Green student. *The New York Times*, April 29. www.nytimes.com/2021/04/29/us/stone-foltz-death-bowling-green.html Accessed 11-4-2024.

7. Gormly, K. B. (2013). Going Greek? College students consider pros and cons of membership. *Pittsburgh Tribune Review*, August 27.

8. For an overview of the IRS exemption for Greek letter organizations, see https://semanchiklawgroup.com/tax-exemption-for-fraternities-sororities/ Accessed 8-26-2026.

9. No author (2024). Kappa Alpha Psi Fraternity, Inc. announces new $2 million fundraining commitment for St. Jude Children's Research Hospital. *South Florida Times*, March 14–20.

10. https://pikes.org/about/philantropy Accessed 8-10-2025.

11. Skorton, D. J. (2011). A pledge to end fraternity hazing. *The New York Times*, August 24.

12. Ibid.
13. Harrington, N. G. & Brigham, N. L. (1999). Alcohol risk reduction for fraternity and sorority members. *Journal of Studies on Alcohol, 60*, 521. https://doi.org/10.15288/jsa.1999.60.521
14. Wechsler, H., Dowdall, G. W., Davenport, A. & Castillo, A. (1995). Correlates of college student binge drinking. *American Journal of Public Health, 85*, 921–926. https://doi.org/10.2105/AJPH.85.7.921
15. DiSalvo, D. (2012). What alcohol really does to your brain. *Forbes*, October 16. www.forbes.com/sites/daviddisalvo/2012/10/16/what-alcohol-really-does-to-your-brain/ Accessed 7-27-2025.
16. For information on the effects of alcohol on human respiration, see https://cyalcohol.com/article/does-alcohol-slow-down-a-person-respiration Accessed 9-28-2025.
17. For information on the lethality of hazing incidents, see www.hazinginfo.org/hazing-death-database-dashboard Accessed 7-31-2025.
18. Storch, E. A. & Storch, J. B. (2002). Fraternities, sororities, and academic dishonesty. *College Student Journal, 36*, 247. See also McCabe, D. L. & Trevino, L. K. (1997). Individual and contextual influences on academic dishonesty: A multicampus investigation. *Research in Higher Education, 38*, 379–396. https://doi.org/10.1023/A:1024954224675
19. Leizinger, A. A., Bather, A. I. & Brady, S. S. (2024). Interpersonal, community, and institutional influences on sexual consent among fraternity and sorority students in the context of a hookup: A qualitative analysis. *Journal of Sex Research*, 1–16. https://doi.org/10.1080/00224499.2024.2438712
20. See Bennett, J. (2014). The problem with frats isn't just rape. It's power. *TIME*, December 4.
21. Guerrero, J. (2021). Fraternities are incubators of sexual assault and other violence. Why is USC defending them? *L.A. Times*, November 11. www.latimes.com/opinion/story/2021-11-11/fraternities-sexual-assault-violence-usc Accessed 7-28-2025.
22. Hartocollis, A. & Heyward, G. (2021). After rape accusations, fraternities face protests and growing anger. *The New York Times*, October 1. www.nytimes.com/2021/10/01/education/fraternities-rape-sexual-assault.html Accessed 6-19-2025.
23. Ibid.
24. For information on Ohio State University's efforts to ensure the safety of students, see https://trustees.osu.edu/code-student-conduct/3335-23-04 Accessed 7-28-2025.
25. The federal protections offered by Title IX can be found at www.ed.gov/laws-and-policy/civil-rights-laws/title-ix-and-sex-discrimination Accessed 6-24-2025.
26. Bouffard, L. A. (2010). Exploring the utility of entitlement in understanding sexual aggression. *Journal of Criminal Justice, 38*, 870–879. https://doi.org/10.1016/j.jcrimjus.2010.06.002
27. See Sidanius, J. & Pratto, F. (1999). *Social Dominance: An Intergroup Theory of Social Hierarchy and Oppression*. Cambridge: Cambridge University Press.

28. McCready, A. M. & Dahl, L. S. (2023). A longitudinal study on the conformity to masculine norms and social dominance hazing motivations of members of a historically white social fraternity. *Innovative Higher Education*, *48*, 39–54. https://doi.org/10.1007/s10755-022-09597-7

29. Jackson, A. & Pelisson, A. (2017). 19 powerful people who were in fraternities and sororities. *Business Insider*, October 7. www.businessinsider.com/famous-fraternity-sorority-members-2017-0 Accessed 8-31-2025.

30. Routon, P. W. & Walker, J. K. (2016). Attitude change and self-perceived skill gains from collegiate Greek organization membership. *Social Science Quarterly*, *97*, 807–822. https://doi.org/10.1111/ssqu.12310

31. Mara, J., Davis, L. &Schmidt, S. (2018). Social animal house: The economic and academic consequences of fraternity membership. *Contemporary Economic Policy*, *36*, 263–276. https://doi.org/10.1111/coep.12249

32. Thomas, E. (2019). White supremacy and white nationalism have re-entered our political conversation. But what do they mean? *ABC News*, August 19. https://abcnews.go.com/Politics/white-supremacy-white-nationalism-entered-political-conversation/story?id=64998396

33. For an overview of the FBI's version of these crimes, see www.fbi.gov/history/famous-cases/mississippi-burning Accessed 7-28-2025.

34. For an analysis of actus reus, see Gorr, M. & Kleinig, J. (1991). The actus reus requirement: A qualified defense. *Criminal Justice Ethics*, *10*, 11–17. https://doi.org/10.1080/0731129X.1991.9991890

35. For the federal government's overview of hate crime, see www.justice.gov/crt/hate-crime-laws Accessed 11-30-2021.

36. For some background, see Southern Poverty Law Center, White Nationalist. www.splcenter.org/resources/extremist-files/white-nationalist/ Accessed 8-31-2025.

37. Ibid.

38. For one study that supports the notion that white supremacists in prison have influence, see Martinez, H. (2024). The effect of incarceration on political beliefs for vulnerable populations. *Social Science Quarterly*, *105*, 2269–2279.

39. As an example of Donald Trump's support for Netanyahu, see Lidman, M. (2025). Trump urges Israel to pardon Netanyahu, sparking concerns over U.S. influence. www.pbs.org/newshour/world/trump-urges-israel-to-pardon-netanyahu-sparking-concerns-over-us-influence Accessed 12-9-2025.

40. Ronayne, K. & Kunzelman, M. (2020). Trump to far-right extremists: "Stand back and stand by" *AP*, September 30. https://apnews.com/article/election-2020-joe-biden-race-and-ethnicity-donald-trump-christ-wallace-0b32339da25fbc9e8b7c7c7066a1dboffb Accessed 9-19-2025.

41. Keegan, M. B. (2017). Trump emboldened white supremacists – and now they know he has their back. *Huffpost*, August 17. www.huffpost.com/entry/trump-emboldened-white-supremacistsand-now-they-know_b_5995e39ee4b033e0fbdec236 Accessed 7-28-2025.

42. https://en.wikipedia.org/wiki/Social_dominance_orientation

43. Ibid.

44. Abusaid, S. & Trubey, J. S. (2020). Man dies after being shot by Atlanta police at Wendy's drive-thru. *Atlanta Journal-Constitution*, June 13. www .ajc.com/news/crime-law/man-shot-killed-atlanta-police-wendy-drive-thru/ rUUFN6yfvgsevglc2Q7ZkJ/ Accessed 3-9-2021.

45. For the background of this case, see No author (2025). Former Columbus police officer Adam Coy sentenced for the 2020 murder of Andre Hill. https:// prosecutor.franklincountyohio.gov/press-releases/1686 Accessed 8-31-2025.

46. Burg, M. (1998). To serve and protect? *Police Magazine*, November 30. www.policemag.com/patrol/article/15350066/to-serve-and-protect   Accessed 9-28-2025.

47. For recent data on law enforcement officers killed in the line of duty, see   https://nleomf.org/memorial/facts-figures/officer-fatalities-by-state/ preliminary-fatalites/ Accessed 8-19-2025.

48. See CBS News (2021). Capitol chaos: Anti-semitic apparel worn during riot traced to website based in New York City. *CBS News*, January 11. www .cbsnews.com/newyork/news/anti-semitic-sweatshirts-camp-auschwitz-6wme-shirt-hate-speech-apparel-us-capitol-protests/ Accessed 8-10-2025.

49. See Pettit, B. & Gutierrez, C. (2018). Mass incarceration and racial inequality. *American Journal of Economic Sociology*, *77*, 1153–1182. https://doi.org/10.1111/ ajes.12241

50. See Jordan, C. H., Nevicka, B. & Sedikides, C. (2021). The many faces of narcissism: Phenomenology, antecedents, and consequences. *Self & Identity*, *20*, 145–151. https://doi.org/10.1080/15298868.2019.1680427

51. For the role of police unions in the aftermath of questionable killings, see https://vcresearch.berkeley.edu/news/after-blitz-police-killings-reformers-focus-power-their-unions Accessed 12-9-2025.

52. Moran R. (2017). Philadelphia mayor bemoans police union chief's "rabid animals" comment. *Philadelphia Enquirer*, September 6.

53. See Levine, K. (2016). Who shouldn't prosecute the police. *Iowa Law Review*, *101*, 1447–1496.

54. Sidanius, J., Lui, J. H., Shaw, J. S. & Pratto, F. (1994). Social dominance orientation hierarchy attenuators and hierarchy enhancers: Social dominance theory and the criminal justice system *Journal of Applied Social Psychology*, *24*, 338–366. https://doi.org/10.1111/j.1559-1816.1994.tb00586.x. See also, Davis, J. A., Baluran, D. A. & Hassan, S. (2024). Support for democratic policing among frontline police officers: The role of social dominance orientation. *British Journal of Criminology*, *64*, 434–451. https://doi .org/10.1093/bjc/azad029

55. This overview of the early Trump business is taken from www.company-histories .com/The-Trump-Organization-Company-History.html Accessed 10-9-2025.

56. Trump, M. L. (2020). *Too Much and Never Enough: How My Family Created the World's Most Dangerous Man*. New York: Simon & Schuster.

57. Reilly, S. (2016). USA TODAY exclusive: Hundreds allege Donald Trump doesn't pay his bills. *USA TODAY*, June 9. www.usatoday.com/story/ news/politics/elections/2016/06/09/donald-trump-unpaid-bills-republican-president-lawsuits/85297274/ Accessed 10-9-2025.

58. Faulders, K. & Carlson, A. (2022). Trump Organization charged Secret Service $1.4 million to stay at his properties, committee says. *ABC News*, October 17. www.abcnews.go.com/US/trump-organization-charged-secret-service-14m-stay-properties/story?id=91640350 Accessed 10-9-2025.

59. NPR Staff (2016). Decades-old housing discrimination case plagues Donald Trump. *NPR*, September 29. www.npr.org/2016/09/29/495955920/donald-trump-plagued-by-decades-old-housing-discrimination-case Accessed 10-8-2025.

60. Duchon, D. & Burns, M. (2008). Organizational narcissism. *Organizational Dynamics*, 37, 354–364. https://doi.org/10.1016/j.orgdyn.2008.07.004

61. For their work on narcissistic leaders, see O'Reilly, C. A. & Chatman, J. A. (2020). Transformational leader or narcissist? How grandiose narcissists can create and destroy organizations and institutions. *California Management Review*, 62, 5–27. https://doi.org/10.1177/0008125620914989; O'Reilly III, C. A., Doerr, B. & Chatman, J. A. (2018). "See you in court": How CEO narcissism increases firms' vulnerability to lawsuits. *The Leadership Quarterly*, 29, 365–378. https://doi.org/10.1016/j.leaqua.2017.08.001; O'Reilly, III, C. A., Chatman, J. A. & Doerr, B. (2021). When "Me" trumps "We": Narcissistic leaders and the cultures they create. *Academy of Management Discoveries* 7, 419–450. https://doi.org/10.5465/amd.2019.0163

6 Narcissistic Crimes of Social Movements and Nation-States

1. Parker, A. (2021). As Trump hints at a 2024 comeback, democracy advocates fear a "worst-case scenario" for the country. *The Washington Post*, September 28. www.washingtonpost.com/politics/as-trump-hints-at-2024-comback-democracy-advocates-fear-a-worst-case-scenario-for-the-country/2021/09/28/ee357558-1a47-11ec-914a-99d701398e5a_story.html Accessed 9-30-2021.

2. Trump, M. L. (2020). *Too Much and Never Enough: How My Family Created the World's Most Dangerous Man*. New York: Simon & Schuster.

3. Lasch, C. (1979). *Culture of Narcissism: American Life in an Age of Diminishing Expectations*. New York: W. W. Norton.

4. For actual experiences, see Segelbaum, D. (2014). Happy 70th birthday, GI Bill. *The Philadelphia Daily News*, June 22.

5. No author. Servicemen's Readjustment Act (1944). National Archives. www.archives.gov/milestone-documents/servicemen-readjustment-act Accessed 5-15-2024.

6. For an early piece on the Baby Boomers and the effects they might have in the US, see Bernstein, P. L. (1961). The Trojan horse of population growth. *Harvard Business Review*, 39 (2), 78–86.

7. Historians divide US history at 1877 due to the Compromise of 1877 and the formal end of Reconstruction. It also represents the time when the tribes of the Northern Plains were forced to surrender and accept life on reservations, facilitating westward expansion.

8. Before 1600, both the Spanish and the French had arrived in parts of North America that later became the United States.

9. Cohen, L. (2021). Vikings landed in North America more than 470 years before Christopher Columbus, new research shows. *CBS News*, October 22. www.cbsnews.com/news/vikings-north-america-470-years-before-christopher-columbus/ Accessed 5-15-2024.

10. The new arrivals, the group that became known as the Pilgrims, and later the Puritans, sought religious freedom.

11. Wakelin, L. (2021). Transportation to the American colonies, execution rates and the "Bloody Code," 1675–1775. *Family & Community History, 24*, 195–219. https://doi.org/10.1080/14631180.2021.2038966

12. HISTORYNET Staff (2006). Powhatan uprising of 1622. HISTORYNET, June 12. www.historynet.com/powhatan-uprising-of-1622/ Accessed 8-22-2024.

13. Hannah-Jones, N. (2021). *The 1619 Project*. New York: One World.

14. For a treatment of Europe's previous experience with African slaves, see Otele, O. (2021). *African Europeans: An Untold History*. New York: Basic Books.

15. To convert the value of a slave to contemporary standards, see www .measuringworth.com/slavery.php Accessed 11-12-2024.

16. Blakemore, E. (2019). The shocking photo of "Whipped Peter" that made slavery's brutality impossible to deny. History.com www.history.com/news/whipped-peter-slavery-photo-scourged-back-real-story-civil-war Accessed 8-12-2024.

17. For a discussion of this issue, see West, E. (2018). Reflections on the history and historians of the black woman's role in the community of slaves: Enslaved women and intimate partner sexual violence. *American Nineteenth Century History, 19*, 1–21. https://doi.org/10.1080/14664658.2018.1429333 See also Feimster, C. (2023). Part 1 – Sexual violence against African American slaves and its legacy today. National Sexual Violence Resource Center, November 10. www.nsvrc.org/blogs/resource-online-magazine/part-1-sexual-violence-against-african-american-slaves-and-its Accessed 7-31-2025.

18. For one female slave's experiences, see Browne, R. M., Lindsay, L. A. & Sweet, J. W. (2022). Rebecca's ordeal, from Africa to the Caribbean: Sexual exploitation, freedom struggles, and black Atlantic biography. *Slavery & Abolition, 43*, 40–67. https://doi.org/10.1080/0144039X.2021.1938399

19. Williams, C. R. (2020). You want a Confederate Monument? My body is a Confederate Monument. *The New York Times*, June 26. www.nytimes .com/2020/06/26/opinion/confederate-monuments-racism.html Accessed 9-30-2021.

20. Davis, M. S. (2006). Crimes mala in se: An equity-based definition. *Criminal Justice Policy Review, 17*, 270–289. https://doi.org/10.1177/0887403405281962

21. Sigurdardottir, S. & Halldorsdottir, S. (2021). Persistent suffering: The serious consequences of sexual violence against women and girls, their search for inner healing and the #MeToo Movement. *International Journal of Environmental Research and Public Health, 18*(4), 1849. https://doi.org/10.3390/ijerph18041839

22. Foley, E. & Planas, R. (2018). 2,000 kids separated from parents under Trump border crackdown. *HuffPost*, June 15. www.huffpost.com/entry/kids-separated-from-parents-under-trump-border-crackdown_n_5b240a7fe4b056 b22639d9d2 Accessed 4-2-2022.

23. For a scholarly analysis of the three-fifths clause, see Levinson, S. (2014). "Who counts?" "Sez who?" *St. Louis University Law Journal, 58*, 937–987.

24. For a discussion of one infamous case, see Foster, E. A., Jobling, M. A. & Taylor, P. G. (1998). Jefferson fathered slave's last child. *Nature, 396*, 27–28. https://doi.org/10.1038/23835 See also Steinberg, N. (2021). A rapist and slaver who did other things. *Chicago Sun-Times*, May 27. www.chicago.suntimes .com/columnists/2021/5/27/22456533/thomas-jefferson-monticello-slaves-sally-hemmings-george-floyd Accessed 9-30-2021.

25. For example, thirty-four of the forty-seven signers of the Declaration of Independence were slaveholders. See Kertscher, T. (2019). Evidence shows that most of the forty-seven men in famous "Declaration of Independence" painting were slaveholders. *POLITIFACT*, September 10. www.politifact .com/factchecks/2019/sep/10/arlen-parsa/evidence-shows-most-47-men-famous-declaration-inde/ Accessed 4-21-2025.

26. Wilentz, S. (2005). *The Rise of American Democracy: Jefferson to Lincoln.* New York: W. W. Norton.

27. Snow, S. (2013). Maps and myths: Consuming Lewis and Clark in the early republic. *Early American Literature, 48*, 671–708. https://doi.org/10.1353/eal,2013,0056

28. Wilsey, J. D. (2017). "Our country is destined to be the great nation of futurity": John L. O'Sullivan's Manifest Destiny and Christian nationalism, 1837–1846. *Religions, 8.* https://doi.org/10.3390/rel8040068

29. Lyons, M. (2023). For 28 May 1830 The Trail of Tears. *History Today, 73*, 26–26.

30. For details about the tragedy known as the Trail of Tears, see www.nps.gov/trte/learn/historyculture/what-happened-on-the-trail-of-tears.htm Accessed 4-21-2025.

31. For information on the Treaty of Guadalupe Hidalgo, see Lopez, L. (1997). Legacy of a land grab. *Hispanic, 10*, 22- and Salvucci, R. J. (2009). Santa Ana never had an iPhone: Some thoughts on the price of peace and the financial misfortunes of the Treaty of Guadalupe Hidalgo in 1948. *Journal of the Historical Society, 9*(1), 67–86. https://doi.org/10.1111/j.1540-5923.2008.01258.x

32. One such merchant was Levi Straus, the producer of heavy cotton trousers, who became very wealthy. See Roth, A. (1952). The Levi's story. *American Heritage, 4*(1), 48–51.

33. See, for example, No author (1851). By telegraph to *The New York Times*. Later from California. Arrival of the Illinois and Brother Johnson. $2,100,000 in gold. https://timesmachine.nytimes.com/timesmachine/1851/09/19/103215745.html Accessed 8-25-2024.

34. See Burge, D. (2016). Manifest mirth: The humorous critique of Manifest Destiny, 1846–1858. *Western Historical Review, 47*, 283–302. https://doi .org/10.1093/whq/whw087

35. John C. Calhoun quote.

36. See *The New York Times*' coverage of the surrender of Ft. Sumter to the Confederacy at www.nytimes.com/1861/04/16/archives/the-coming-struggle-prompt-answers-to-the-call-for-volunteers-list.html Accessed 8-25-2024.

37. Gugliotta, G. (2012). New estimate raises Civil War death toll. *The New York Times*, April 2. www.nytimes.com/2012/04/03/science/civil-war-death-toll-up-by-20-percent-in-new-estimate.html Accessed 8-28-2024.
38. See Bartlett, J. (1980). *Bartlett's Familiar Quotations, 15th Edition*. Boston: Little, Brown & Co.
39. No author. (1862). A Proclamation by the President of the United States. *The New York Times*, September 23. https://timesmachine.nytimes.com/timesmachine/1862/09/23/79178161.html Accessed 9-30-2021.
40. Northern support of slavery is discussed at www.tracingcenter.org/resources/background/northern-involvement-in-the-slave-trade/ Accessed 10-12-2024. See also Wilson Moore, S. A. (no date). Chapter 1: Race, slavery, and freedom – Northern "unfreedom." National Park Service. www.nps.gov/articles/000/chapter-1-race-slavery-and-freedom-northern-unfreedom.htm Accessed 6-19-2025.
41. For an updated, revised version of Sherman's infamous march to the sea, see Blinder, A. (2014). 150 years later, wrestling with a revised view of Sherman's march. *The New York Times*, November 14. www.nytimes.com/2014/11/15/us/150-years-later-wrestling-with-a-revised-view-of-shermans-march.html Accessed 8-28-2024.
42. Gandhi, L. (2021). The Transcontinental Railroad's dark costs: Exploited labor, stolen lands. *History.com*, December 8. www.history.com/news/transcontinental-railroad-workers-imact Accessed 11-21-2024.
43. Hiltzik, M. (2020). *Iron Empires: Robber Barons, Railroads, and the Making of Modern America*. Boston & New York: Houghton Mifflin Harcourt.
44. Harrod, R. P. & Crandall, J. J. (2015). Rails built of the ancestors' bones: The bioarcheology of the overseas Chinese experience. *Historical Archeology*, *49*, 148–161. https://doi.org/10.1007/BF03376965
45. Weber, K. T. (2001). Historic bison populations: A GIS-based estimate. *Proceedings of the 2001 Intermountain GIS Users' Conference*. https://giscenter.isu.edu/Research/Projects/BisonPaper.pdf Accessed 8-7-2025.
46. Taschereau Mamers, D. (2020). Historical photo of mountain of bison skulls documents animals on the brink of extinction. *The Conversation*, December 2. https://theconversation.com/hisorical-mountain-of-bison-skulls-documents-animals-on-the-brink-of-extinction-148780 Accessed 8-29-2024.
47. Phippen, J. W. (2016). "Kill every buffalo you can! Every buffalo dead is an Indian gone" *The Atlantic*, May 13. www.theatlantic.com/national/archive/2016/05/the-buffalo-killers/482349/ Accessed 7-28-2025.
48. For a history of treaties with Native Americans, see Calloway, C. G. (2013). *Pen and Ink Witchcraft: Treaties and Treaty Making in American Indian History*. New York: Oxford University Press.
49. Riddle, W. A. (1995/1996). The origins of black sharecropping. *Mississippi Quarterly*, *49*, 53–71.
50. Stiles, T. J. (2015). *Custer's Trials: A Life on the Frontier of a New America*. New York: Alfred A. Knopf.
51. Ibid.

52. Ibid.
53. Budiansky, S. (2011). Judging George Custer. *Civil War Times, 50*, 37–43.
54. Stiles, T. J. (2015). See Note 50.
55. See, for example, No Author (1869). The Indians. More Indian depredations-a government train attacked-General Carr's expedition. *The New York Times*, July 7. https://timesmachine.nytimes.com/1868/07/08/79899217.pdf Accessed 9-22-2024.
56. Stiles, T. J. (2015). See Note 50.
57. Custar (sic), G. A. (1868). The Indian war. Battle of the Washita – Gen. Custar's report to Gen. Sheridan. *The New York Times*, December 9. https://timesmachine.nytimes.com/timesmachine/1868/12/09/issue.html Accessed 11-24-2024. See also Hoig, S. (1976). *The Battle of the Washita: The Sheridan-Custer Indian Campaign of 1867-69*. New York: Doubleday.
58. No author. (1876). The Sioux Indians. Message of the President on the deficiency of supplies at Red Cloud Agency – Necessity of an early appropriation – An expedition moving against Sitting Bull. *The New York Times*, March 1. https://timesmachine.nytimes.com/timesmachine/1876/03/01/81686097.pdf Accessed 9-22-2024.
59. For an analysis of this issue, see Michno, G. (2006). Battle of Little Bighorn: Were the weapons the deciding factor? HISTORYNET, June 12. www.historynet.com/battle-of-little-bighorn-were-the-weapons-the-deciding-factor/ Accessed 4-19-2025.
60. The New York Times. (1876). The Little Big Horn Massacre. *The New York Times*, July 7. https://timesmachine.nytimes.com/timesmachine/1876/07/07/84623481.html Accessed 2-28-2022.
61. Ibid.
62. Elizabeth "Libby" Bacon Custer's books included: Custer, E. B. (1885). *Boots and Saddles, or Life in Dakota with General Custer*. New York: Harper & Brothers; Custer, E. B. (1994). *Following the Guidon*. Lincoln: University of Nebraska Press; Custer, E. B. (1971). *Tenting on the Plains: Or, General Custer in Kansas and Texas*. Norman: University of Oklahoma Press.
63. See Madley, B. (2015). Reexamining the American genocide debate: Meaning, historiography, and new methods. *American Historical Review, 120*, 98–139. https://doi.org/10.1093/ahr/120.1.98
64. Stewart, E. I. (1971). A psychoanalytic approach to Custer: Some reflections. *Montana: The Magazine of Western History, 21*, 74–77.
65. Stiles, T. J. (2015). See Note 50.
66. Russell (1867). From the plains, the trial and sentence of Gen. Custer – His defense before the court-martial – surprise and regret at the result. *The New York Times*, December 7. https://timesmachine.nytimes.com/timesmachine/1867/12/07/80422523.html Accessed 5-15-2024.
67. Stark, P. (2023). *Gallop Toward the Sun: Tecumseh and William Henry Harrison's Struggle for the Destiny of a Nation*. New York: Random House.
68. Roberts, D. (2000). *A Newer World: Kit Carson, John C. Fremont, and the Claiming of the American West*. New York: Simon & Schuster.

69. Guelzo, A. C. (2021). *Robert E. Lee: A Life*. New York: Alfred A. Knopf. See also Gallagher, G. W. (2011). Robert E. Lee's conflicted loyalties. *Civil War Times, 50*(5), 23–25.

70. Prothero, S. R. & Queen, II, E. L. (2018). Church of Jesus Christ of Latter-Day Saints. *Encyclopedia of American Religious History, Fourth Edition*.

71. Ibid.

72. Martin, N. (2024). The Indian, Chinese, and Mormon questions: The American home and Reconstruction politics in the West. *Pacific Historical Review, 93*, 445–474. https://doi.org/10.1525/phr.2024.93.3.445

73. This phrase has been attributed to General Phil Sheridan. For an analysis of its origins, see Mieder, W. (1993). "The only good Indian is a dead Indian" History and meaning of a proverbial stereotype. *Journal of American Folklore, 106*, 38–60. https://doi.org/10.2307/541345

74. For the definitive account of this story, see Brown, D. (1970). *Bury My Heart at Wounded Knee*. New York: Holt, Rinehart & Winston. See also Trever, D. (2019). *The Heartbeat of Wounded Knee: Native America from 1890 to the Present*. New York: Riverhead Books.

75. American Battlefield Trust (2023). American Battlefield Trust, September 15. www.battlefields.org/learn/articles/civil-war-casualties Accessed 4-21-2025.

76. This account of more recent American history is also admittedly selective and biased.

77. See Starna, W. A. (1992). The biological encounter: Disease and the ideological domain. *American Indian Quarterly, 16*, 511–519. https://doi.org/10.2307/1185296

78. Hall, R. (2024). Patterns of plunder: Corruption and the failure of the Indian reservation system, 1851–1887. *Western Historical Quarterly, 55*, 21–38. https://doi.org/10.1093/whq/whad124

79. Hibbard, A. (2023). Investigating the smallpox blanket controversy. American Society for Microbiology, November 15. https://asm.org/articles/2023/November/Investigating-the-Smallpox-Blanket-Controvery Accessed 12-6-2024.

80. See Grinde, Jr., D. A. (2004). Taking the Indian out of the Indian: U.S. policies of ethnocide through education. *Wicazo Sa Review, 19*(2), 25–32. https://doi.org/10.1353/wic.2004.0018

81. See Holm, T. (2009). *The Great Confusion in Indian Affairs: Native Americans and Whites in the Progressive Era*. Austin: University of Texas Press.

82. Senate Select Committee on Indian Affairs. (1989). *A Report of the Special Committee on Investigations of the Select Committee on Indian Affairs. Final Report and Legislative Recommendations. Senate, 101st Congress, 1st Session*. Washington, DC: U.S. Government Printing Office.

83. See, for example, Showalter, D. (2012). Fear! *Military History, 28*, 40–43.

84. To see the extent to which a public lynching was a community event, see www.pbs.org/wgbh/americanexperience/features/emmett-lynching-america/ Accessed 8-6-2025.

85. For a discussion of some of the manifestations of Jim Crow, see Lessenberry, J. (2022). An unforgettable forgotten story. *USA Today*, July, 30–31.

86. For an analysis of the murder and its aftermath, see Thornton, B. (2010). The murder of Emmett Till. *Journalism History, 36*, 96–104. https://doi.org/10.10 80/00947679.2010.12062820

87. For an overview of how the railroads benefitted from free land, see www .loc.gov/collections/railroad-maps-1828-to-1900/articles-and-essays/ history-of-railroads-and-maps/land-grants/ Accessed 4-22-2025.

88. Folsom, B. W. (1988). John D. Rockefeller and the oil industry. Foundation for Economic Education, October 1. https://fee.org/articles/john-d-rockefeller-and-the-oil-industry/ Accessed 8-31-2025.

89. For an overview of these early challenges, see Rosner, D. & Markowitz, G. (2020). A short history of occupational safety and health in the United States. *American Journal of Public Health, 110*, 622–628. https://doi.org/10.2105/ AJPH.2020.305581

90. Kiger, P. J. (2022). How robber barons flaunted their money during the Gilded Age. History.com, January 24. www.history.com/articles/robber-barons-gilded-age-wealth Accessed 8-31-2025.

91. See Rosner, D. & Markowitz, G. (2020). A short history of occupational safety and health in the United States. *American Journal of Public Health, 110*, 622–628. https://doi.org/10.2105/AJPH.2020.305581

92. Bobinski, G. S. & Falgione, J. F. (1990). Carnegies. *American Libraries, 21*, 296–303.

93. Chernow, R. (2004). *Titan: The Life of John D. Rockefeller, Sr.* New York, Vintage Books.

94. The New York Times. (1945). Museum building to rise as spiral. *The New York Times*, July 10. https://timesmachine.nytimes.com/timesmachine/ 1945/07/10/issue.html Accessed 6-24-2025.

95. See, for example, Konrath, S., Ho, M-H & Zarins, S. (2016). The strategic helper: Narcissism and prosocial motives and behaviors. *Current Psychology, 35*, 182–194. https://doi.org/10.1007/s12144-016-9417-3

96. Zucchino, D. (2020). *Wilmington's Lie: The Murderous Coup of 1898 and the Rise of White Supremacy*. New York: Atlantic Monthly Press.

97. Ibid.

98. Madigan, T. (2021). *The Burning: The Tulsa Race Massacre of 1921*. New York: St. Martin's Griffin.

99. Ibid.

100. Ibid.

101. Ibid.

102. Murphy, S. (2024). What we know about the lawsuit filed by the last survivors of the 1921 Tulsa Race Massacre. *AP News*, June 13. https://apnews .com/article/tulsa-race-massacre-1921-lawsuit-40c086865f644568e9525394f3 d4743d Accessed 12-7-2024.

103. Rose, A. & Jimenez, O. (2024). Oklahoma Supreme Court dismisses lawsuit brought by survivors of Tulsa Race Massacre. *CNN*, June 12. www.cnn .com/2024/06/12/us/tulsa-race-massacre-lawsuit-dismissed-reaj/index.html Accessed 12-5-2024.

104. Davis-Marks, I. (2020). The little-known story of America's deadliest election day massacre. *Smithsonian Magazine*, November 13. www.smithsonianmag.com/smart-news/new-exhibition-florida-honors-victims-bloodiest-election-massacre-american-history-180976283/

105. Rutherford, A. (2023). *Control: The Dark History and Troubling Present of Eugenics*. New York: W. W. Norton.

106. Berveling, J. (2021). "My God, here is the skull of a murderer!" Physical appearance and violent crime. *Journal of the History of the Neurosciences, 30,* 141–154. https://doi.org/10.1080/0964704X.2020.1789937

107. For an overview of the Pennhurst expose, see https://disabilityjustice.org/halderman-v-pennhurst-state-school-hospital/ Accessed 9-19-2025.

108. Morse, A. D. (1968). *While 6 Million Died: A Chronicle of American Apathy*. New York: Ace Publishing Co.

109. For an overview of the FBI's version of these crimes, see www.fbi.gov/history/famous-cases/mississippi-burning Accessed 7-28-2025.

110. Alexander, M. (2012). *The New Jim Crow: Mass Incarceration in the Age of Colorblindness*. New York: New Press.

111. Gregorian, D. (2020). Trump told Bob Woodward he knew in February that Covid-19 was "deadly stuff" but wanted to "play it down" *NBC News*, September 9. www.nbcnews.com/politics/donald-trump/trump-told-bob-woodward-he-knew-february-covid-19-was-n1239658 Accessed 7-25-2025.

112. Sanger, D. E. (2020). Trump seeks push to speed vaccine, despite safety concerns. *The New York Times*, April 29. www.nytimes.com/2020/04/29/us/politics/trump-coronavirus-vaccine-operation-warp-speed.html Accessed 12-7-2024.

113. Hernandez, A. (2024). As Trump courts their vote, comedian at his rally makes racist jokes about Latinos and Puerto Rico. *NBC News*, October 27. www.nbcnews.com/politics/2024-election/comedian-trump-rally-makes-racist-jokes-latinos-puerto-rico-rcna177514 Accessed 11-22-2024.

114. Fossum, S. & Lee, M. J. (2024). Biden seeks to clean up "garbage" comment about Trump supporters denigrating Latinos. *CNN*, October 29. www.cnn.com/2024/10/29/politics/biden-trump-supporters-garbage/index.html Accessed 11-22-2024.

115. Reilly, K. (2016). Read Hillary Clinton's "basket of deplorables" remarks about Donald Trump supporters. *TIME*, September 10. https://time.com/4486502/hillary-clinton-basket-of-deplorables-transcript/ Accessed 11-22-2024.

7 Reflecting on the Nefarious Side of Narcissism

1. See, for example, Robinson, E. (2016). Donald Trump's shocking ignorance, laid bare. The Washington Post, March 24. www.washingtonpost.com/opinions/donald-trumps-shocking-ignorance-laid-bare/2016/03/24/b66d2b6c-f1f7-11e5-89c3-a647fcce95e0_story.html Accessed 3-11-2024. See also, Bolton, J. (2020). *The Room Where It Happened: A White House Memoir*. New York: Simon & Schuster.

2. Lehrer, L. & Gold, M. (2024). Trump escalates threats to political opponents he deems the "enemy." The New York Times, October 15. www.nytimes .com/2024/10/15/politics/trump-opponents-enemy-within.html   Accessed 11-23-2024.

3. For an analysis of Giuliani's downfall, see Barry, D. (2023). From America's Mayor to criminal defendant: Giuliani's long tumble. *The New York Times*, August 15. www.nytimes.com/2023/08/15/nyregion/rudy-giuliani-trump-indictment.html Accessed 5-15-2024.

4. Feuer, A. (2023). Giuliani concedes he made false statements Georgia election workers. *The New York Times*, July 26. www.nytimes.com/2023/07/26/us/politics/giuliani-georgia-election-workers.html Accessed 4-22-2025.

5. Haberman, M. (2021). McCarthy to meet Trump after rift over his assertion that the former president "bears responsibility" for the Capitol attack. *The New York Times*, January 27. www.nytimes.com/2021/01/27/us/trump-mccarthy-capitol.html Accessed 4-21-2025.

6. Sullivan, K. (2024). Trump's allies flock to Manhattan courthouse to show support and curry favor with the former president. *CNN News*, May 14. www.cnn.com/2024/05/14/politics/trump-allies-court-appearances/index .html Accessed 5-27-2024.

7. Lilienfeld, S. O. & Watts, A. L. (2015). The narcissist in chief. *The New York Times*, September 4. www.nytimes.com/2015/09/06/opinion/the-narcissist-in-chief.html Accessed 1-23-2024.

8. For the rationales for the genocide of Native Americans, see www.history .com/news/native-americans-genocide-united-states Accessed 1-28-2024.

9. American history records numerous massacres of whites by various Native American tribes. Likewise, there were many instances of Native Americans killing whites in large numbers. See https://native-americans.com/timeline-of-us-indian-massacres/ Accessed 4-1-2022.

10. See Madley, B. (2015). Reexamining the American genocide debate: Meaning, historiography, and new methods. *American Historical Review, 120*, 98–139. https://doi.org/10,1093/ahr/120.1.98

11. One example is the way the US government separated Native American families after the Sioux uprising of 1862, discussed in Chapter 6. A more recent example is how the first Trump administration separated the families of immigrants arriving at the southern border of the US. See Haberman, M. (2023). 5 moments that defined Trump's record on immigration. *The New York Times*, May 14. www.nytimes.com/2023/05/14/us/politics/trump-immigration-record.html Accessed 3-11-2024.

12. For a discussion of the role of politics in the COVID-19 pandemic, see Cheatham, M., Hancher-Rauch, H., Brookins-Fisher, J., Blavos, A. & Thompson, A. (2022). Politics spread COVID: Developing a public health response. *Health Promotion Practice, 23*, 729–734. https://doi .org/10.1177/15248399221118012

13. For an overview of the effects of climate change, see www.noaa.gov/education/ resource-collections/climate/climate-change-impacts Accessed 10-29-2021.

14. Thomas, S. P. (1998). Editorial: Information fatigue syndrome – Is there an epidemic? *Issues in Mental Health Nursing*, *19*, 523–524. https://doi .org/10.1080/016128498248818
15. The concept of social glue comes from Kleinig, J. (1978). Crime and the concept of harm. *American Philosophical Quarterly*, *15*, 27–36. www.jstor.org/ stable/20009692
16. Blake, P. R., McAuliffe, K., Corbit, J., Callaghan, T. C., Barry, O., Kleutsch, L., Kramer, K. L., Ross, E., Vongachang, H., Wrangham, R. & Warneken, F. (2015). The ontogeny of fairness in seven societies. *Nature*, *528*, 258–261. https://doi.org/10.1038/nature15703
17. For a discussion on crime for which true restoration is not possible, see Davis, M. S. (2006). Crimes mala in se: An equity-based definition. *Criminal Justice Policy Review*, *17*, 270–290. https://doi.org/10.1177/0887403405281962
18. For a description of obsessive-compulsive symptoms, see www.ncbi.nlm.nih .gov/pubmedhealth/PMHT0024922/ Accessed 6-16-16.
19. Thanks to the anonymous reviewer who reminded the author of this.
20. Clayton, D. M., Moore, S. E. & Jones-Eversley, S. D. (2021). A historical analysis of racism within the US presidency: Implications for African-Americans and the political process. *Journal of African American Studies*, *25*, 383–401. https://doi.org/10.1007/s12111-021-09543-5
21. See Levin, B. (2020). The Trump administration wanted to use a weapon on protesters to make their skin "feel like it was on fire" *Vanity Fair*, September 17. www.vanityfair.com/news/2020/09/trump-administration-protestors-skin-on-fire Accessed 10-29-2021.
22. Silva, D. (2017). Trump defends throwing paper towels to hurricane survivors in Puerto Rico. NBC News, October 8. www.nbcnews.com/politics/ politics-news/trump-defends-throwing-paper-towels-hurricane-survivors-puerto-rico-n808861 Accessed 5-31-2025.
23. Details of President Ford's pardon of Richard Nixon can be found at www .fordlibrarymuseum.gov/digital-research-room/library-collections/topic-guides/nixon-pardon Accessed 5-29-2025.
24. See the description of sociology's concerns at www.asanet.org/about/what-sociology Accessed 9-11-2021.
25. For an overview of this collapse, see Egan, M. (2018). The stunning downfall of Bear Stearns and its bridge-playing CEO. *CNN Business*, September 30. www.cnn.com/2018/09/30/investing/bear-stearns-2008-crisis-jimmy-cayne/ index.html Accessed 4-20-2025.
26. *Final Report of the Select Committee to Investigate the January 6th Attack on the United States Capitol* (2022).
27. Schlosser, E. (1997). More reefer madness. *Atlantic Monthly*, *279*(4), 90–100.
28. See Davis, M. S. & Berry, B. (2018). *Scholarly Crimes and Misdemeanors: Violations of Fairness and Trust in the Academic World*. Abingdon, Oxon, and New York: Routledge.
29. Ibid.

30. Sellin, T. (1938). *Culture Conflict and Crime: A Report of the Subcommittee on Delinquency of the Committee on Personality and Culture.* New York: Social Science Research Council.

31. See www.cdc.gov/pictureofamerica/pdfs/picture-of-america-prevention.pdf Accessed 9-11-2021.

32. For a discussion of this common assertion, see Gerber, L. (2013). Is there a parenting manual? *HuffPost*, January 22. www.huffpost.com/entry/is-there-a-parenting-manu_b_2490934 Accessed 4-1-2022.

33. Some popular parenting books include: *Live Love Now* by Rachel Macy Stafford; *Mindset: The New Psychology of Success* by Carol S. Dweck; *How to Talk So Little Kids Will Listen* by Julie King and Joanna Faber, and; *The Whole-Brain Child* by Daniel J. Siegel and Tina Payne Bryson.

34. See Dalrymple, S. (2010). Making a difference for 50 years: A letter from the Lamaze president. *GENESIS, 7,* 1.

35. For an overview of delinquency prevention, see https://modelsforchange.net/publications/333/ Accessed 12-9-2025.

36. See, for example, Asare, J. G. (2021). The war on critical race theory continues as some call it anti-white. *Forbes*, May 9. www.forbes.com/sites/janicegassam/2021/05/09/the-war-on-critical-race-theory-continues-as-some-call-it-anti-white/?sh=6b23b03673a7 Accessed 11-30-2021.

37. The actual quote, "Those who cannot remember the past are condemned to repeat it," can be found in Bartlett, J. (1980). *Bartlett's Familiar Quotations, 15th Edition.* Boston: Little, Brown & Co.

38. Rowe, M., Kimmel, Jr., J., Pavlo, A. J., Antunes, K. D., Bellamy, C. D., O'Connell, M. J., Ocasio, L., Desai, M., Bal, J. & Flanagan, E. H. (2018). A pilot study of motive control to reduce vengeance cravings. *Journal of the American Academy of Psychiatry and the Law, 46,* 486–497. https://doi.org/10.29158/JAAPL.003792-18

39. For a clinical discussion on narcissism and humiliation, see Bernardi, R. & Monica, E. (2018). Thin-skinned or vulnerable narcissism and thick-skinned or grandiose narcissism: similarities and differences. *International Journal of Psychoanalysis, 99,* 291–313. https://doi.org/10.1080/00207578.2018.1425599

40. Braithwaite, J. (1989). *Crime, Shame and Reintegration.* Cambridge: Cambridge University Press.

41. Jones, C. M. (2014). Why persistent offenders cannot be shamed into behaving. *Journal of Offender Rehabilitation, 53,* 153–170. https://doi.org/10.1080/10509674.2014.887604

42. Davis, M. S. & Berry, B. (2018). *Scholarly Crimes and Misdemeanors: Violations of Fairness and Trust in the Academic World.* Abingdon, Oxon and New York: Routledge.

43. See, for example, Bergman, J. Z., Westerman, J. W., Bergman, S. M., Westerman, J. & Daly, J. P. (2014). Narcissism, materialism, and environmental ethics in business students. *Journal of Management Education, 38,* 489–510. https://doi.org/10.1177/1052562913488108

44. Burton, J. P. & Hoobler, J. M. (2011). Aggressive reactions to abusive supervision: The role of interactional justice and narcissism. *Scandinavian Journal of Psychology, 52,* 389–398. https://doi.org/10.1111/j.1467-9450.2011.00886.x

45. See Natoli, Jr., V. J. (2001). Organizational personality. *Executive Excellence, 18,* 7.

46. For the consequences of CEO narcissism, see Kashmiri, S., Nicol, C. D. & Aurora, S. (2017). Me, myself, and I: Influence of CEO narcissism on firms' innovation strategy and the likelihood of product-harm crises. *Journal of the Academy of Marketing Science, 45,* 633–656. https://doi.org/10.1007/s11747-017-0535-8

47. To assess the AACU's possible role in addressing organizational narcissism, see https://aacu.org/

48. To assess the AACU's President's Trust in addressing organizational narcissism, see https://aacu.org/presidentstrust

49. Russonello, G. (2020). Teachers push back against reopening in Florida. *The New York Times,* July 21. www.nytimes.com/2020/07/21/us/politics/teachers-reopening-florida-desantis.html Accessed 3-1-2022.

50. Finn, T. (2022). DeSantis asks students to remove masks and "stop with this COVID theater." *NBC News,* March 2. www.nbcnews.com/politics/politics-news/desantis-asks-students-remove-masks-he-says-are-doing-nothing-n1290693 Accessed 4-1-2022.

51. For detailed information about Add Health, see https://addhealth/cpc/unc.edu/

52. For a list of the many studies that have used the Add Health dataset, see www.icpsr.umich.edu/web/ICPSR/search/studies?q=add+health

53. Davis, M. S. & Brunell, A. B (2012). Measuring narcissism within Add Health: The development and validation of a new scale. *Journal of Research on Adolescence, 22,* 632–645. https://doi.org/10.1111/j.1532-7795.2012.00833.x

54. For information on the role of SPSP, see https://spsp.org Accessed 9-14-2021.

55. See Raudenbush, S. W. & Bryk, A. S. (2001). *Hierarchical Linear Models: Applications and Data Analysis Methods,* 2nd Edition. Thousand Oaks, CA: Sage Publications.

56. See, for example, Joyner, B. & Beaver, K. M. (2021). Examining the potential link between child maltreatment and callous-unemotional traits in children and adolescents: A multilevel analysis. *Child Abuse & Neglect, 122,* https://doi.org/10.1016/j.chiabu.2021.105327

57. Vaughn, D. (1996). *The Challenger Launch Decision: Risky Technology, Culture and Deviance at NASA.* Chicago: University of Chicago Press.

58. For details about the General Social Survey, seewww.gss.norc.org/about-the-gss.html Accessed 11-30-2021.

59. The Associated Press (2009). K-G-Beefcake: Putin bares his chest in Siberia. *NBC News,* August 5. www.nbcnews.com/id/wbna32299822 Accessed 7-29-2025.

60. Impelli, M. (2022). Where does Putin live? A look at the Russian President's residences. *Newsweek,* March 17. www.newsweek.com/russian-president-vladimir-putins-residences-1689185 Accessed 7-29-2025.

61. Gupta, G. (2024). Several of Putin's other critics have been poisoned or have met violent ends. *The New York Times*, February 16. www.nytimes.com/live/2024/02/16/world/aleksei-navalny?searchResultPosition=46#several-of-putins-others-critics-have-been-poisoned-or-have-met-violent-ends Accessed 4-1-2024.

62. Haberman, M. (2016). Donald Trump, in upstate New York, tries another label for Hillary Clinton. *The New York Times*, April 16. www.nytimes.com/politics/first-draft/2016/04/16/donald-trump-in-upstate-new-york-tries-another-label-for-hillary-clinton/ Accessed 4-1-2022.

63. For information on how Trump solicited Russia's help, see www.cnbc.com/2016/07/27/trump-hope-russia-finds-the-30000-emails-that-are-missing.html Accessed 4-1-2022.

64. Rappeport, A. (2015). Vladimir Putin praises Donald Trump, sealing a long-distance bromance. *The New York Times*, December 17. https://archive.nytimes.com/www.nytimes.com/politics/first-draft/2015/12/17/vladimir-putin-praises-donald-trump-sealing-a-long-distance-bromance/ Accessed 8-23-2024.

65. Satter, R., Donn, J. & Day, C. (2017). Inside story: How Russians hacked the Democrats' emails. *AP News*, November 4. www.apnews.com/article/technology-europe-russia-hacking-only-on-ap-dea73efc01594839957c3c9a6c962b8a Accessed 5-27-2024.

66. Ruiz, R. R. & Landler, M, (2017). Robert Mueller, former F.B.I. director, is named special counsel for Russia investigation. *The New York Times*, May 17. www.nytimes.com/2017/05/17/us/politics/robert-mueller-special-counsel-russia-investigation.html Accessed 2-28-2022.

67. Apuzzo, M. & LaFraniere, S. (2018). 13 Russians indicted as Mueller reveals effort to aid Trump campaign. *The New York Times*, February 16. www.nytimes.com/2018/02/16/us/politics/russians-indicted-mueller-election-interference.html Accessed 2-28-2022.

68. See Dawisha, K. (2014). *Putin's Kleptocracy: Who Owns Russia?* New York: Simon & Schuster.

69. Robbins, L. (2004). Olympic; "cheaters" subculture is cited. *The New York Times*, July 7. www.nytimes.com/2004/07/07/sports/olympics-cheaters-subculture-is-cited.html Accessed 1-22-2024.

70. Ruiz, R. R. (2016). Dissecting the Russian doping inquiry. *The New York Times*, July 17. www.nytimes.com/2016/07/18/sports/olympics/world-antidoping-agency-russian-doping-inquiry.html Accessed 4-1-2022.

71. Isikoff, M. (2017). As Putin seethes over Olympic ban, doping whistleblower fears for his life. *Yahoo! News*, December 26. www.yahoo.com/news/putin-seethes-olympic-ban-doping-whistleblower-fears-life-100019751.html Accessed 5-27-2024.

72. Williams, M. & Emmott, R. (2021). Ukraine says Russia will soon have over 120,000 troops on its borders. *Reuters*, April 20. www.reuters.com/world/europe/russia-reach-over-120000-troops-ukraines-border-week-ukraine-says-2021-04-20/ Accessed 4-1-2022.

73. Hopkins, V. (2022). Poised on border, Russia may be seeking pretext for Ukraine invasion, officials say. *The New York Times*, February 20. www.nytimes.com/2022/02/20/world/europe/ukraine-russia-belarus-putin.html Accessed 2-28-2022.

74. Kingsley, P. (2022). The Ukraine crisis: What to know about why Russia attacked. *The New York Times*, February 24. www.nytimes.com/article/ukraine-russia-putin.html Accessed 2-28-2022.

Index

Page numbers refer with "n" indicate endnotes.

Lanza, Adam, 13
Lasch, Christopher, 5, 42, 44, 46, 112, 184
Lauer, Matt, 69
Laundrie, Brian, 65
Lee, Robert E., 123, 132
Lehman Brothers, 44
Lehrer, Jonah, 78
Lemp, Zeke, 142
Leopold and Loeb, 72
Lewis and Clark expedition, 118–119
LGBTQ+ community, 142
Lincoln, Abraham, 122–123
Little Bighorn, Battle of the, 129
Little St. James, 84
Lombroso, Cesare, 141
Loughlin, Lori, 81
Louisiana Purchase, 118
lynchings, of black people, 15, 127, 136, 140

MAGA Movement, 151–152, 160
Malesza, Marta, 52
Manifest Destiny, 120, 122, 130, 154–155
Marcus, David, 59
Martin, Trayvon, 62
Marx, Karl, 53
mass incarceration, 145
mass shootings, 8–9, 11–13, 29, 196n20
Maxwell, Ghislaine, 84
McCarthy, Kevin, 159
McConnell, Mitch, 147
McFaul, Michael, 186
McMichael, Greg, 14
McMichael, Travis, 14
Meili, Trisha, 86
Mein Kampf (Hitler), 143
Mellon, Andrew, 137
Merton, Robert K., 57
#MeToo movement, 68–70, 95
Mexican War, 120
Michigan State University, 16
Milley, Mark A., 66
misfeasance, 149
Monahan, John, 196n17
Mormons, 133
Mueller, Robert, 187

narcissism. *See also* arrogance; entitlement;
  exploitation; narcissistic personality
  disorder (NPD); Narcissistic Personality
  Inventory (NPI); retaliation; superiority;
  specific narcissists
  and AI, 191
  in American society, 111–113
  collective, 6, 46–47, 133, 165
  communal, 45

comparison with other disorders, 163
as a contagious virus, 44, 47, 49, 90, 110–111,
  158, 161, 168
and crime, 72, 77, 89–90, 158, 168, 182
diagnosis, 34
in entertainment, 46
and environment, 31, 43
and fairness, 61, 70
fascination with, 44
grandiose, 165
harm caused by, 161, 166–167, 174
and humiliation, 173
maladaptive, 89, 149, 158
measurements of, 47
as a mindset, 48
in non-narcissists, 47, 77, 168
organizational, 4, 17, 19, 28, 46, 92, 106–111,
  154, 158, 165, 174–178, 182–184
and parenting, 42, 89, 170–171
and pathology, 36
and power, 21
prevention, 169
  democracy, 180
  in education, 171–172, 175, 178–179
  in organizations, 174–178
  parenting, 170–171, 173
  primary, 169
  prosocial gossip, 174
  secondary, 169, 172
  showing harm, 174
  in society, 178–180
  tertiary, 169
  universal approach, 171
and psychoanalysis, 30–32
research on, 3, 5, 38–43, 162, 181–185
rise of, 44
as romantic partners, 42
saturation of, 48
and social media, 43, 166
societal, 155–157, 160–161, 166, 178–180,
  184–185
subclinical, 36
traits of narcissists, 2, 5–6, 34, 42, 47
vulnerable, 45, 165
as a worldview, 166
in young people, 178
narcissistic personality disorder (NPD), 30–32,
  34–38, 44, 54, 181
Narcissistic Personality Inventory (NPI), 5,
  165, 181
development, 38
importance, 39–41
limitations, 39–41
reductions of, 40
subscales, 38

For EU product safety concerns, contact us at Calle de José Abascal, 56–1º,
28003 Madrid, Spain or eugpsr@cambridge.org.

www.ingramcontent.com/pod-product-compliance
Ingram Content Group UK Ltd.
Pitfield, Milton Keynes, MK11 3LW, UK
UKHW022053020626
471784UK00009B/372